DAUGHTER
OF THE
BOYCOTT

CARRYING ON
A MONTGOMERY FAMILY'S
CIVIL RIGHTS LEGACY

KAREN GRAY HOUSTON

Lawrence Hill Books

Chicago

Published by Lawrence Hill Books
an imprint of Chicago Review Press Incorporated
814 North Franklin Street
Chicago, Illinois 60610
ISBN 978-1-64160-303-4

Library of Congress Cataloging-in-Publication Data
Names: Houston, Karen Gray, 1951– author.
Title: Daughter of the boycott : carrying on a Montgomery family's civil
    rights legacy / Karen Gray Houston.
Description: Chicago : Lawrence Hill Books, 2020. | Summary: "Award-winning
    broadcast journalist Karen Gray Houston tells the story of the key roles
    played by her father, Thomas Gray, and her uncle, Fred D. Gray, in the
    historic Montgomery bus boycott, the action that kick-started the civil
    rights movement"—Provided by publisher.
Identifiers: LCCN 2019059100 (print) | LCCN 2019059101 (ebook) | ISBN
    9781641603034 (hardcover) | ISBN 9781641603041 (Adobe pdf) | ISBN
    9781641603065 (epub) | ISBN 9781641603058 (Kindle edition)
Subjects: LCSH: Gray, Fred D., 1930– | Gray, Thomas W., 1924–2011. |
    Montgomery Bus Boycott, Montgomery, Ala., 1955–1956. | Civil rights
    demonstrations—Alabama—Montgomery. | Segregation in
    transportation—Alabama—Montgomery—History—20th century. |
    Montgomery (Ala.)—Race relations—History—20th century.
Classification: LCC F334.M79 H68 2020 (print) | LCC F334.M79 (ebook) |
    DDC 305.8009761/47—dc23
LC record available at https://lccn.loc.gov/2019059100
LC ebook record available at https://lccn.loc.gov/2019059101

All photos are from the author's collection unless otherwise indicated

Typesetting: Nord Compo

Printed in the United States of America
5 4 3 2 1

In loving memory of my parents, Thomas and Juanita Gray

With special gratitude to my dear husband, Robert Nesbitt,
for the laughter, joy, and unwavering support

CONTENTS

FOREWORD

A LOT HAS BEEN WRITTEN about the Montgomery bus boycott, Dr. Martin Luther King Jr., and Rosa Parks, including what I wrote in my own book, *Bus Ride to Justice,* recounting my involvement as the boycott attorney. So when Karen came to me to let me know she was working on a manuscript about that pivotal moment in our nation's history, I was curious about the approach she would take, though confident it would be interesting, engaging, and informative.

As her uncle, I admit to being somewhat biased. Karen is the daughter of one of my older brothers, the late Judge Thomas W. Gray Sr., and his wife, Juanita. The two of them didn't live to see this book published, but you will meet them on the pages of *Daughter of the Boycott,* and you will understand how they produced an offspring who appreciates how they lived their lives, becoming displaced refugees as they fought back against a segregated system that tried to hold them down.

Our entire family was touched in some way by that historic boycott. Karen was only four years old in 1955, when Montgomery's African American citizens stopped riding city buses for 382 days to protest the way we were treated, seeking an end to racial discrimination. Her father was one of the original members of the board of the Montgomery Improvement Association, which coordinated the boycott. Tom also drove his car to pick up African American passengers and was later arrested along with eighty-eight other activists, including myself. They were charged with violating the state's anti-boycott laws. I was accused of representing one of the plaintiffs without her consent in the federal case that desegregated busing, *Browder v. Gayle*. That indictment was dismissed.

Tom's daughter and two sons were probably too young to understand the magnitude of what was happening, but they were old enough to feel the slights of being told to drink from colored water fountains, to know they wouldn't be served inside some stores and restaurants, to be called the *n*-word by strangers.

I'm certain many of Karen's friends and former work colleagues will be surprised to learn that her family didn't just move to Cleveland as part of the Great Migration, when African Americans sought a better life up north. The reason comes alive in the book, along with many other stories Karen came across as she went digging for tales she never knew about the boycott. At the outset, I spent many hours talking to her about what I knew and my experiences. She tagged along with me on many of my speaking engagements around the country as she formed an opinion about the boycott legacy.

Inquisitive, intrepid reporter that she is, during her research Karen discovered information that had been locked away for years in a closet—angry, hateful letters written to white city officials and the bus company being boycotted, now being kept in the Alabama Department of the Archives and History. She combed Rosa Parks's personal papers, now housed at the Library of Congress in Washington, DC, for new insight. A white woman introduced her to the maid she employed during the boycott. Struggling to understand what the yearlong protest meant to her, my niece talked to the daughter of Montgomery's police commissioner, known for his rabid efforts to keep segregation in place. She traveled to New York City to an auction of boycott financial papers, long hidden from view.

Karen is a great storyteller. The tone of *Daughter of the Boycott* is comfortable and conversational. It goes behind the scenes to look at whites who fought along with us, and at white enemies who used bombs, rhetoric, and other tactics against us. She also spoke to one boycott insider, once labeled a traitor by the movement. I found the book to be enlightening and educational with a view of the boycott you haven't seen before and will not see hereafter.

As a civil rights attorney whose career has spanned sixty-four years, I am often asked about the progress African Americans have made. People want to know if the civil rights movement was a success. How far have we come and how far do we have to go?

My activities in connection with the Montgomery bus boycott were just the beginning of my career in the legal profession, which included cases that eliminated racial discrimination in almost every aspect of American life, including the right to public transportation, to vote, to protect the membership of organizations, and to public education without discrimination, as well as equal access to farm subsidies, health care, and the right to serve on civil juries.

Yes, we have made substantial progress. Yet, as *Daughter of the Boycott* points out, desegregated schools are, years after the battle, largely resegregated. Racial profiling and police brutality remain as challenges. In addition, the National Urban League's "2018 State of Black America" report states that the equality index can be interpreted as the relative status of blacks and whites in American society measured according to five areas: economics, health, education, social justice, and civic engagement. In each there is substantial disparity having a negative effect on African Americans as compared to white Americans. The report also states that African Americans are twice as likely as whites to be unemployed, three times more likely than whites to live in poverty, and more than sixteen times as likely to be incarcerated.

I agree with this report. It demonstrates as well as *Daughter of the Boycott* the fact that the struggle for equal justice continues.

FRED D. GRAY, ATTORNEY AT LAW
GRAY, LANGFORD, SAPP, MCGOWAN,
GRAY, GRAY & NATHANSON
AUTHOR, *BUS RIDE TO JUSTICE* AND
THE TUSKEGEE SYPHILIS STUDY

PREFACE

THE 1955 MONTGOMERY BUS BOYCOTT was a powerful example of how extraordinary results can spring from the efforts of ordinary people. For 382 days, forty-two thousand African American citizens stood up to the ruling white majority and white supremacists in Alabama's capital city to demand the simple right to sit where they wanted to, instead of having to endure the daily humiliation of being segregated in the back of city buses. Two of the leaders of that boycott were my father and my uncle.

Daughter of the Boycott is a memoir. It's a collection of narratives that came out of my journey to discover details about their roles in the protest and what motivated them to stop their ordinary lives to pursue racial justice. In my quest I discovered some remarkable untold stories. Fred D. Gray, my uncle, was fresh out of law school when he represented Rosa Parks and Martin Luther King Jr. during the bus protest. But his first civil rights case involved a lesser-known name and often-unsung heroine, Claudette Colvin.

When people think about the Montgomery bus boycott, they think Rosa Parks. What most don't know is that Mrs. Parks was not a plaintiff in the lawsuit Fred Gray filed that went all the way to the US Supreme Court, which struck down segregated seating as unconstitutional. There were four women plaintiffs in that case, *Browder v. Gayle*, which challenged the city's bus segregation laws: Aurelia Browder, Claudette Colvin, Susie McDonald, and Mary Louise Smith, against Montgomery's then mayor, W. A. "Tacky" Gayle. While Colvin has chosen not to speak out much about the matter over the years, as she approached her eightieth birthday she wanted people to know she played a part in a momentous historical event.

My father, Thomas W. Gray Sr., was a founding member of the executive board of the Montgomery Improvement Association, which coordinated the activities of the protest. Dad was a businessman who drove his car to pick up black passengers to keep them off the buses to make the boycott a success. He was arrested for his activism. He later became a lawyer and a judge.

The two Gray brothers may have been born in the Jim Crow South, but they refused to accept the hand dealt to them. Their efforts to wipe out segregation in public transportation in Montgomery unfolded right in front of my eyes. I was four when the boycott started. I grew up not understanding the far-reaching significance of the boycott until I was an adult. My parents didn't bring it up often. But, before my father died of cancer in 2011, my brother Thomas Jr. and I videotaped an interview with him, in which he talked in depth about his experiences in the boycott. He also revealed amazing stories about civil rights activism years before and combat duty in the segregated US Navy during World War II.

After the boycott, Thomas Gray had a remarkable, decades-long career as a lawyer in Cleveland, Ohio, recognized for his practice of civil rights, fair housing, and poverty law. After moving to Cleveland from Montgomery, he encountered and litigated against a stubborn pattern of racial segregation in housing maintained by pervasive practices of discrimination. He used the law to tackle steering and redlining aimed at keeping black people segregated into ghettos. He served as director of Law in Urban Affairs, director of the local Lawyers' Committee for Civil Rights Under Law, and director of Lawyers for Housing. He headed up a neighborhood law office of the Legal Aid Society.

For many of his early years he worked in private practice and later was chief assistant general counsel for the Greater Cleveland Regional Transit Authority. But much of his work over the years involved civil rights litigation and promoting better housing opportunities for poor people.

He later returned to Montgomery after receiving an appointment as a federal administrative law judge, ironically to the state that would not have allowed him to attend law school in the 1950s because of the color of his skin. My father also left a wealth of written materials that helped me tell this story.

Fred Gray is a nationally recognized civil rights attorney, whose landmark civil rights cases can be found in most constitutional law textbooks. In addition to *Browder v. Gayle,* which integrated Montgomery's buses, they include the *Gomillion v. Lightfoot* voting rights case and *William v. Wallace,* which ordered the protection of protesters in the 1965 Selma-to-Montgomery march. He represented victims who received a settlement in the US government's nefarious Tuskegee syphilis experiment and was one of the first African American lawmakers to serve in the Alabama legislature since Reconstruction. He was the first black president of the Alabama Bar Association. During a distinguished career, his legal cases desegregated transportation, schools, housing, and public accommodations, and expanded voting rights. He is the recipient of numerous awards and honorary doctorate degrees. Lipscomb University in Nashville has named an undergraduate legal program after him.

The Gray brothers' successes came despite efforts by white officials in Alabama as high up as then governor George Wallace to thwart their attempts to fight discrimination. Their lives were molded and shaped by what happened in Montgomery in 1955. So was mine. I was born in Montgomery in a hospital for Negroes. As a child I witnessed firsthand the segregation in schools, on trains, in restaurants and gas stations, and at water fountains. I believe the successful dismantling of Jim Crow on the buses proved there was strength in numbers as a strategy. The boycott, under the tutelage of Dr. King and his advocacy of nonviolent civil disobedience, gave African Americans the courage to continue to use mass protest as a tactical maneuver in the sit-ins, freedom rides, marches, and boycotts that led to the Civil Rights Act of 1964 and the Voting Rights Act of 1965.

I was a personal beneficiary of their struggles and sacrifices, and when I retired from a forty-one-year career as a radio and TV journalist, I decided to take a closer look at the bus boycott, how it affected me, and what inspired my father and uncle. I took a trip back to the city where I was born, met some interesting people, and uncovered some fascinating stories. My research unearthed confessions from Claudette Colvin, surprising revelations about the life and activism of Rosa Parks, and little-known tales about white allies. I videotaped many of my interviews with some of the few surviving participants in the boycott and people who lived through the ordeal. I thought it was crucial to have an oral record from the survivors of such an important protest, many of whom are now in their eighties and nineties. To better tell the story, I have taken the liberty of creating some conversations based on fact, what I know, and what others have told me.

The boycott, backed by the power of the law, is what turned the tide in Montgomery. I heard that from both my uncle and my father, and I believe that's true. Except for Dr. King's account, *Stride Toward Freedom*, published in 1958, many of the books documenting the event came out thirty to forty years later. That includes my uncle's book, *Bus Ride to Justice*, first published in 1995. That could help explain the lack of knowledge of many younger people and even baby boomers who live outside Montgomery about the complexity of that important racial justice protest. What stands out in the minds of most Americans, including African Americans, is the incident on the bus involving Rosa Parks. But the boycott was born of a lot of behind-the-scenes strategizing. It is only recently that we received official documentation of the significant role of women in the boycott, when in 1987 Jo Ann Robinson published her memoir, *The Montgomery Bus Boycott and the Women Who Started It*.

My book looks at two brothers and the separate paths they took in their fight against racial inequality. It talks about the legacy they left me and the impact their activism had on my upbringing and career. Along the way, I reveal what life was like for black people in Montgomery in the days leading up to and during the boycott, which catapulted a young Martin Luther King Jr. into the national spotlight and kicked off the modern-day civil rights movement.

INTRODUCTION

THE YEAR WAS 2018. One summer day I was sitting at home in the den watching one of my favorite TV shows, *Jeopardy*. Alex Trebek had read a clue about Rosa Parks, asking what her occupation was the year she refused to surrender her seat to a white passenger on a bus in Montgomery, Alabama. The first contestant ringing in gave the response "What is a domestic worker?" The correct answer, of course, and the one I thought would be embedded into the American psyche by then, was "What is a seamstress?"

Another time, I saw a television news anchor refer to the famous 1955 bus boycott, which she said was in Birmingham, Alabama. She was young, but I found that unforgiveable. I have heard other people, including some friends of mine, say they thought the boycott happened in Mobile. What would seem to be relatively recent American history is either not being taught in school or not being remembered. A momentous civil rights action seems to be fading into the recesses of the nation's collective memory. But not for me.

What made an indelible impression on my young mind, and is still vivid to this day, is a neighborhood adventure I can thank my mother for. Juanita Emanuel Gray was a nurturer who loved her own children and the elementary school children she educated throughout a long career as a public school teacher. On that day she would teach us a lesson we would never forget about the importance of standing up for what you believe in, and how sweet the payoff could be.

My mother had disrupted our usual routine. She was getting me and my two younger brothers dressed up to go somewhere. No small feat. A bustle of activity in our tiny two-bedroom house. A handful of hassle for Mom, who had the presence of mind to pull herself together first. She stepped into one of her favorite "going out" dresses: a floral print swing dress with a full skirt, not too wide, cinched at the waist, with a hemline that stopped right around the knee.

Nothing too unusual about that. Tommy and I were accustomed to wearing Sunday-go-to-meeting clothes for church or just plain nice clothes for nursery and kindergarten classes. Putting on my black patent leather flats with lacey white anklet socks always made me a little giddy. Somehow, we sensed this day we were headed someplace we had probably never been before.

Dad had left for work hours earlier, leaving a light cloud of dust as he backed out of our gravel driveway in his green Plymouth. In my six-year-old mind, I anticipated he would come back for us, wherever we were going. Instead, Mom picked up my baby brother Frederick, who was then a toddler, left his stroller behind, and coaxed Tommy and me out the front door. "We're going to the bus stop," she said.

I still remember that first ride on a bus. My mother marched my brothers and me down Mobile Drive, which had no sidewalk then, and plopped us down in the seats of a city bus in the sleepy southern town where I grew up. This would have been an unremarkable memory, except the town where I took that first bus ride was Montgomery, Alabama—and the day I rode occurred when the dust had settled after the historic 1955 bus boycott. Mom wanted us to know what it felt like for Negroes to sit in the front of a bus.

We called ourselves Negroes then, sometimes "colored." We have evolved over the years with how we refer to ourselves—I remember a time when calling somebody black was fighting words. My memories of growing up in Montgomery have also evolved. Yet I am so happy to have a memory of that first bus ride and getting to witness the pride my mother felt in simply sitting down in seats previously reserved for whites. It was probably more powerful than my young brain could grasp. But powerful, too, because my father, Thomas W. Gray Sr., and his youngest brother, Fred D. Gray, helped make that moment possible. They were both leaders of the boycott that forced the integration of city buses in Montgomery.

The "problems on the buses" had been festering for years. Negro passengers suffered the humiliation of having to board the front of the bus, pay their fares, exit the front door, and then go around to board the bus again at the side door, so they could sit in the back. The first ten seats on every bus, including the two that faced each other in the front, were reserved for white people, whether they were on the bus or not.

The very idea of the practice was repulsive, but Negro riders endured it. In 1950 a white police officer, M. E. Mills, shot and killed Hilliard Brooks, a Negro man, who was just trying to get a ride on a bus. My father knew that man. He and Brooks played street football together when they were growing up.

In the months before Rosa Parks famously refused to budge from her seat on a bus, a string of black women had been arrested for resisting the status quo. One of them was fifteen-year-old high school student Claudette Colvin, who made headlines when she was handcuffed and arrested for refusing to give up her seat to a white person. It was my uncle Fred Gray's first civil rights case, before he took up the cause of Rosa Parks just a few months later. The idea of a bus boycott had been bandied about, but many of the city's black leaders didn't think Colvin was the proper face, or had the right temperament, to build one around. And in the end, she was convicted of the charges against her, which included assault against a police officer, and was sentenced to unsupervised probation.

On the day I took my first bus ride, I knew very little about the bus boycott. Even though the memory of that event is very sharp, I don't remember the exact day my mother took my brothers and me on that bus ride. It was probably sometime in 1957, perhaps during the middle of the afternoon, when the bus wasn't crowded, so we could be sure there would be room for the four of us in one of the ten seats in the front that used to be for whites only. We were headed for my father's electronics store. I'm sure the trip was Dad's idea.

Thomas Jr., Frederick, and me in front of
the family house on Mobile Drive.

It was rare to see anyone in our middle-class black neighborhood
of Mobile Heights board a bus. Most families were headed by veterans,
from World War II or the Korean War, whose wives were home raising
children. Most of those families had cars.

My brother Tommy was not quite five years old. It was a steep
climb into the bus stairwell for our little legs. He and I got on first. My
mother, who had let Freddie toddle a few steps across our front lawn,
was now carrying him. He was almost two. Mom paid our fares. Then
we sat on the left side of the bus. Tommy and I in the first two seats
facing the front. I sat next to the window. Mom sat directly across from
us, with Freddie on her lap. More than anything else, it was exciting to
me because I had never been on a bus before.

"I want you to remember this day," she said to us as the white bus
driver pulled away from the curb. "This is really special, because now

Negroes don't have to sit in those seats in the back," she stated emphatically.

I'm going to guess my first ride came after the glare of the cameras had dimmed and after the fear was gone. Those first few days after the boycott ended in late December 1956, blacks and whites coexisted peacefully on the buses. Then the violence erupted. According to newspaper reports, shots were fired at buses. A pregnant Negro woman was struck in the leg. There was a rash of bombings. Rev. Ralph Abernathy's house and his First Baptist Church were bombed. The parsonage of Trinity Lutheran Church, where white Lutheran minister Rev. Robert Graetz and his family lived, was bombed. Other churches were bombed.

Then, the Negro community was stunned when, amazingly, seven white suspects were rounded up by police. Five were indicted. In the end, however, a jury failed to convict anyone. Eventually, the shootings and bombings ceased. Black people returned to the buses. And one day, when my family felt it was safe enough, my mother took my brothers and me for a ride.

The memory of my first bus ride has led me to reflect on what has changed—as well as what has not changed—since that afternoon in 1957.

Despite that memory, it was years before I knew that my uncle and Rosa Parks were active planners of the boycott, before I learned that my father helped organize a mass protest after that white policeman, Officer Mills, shot Hilliard Brooks, who was just trying to ride a Montgomery bus.

Fred and Thomas Gray left a legal legacy and trail of political activism. Now I plan to reclaim that legacy and its lessons, as well as reflect on their relevance to the world today, a world that is still learning that black lives matter.

1

HILLIARD BROOKS

FIVE MONTHS BEFORE I WAS BORN, my father, Thomas Gray, was plotting to take on the white establishment in Montgomery, Alabama, to protest the shooting of a black man by a white police officer. It must have been a scary time for my mother. She and Dad had barely been married a year and were just starting their new family.

"Hilliard Brooks may have been drunk and disorderly, but that was no reason to kill him!" my father exclaimed—to his business partner, to his other friends, to the veterans he taught math to in night school, to my mother, to anybody who would listen. He was furious.

It was August 1950, long before many people had ever heard of Rosa Parks. Martin Luther King Jr. was attending seminary school in Pennsylvania. It was five years before Dad drove his car every day to pick up passengers during the bus boycott.

Society was segregated. Separation of the races on city buses was just one way to keep black people in their place. My father's youngest brother, Fred, was finishing his undergraduate studies at Alabama State College. Dad had just teamed up with a former high school and college classmate, William Singleton, to own and operate Dozier's Radio, TV and Appliances Sales and Service.

Then came the news. Their buddy Hilliard Brooks had been killed. The headlines screamed out from the pages of the *Montgomery*

Advertiser, the city's daily newspaper: GUNSHOT WOUND FATAL TO NEGRO; 3 WOUNDED AS POLICEMAN FIRES AT NEGRO.

When Thomas Gray read that a fellow veteran and former neighborhood football pal had been fatally shot by a white police officer, he flew into a rage, not afraid of confrontation. It was time for action. He showed the article to his friend Ronald Young, insisting, "We can't let those jokers get away with that."

The incident occurred August 12, 1950. Nobody doubted that Hilliard Brooks was inebriated. Witnesses agree he was unruly when he tried to board a bus on Dexter Avenue, the main street in downtown Montgomery. But there are several versions of what happened next. One was that Brooks was shot when he got off the bus after exchanging words with the white driver for refusing to pay his dime bus fare. Another has it that Brooks had been drinking and dropped his money on the floor. When the bus driver told him to pick it up, Brooks said, "You pick it up."

Whatever happened, the bus driver summoned a nearby police officer to deal with a "disturbing the peace" complaint. Brooks must have gotten off the bus. As historian J. Mills Thornton tells the story in his book *Dividing Lines*, "Police Officer M.E. Mills pushed Brooks to the sidewalk and shot him to death after he struggled back to his feet." According to at least one account, Brooks was coming toward the officer, but other witnesses reported that Brooks was standing with his arms at his side.

An article in the newspaper the day after the shooting said Brooks was drunk and cursing. The *Advertiser* said there were hundreds of witnesses, and some of them called the shooting "reckless and needless." The newspaper quotes a detective as saying the bullet went through Brooks's stomach and injured two bystanders. A man and a woman were struck in the leg. According to the *Advertiser*, Officer M. E. Mills said Brooks hit at him and pulled the whistle and chain from his shirt. The officer pushed Brooks away. That's when he fell, got up, and allegedly advanced toward the policeman. The officer shot him. Brooks later died in the hospital.

Not a big man, Brooks weighed about 145 pounds. One female witness was quoted as saying, "The boy appeared to be so intoxicated that he could have been subdued easily. I do not think the policeman shot in self-defense. I think he took the law into his own hands."

It was the beginning of one of many sagas predating the 1955 bus boycott that my father recounted to me, late in his life.

––––––––––

In August 1950 my father was twenty-six, about the same age and, at five foot eight and around 160 pounds, not that much bigger than Brooks. Dad wore his dense black hair closely cropped, sharply parted on the right side. His mustache was always neatly trimmed, with a few hairs that always seemed to curl down around both sides of his lips, dressing up his smile.

He was teaching math and civics classes at St. Jude Educational Institute. St. Jude was a new private Catholic elementary-through-high-school for Negroes on a campus of beautiful redbrick buildings that included a church and Montgomery's first hospital for African Americans. The sprawling fifty-six-acre site, founded by a Catholic priest who wanted to improve the plight of the downtrodden, was called the City of St. Jude. The Catholics named it after Saint Jude Thaddeus, one of the twelve apostles of Christ, the patron saint of difficult and impossible causes.

When my mother, Juanita, was working there, she taught English. Both she and my father were recent graduates of Alabama State College for Negroes (today Alabama State University). Both were helping vets who were trying to complete their high school equivalency work under the auspices of American Veterans Inc. (AMVETS), which has a long history of sponsoring programs to assist veterans in specialized training. Hilliard Brooks also belonged to that AMVETS post. Ronald Young, a neighbor and friend of my father, was the post commander.

The day the article about Hilliard was published in the *Advertiser*, Dad took the paper with him to St. Jude. The news was all the buzz in the hallways as teachers and students headed to class that evening. Many of them knew Hilliard.

"Do you believe this?" my father said, holding the paper above his head and shaking it in the air. "I used to play sandlot football with Hilliard when we were kids."

On his way to teach his math class, Dad bumped into his AMVETS commander. "Look," Dad told Young, "these guys think they can get away with murder." They both decided something had to be done. Young lived a few blocks from our house, and Dad told him to stop by after classes were over that evening so they could talk.

————————

My parents purchased their first home not long after they married in August 1949. The house was in the Mobile Heights section of the city. Mobile Heights was designed for Negro veterans returning home after serving in World War II and later the Korean War. As Montgomery expanded, it became an ideal location for vets to use the GI Bill to buy a new house. A tract house development, it was the first of its kind in the city—suburban living for many people of color who had previously lived in low-income neighborhoods in the inner city and for some who had moved in from rural areas and farms.

LEFT: Willie Lee Dyer Martin Emanuel, my grandmother, visiting our family home in Montgomery on the birth of her youngest daughter's second child, Thomas Gray Jr., in June 1952. RIGHT: Fred D. Gray, my uncle, was a frequent visitor to our home in Mobile Heights and sometimes babysat me and my brothers.

There were 511 homes in Mobile Heights. They were two- and three-bedroom ranch houses made of stucco, in white and pastels. Some of the homes were brick. Some had car ports. Predictably, the cookie-cutter design was a single floor with low-pitched roofs and shuttered windows. Our house was on Mobile Drive at the corner of Tuskegee Circle, and it still stands. I drive by to see it whenever I'm in Montgomery. There are sidewalks there now. In front of our tiny stucco home, someone carved OBAMA on the concrete while it was still wet.

Mom was popular, pretty, and a petite five foot three. She and my father met and courted in college. Fair-skinned, with a coquettish twinkle in her eye, she had a way of walking that made people take notice. When my two brothers and I were older, we called her "swivel-hips." I was slightly taken aback one day as a teenager when she told me I should put a little more "bounce" in my walk.

The way the story goes, my mother, attractive and sassy, was sashaying down a street on campus one day, right past my dad and some of his friends, who were just hanging out. He whistled. She turned around, and the rest, as they say, is history. Dad helped Mom with her math homework and taught her to play chess. He was a real catch. He played football and was also president of his campus chapter of the Omega Psi Phi fraternity.

After graduation, they married in a small ceremony with just a couple of witnesses at St. John the Baptist Catholic Church.

"Gray, I know you and your family like attending church at Holt Street Church of Christ, but you know I like the organ music at St. John's. It's a beautiful church, and I would love it if we could have our special ceremony there," she cooed. If Dad thought it would upset his mother that no family would be in attendance, he didn't say; he just went along with the program.

That tells you something about Juanita. She married a man who, like most of the males of his generation, played the dominant role in their relationship. Dad's church was very important to him. But on one of the most important days of his life, he succumbed to the wishes of

LEFT: Juanita Emanuel as a student at Alabama State College for Negroes around 1948, when she and Thomas Gray were courting. RIGHT: Thomas Gray sporting one of the apple caps he was known for wearing in college.

my mother: they would tie the knot in her church. Juanita might have appeared submissive, but when she wanted something, she had a way of getting it. She made her point that day, but to keep the peace, for the rest of her life, she attended my father's church.

On a very cold day in January 1951, I was born at Hale Infirmary, 325 Lake Street in the middle of town. It was the closest thing black people had to a hospital in the city then. It was for Negro patients, staffed by caring Negro physicians and Negro nurses. Hale was a gift. At the time, Negroes were either denied admission to white hospitals or accommodated in segregated, subpar units, sometimes in basements or attics.

From the outside, the infirmary had none of the appearance of modern-day hospitals. It was an old two-story white wood-frame building with steeples. It looked more like an old antebellum mansion in need of a touch of paint and a tad more maintenance. My mother and another young woman, who was to become a local civil rights notable, Johnnie Carr, were both patients at Hale that week having babies. Mom and I went home to our new house in Mobile Heights.

"You been in touch with Bruh Nixon?" Young asked Dad the evening he stopped by to talk about the Hilliard Brooks situation.

"You know I have," my father replied, smiling an impish grin.

E. D. Nixon (Edgar Daniel Nixon) was affectionately and respectfully known as "Brother Nixon," or in the vernacular of the time, "Bruh." Before he died in 1987, he was the go-to guy in Montgomery for all things civil rights. Nixon was a Pullman porter who worked trains from Montgomery to Chicago. He was heavily influenced by A. Philip Randolph, who organized Negro sleeping car porters into the nation's first black union. Randolph inspired Nixon to become leader of a branch of the union in Montgomery. According to historians, Nixon was impressed with Randolph's special brand of civil rights activism. He used collective bargaining and nonviolent direct action to get better benefits and treatment for black workers, who were overworked and underpaid.

Nixon was a bundle of contradictions. He was a big, tall, dark-skinned man with a booming voice and more connections than just about any other black man living in Montgomery. But he was an uneducated man who often misconjugated his verbs when he spoke. His lack of education and fractured speech may have cost him the recognition and honor he felt he deserved later for the large role he played in the success of the bus boycott.

In the 1940s and '50s, Nixon selflessly struggled to fight racial discrimination and increase black voter registration. He was Mr. It in Montgomery. Nixon knew people—white people—such as judges and lawyers and police officers and newspaper reporters. If you had a complaint that needed resolving, you went to him for assistance. Dad had a lot of respect for E.D.

I remember when we were old enough to go for Sunday drives, Dad would take the family to Nixon's house on Clanton Street for what he called a "pop call." We didn't stay long. Sometimes Mom and we kids would stay in the car. Dad would have a brief visit with Nixon, who would come out to greet us as Dad left. "How y'all doing?" I remember him saying in that deep voice of his. Nixon and his wife lived in one of the nicest houses in his neighborhood on the west side of Montgomery. It was all brick, rather stately looking.

Notably, it was Nixon, along with white attorney Clifford Durr and his activist wife, Virginia, who helped bail Rosa Parks out of jail after she was arrested in December 1955. Eleven years earlier, as chief of the Alabama Voters League, Nixon organized a huge protest of racist policies against black voters. He was probably the one person in town who could get 750 demonstrators to turn out to march on the Montgomery County courthouse. It was the first major protest march in Montgomery since Reconstruction. So after Hilliard Brooks was killed in 1950, Dad did the logical thing and turned to Nixon for advice.

Dad would drive over to Nixon's house to talk to him because you couldn't trust conversations on the telephone. Those were the days when most private residences shared party lines. You got a discount on your telephone bill by sharing your phone line with two to four other residences. Any of your phone conversations could be overheard by the other people on your line.

"Look, Gray," Nixon told him in a face-to-face conversation, "I'mo stay in the background on this thing. But you know the police department is already in trouble, 'cause those clowns on the force have beat up a bunch of other Negroes. But you can round up a heap of veterans and make a big stink about this Hilliard case and it could hurt 'em."

One of the other cases he was referring to happened on September 26, 1947. Two white police officers beat a Negro man unmercifully. Robert Felder was taken to the hospital unconscious and partially paralyzed. His crime? Felder and his sixty-five-year-old father were unable to produce the moonshine police suspected was inside their car during a vehicle stop.

The black community was angry and agitated. Local leaders like E. D. Nixon had demanded that the department add black officers to the police force. It was in that climate that Dad swung into action after the Brooks shooting.

The night his AMVETS commander stopped by for a beer, Dad and Young came up with a plan. They would write a letter to top city officials, including the mayor and police chief. They'd send a copy of the letter to the editor of the newspaper. "We should at least make some noise and let those white folks know, cops can't keep beating and killing Negroes and get away with it!" my father said.

2

ROAD TRIP

As I sought to fill in blanks about my family's fight for civil rights, my father's plan to seek justice in the death of Hilliard Brooks was a starting point. I took one of many trips south from my home in Silver Spring, Maryland, to discover more details about the Montgomery of the 1950s. It was the summer of 2014, and America was a hotbed of racial turmoil and political chaos. A yearlong string of high-profile fatal killings of unarmed black men by white police officers touched off unrest around the country. It began with the shooting of Michael Brown in Ferguson, Missouri, and was followed by the chokehold death of Eric Garner in New York City, the death of Freddie Gray in police custody in Baltimore, the killing of Ezell Ford by multiple gunshots in Los Angeles, and others.

As the violence unfolded, Donald Trump became the Republican front-runner in the 2016 presidential campaign, unashamedly touting a racist agenda. He visualized "Making America Great Again" by building a wall to keep Latino immigrants out. He called for a total ban on Muslims entering the United States, and amazingly condoned the violence that played out at his political rallies. The summer after assuming office in 2017, President Trump was roundly criticized for refusing to call out white nationalists, neo-Nazis, and other white supremacists after a woman counterprotester was killed and thirty others injured during a bloody demonstration in Charlottesville, Virginia, over removal of a

Confederate statue. Trump said there was blame on "many sides" for the bigotry, hatred, and violence.

The police shootings and Donald Trump's candidacy and eventual ascendency to the presidency exposed the hidden anxieties of many white people—making me wonder how deeply racism is still embedded in our society. Or were we simply coming back full circle? All of that was in the back of my head as I took up residence in my grandmother's old house in the city where I was born.

I had just retired from nearly twenty years as a local DC news reporter. It wrapped up forty-one years altogether in radio and TV news. Finally, I was free from the shackles of the daily work grind, awash in my new-found freedom.

My career had been a roller-coaster ride. I took advice to follow my dreams from professors at Columbia University's School of Journalism. There was no forgetting the frequent reminders from professor Fred Friendly, my adviser and former president of CBS News, that "you need a fire in your belly" to succeed in the highly competitive world of broadcast news.

Ignoring my fears and others' admonitions to start in the boonies, I reached for jobs I was sometimes not quite qualified for. In the 1970s, white newsrooms around the country were beginning to open up to young African Americans like me—not because they wanted to, but because news executives were pressured to, partially by the crush of events.

Race riots swept across America from the mid-1960s through the early '70s. Violence erupted in Watts in August 1965 after a white police officer used excessive force in the arrest of a black man accused of drunk driving. Three years later, the assassination of Dr. Martin Luther King Jr. prompted a rash of riots that escalated into looting and arson in black neighborhoods around the country. Some of the worst clashes were between white police and black residents in Chicago and Washington, DC.

Newspapers and radio and TV newsrooms that wanted to cover the social upheaval needed black reporters who could venture into the urban neighborhoods to help get the stories. During an emerging black power movement, there was pressure on managers to hire minorities, to

Me at my first radio job in the newsroom at WHDH-AM in Boston. *Courtesy of Nick Mills*

get more black faces on television. Community groups like the Southern Christian Leadership Conference's Operation Breadbasket and Jesse Jackson's Operation Push threatened boycotts. There were calls for parity in employment, the hiring of nonwhites in proportion to their representation in a community. Lucky for me, I made it through previously unopened doors and worked hard.

My first job was in Massachusetts. An unsolicited letter from United Press International, no doubt spurred by a recommendation from somebody at Columbia, landed me my first job in Boston, as a writer/editor/reporter. The news director of popular station WHDH gave me my first shot at a job as a radio news reporter. An ABC Radio network executive heard me on the air as he drove through New England one Christmas season. I ended up with a five-year contract anchoring news out of New York broadcast over hundreds of FM radio stations around the country owned by or affiliated with ABC.

Inexperience aside, that job led to one at NBC News as a radio and television correspondent, mostly assigned to the White House when

Covering the aftermath of the horrific plane
crash into the Pentagon on 9/11.

Ronald Reagan was president. I also covered the John Hinckley trial,
where he was found not guilty by reason of insanity for gunning down
Reagan outside a Washington, DC, hotel. I reported news from the US
Capitol and covered the horrific Air Florida plane crash that left only
five survivors the snowy day it clipped the Fourteenth Street Bridge and
smashed into the icy waters of the Potomac River.

There were a few years as a writer/associate producer at WCBS-
TV in New York; seven years at WTOP, the all-news radio station in
Washington, as a reporter and anchor; followed by almost twenty years
at WTTG-TV, the Fox station in DC. It was a long ride and a rather
charmed career as stints in journalism go.

Retirement was freeing in so many ways. Free from waking in the
middle of the night to report yesterday's news stories or early-morning
fires and shootings every half hour during the ungodly early hours
between 4:30 and 9:00 AM. Or, from starting my day at four in the
afternoon and finishing after midnight. Free from smiling through a

windy, cold snowstorm to tell viewers to stay home where it's safe and warm. Television news was interesting and fun for a while, but it was a lot more glamorous from the outside looking in.

I had to give partial credit for many of the opportunities I had, which had not previously been available to people of color, to my father and uncle and their fight for racial justice. They were opportunities many young black people like myself took for granted. It was why I wanted to explore more deeply what life for them had been like. I was curious about what drove them to take part in a first-of-its-kind show of civil disobedience that became a model for future protests and changed our country.

3

VETERANS PROTEST

MY FATHER AND AMVETS COMMANDER RONALD YOUNG were disappointed, though not surprised, that Montgomery's leaders refused to hold the white police officer accountable for the death of Hilliard Brooks. Their letter to the mayor and city officials that was printed on the op-ed page of the *Advertiser* demanding that the policeman be prosecuted to the full extent of the law fell on deaf ears. A police board found the shooting justifiable.

"Justifiable my eye," Dad said at the time. He and Ron Young started organizing a protest march. The idea was for it to take place over several days. With behind-the-scenes guidance from political guru E. D. Nixon, they put the word out, mostly to veterans, during and after their night classes at St. Jude. According to my father, the protest wasn't always an easy sale.

"Man, what makes you think those white boys are gonna lock up one of their own for killing a Negro?" a vet shouted out during one of the planning sessions.

"We've got the law on our side and a lot of witnesses," Ron answered. Like my father, he was not one to back down from a fight.

"Just remember, what we're planning is in memory of one of our guys," Ron told the group.

"Yeah," somebody yelled out. "Yeah!"

"Hilliard did not deserve that," said another.

"We're going to need some volunteers to help us make some signs," said Dad.

"No problem."

And here's where you could hear the imprint of E. D. Nixon.

"The signs will say 'Ballots Will Stop Bullets,'" said my father. "How many of you are registered to vote?"

Maybe a dozen hands went up.

"We're going to protest the murder of Brooks, but we need an excuse to have hundreds of people walking down the street downtown. We're going to need a destination to march to, so they can't accuse us of loitering. So we're going to march toward the courthouse, and those of you who aren't registered to vote, go inside and register. Spread the word, and anybody who can help with the signs, stick around and help."

One of the volunteer organizers was Dad's business partner, William "Chink" Singleton. Singleton was also a World War II veteran, and as a skilled electronics expert he trained vets at St. Jude. His wife, Bernice, was a schoolteacher who had also attended 'Bama State.

Mr. Singleton was mixed race. According to his kids, and there were eight of them, Singleton's grandfather was half Indian and half Negro. Marsha, his oldest, says his grandmother was half Jewish and half Negro. But as we all know, one drop of black blood determines your destiny. At first glance Mr. Singleton, which is what I called him until he died, appeared to be of Asian descent. His buddies thought he looked Chinese and called him "Chink." Oh, the irony of a group of African Americans battling discrimination resorting to racially offensive language. But back then, nobody thought about it twice.

Early in 1950, Singleton spent some of his time as an assistant to a guy named Charlie Dozier. A fellow veteran, Dozier had a service-related disability that left him using a wheelchair. Dozier was a businessman, the first owner of the small radio and TV repair shop on West Jeff Davis Avenue, which Singleton worked in. Dozier died by suicide, leaving the store to Singleton.

After Dozier died, Singleton needed someone to help him run the business, so he partnered with my father. They moved from the tiny shop on West Jeff Davis to a bigger space a few doors down, with large front picture windows. Both stores were full of radios and black-and-white televisions. I still can see my father and Mr. Singleton in the back of the store, working on radios that were broken. When the back frames of the radios were removed, they revealed guts full of copper wire and coils that were all a mystery to me. It had the feel of a science lab.

Sometimes my mother would work in the store answering phones, and when my younger brother Tommy and I were old enough, she'd take us with her and let us roam around the shop. I would watch Dad and Mr. Singleton use a soldering iron to splice wires together. The smell was a mix of burning metal with the thick sweetness of whatever aftershave the men were wearing.

My father and William Singleton not only repaired radios and television sets, they also sold them, as well as large appliances such as refrigerators and washing machines. Their store wasn't fancy, but Negroes who wanted to buy from a black-owned store in the early '50s could buy their TVs from Dozier's. My father would brag years later

Gray family photo around 1954. From left to right, Juanita, Thomas Jr., Karen, and Thomas Sr.

about selling two television sets and a washing machine to Dr. Martin Luther King Jr. and his wife, Coretta, when they were new in town. "Martin told me he was ready to purchase a television but was not interested in the largest or most expensive set," Dad used to tell people. "He wanted to know which sets were giving less trouble. I told him we sold more Zenith, RCA, Philco, and Admirals, in about that order, but Emerson sets gave the least trouble. Ralph Abernathy and I had been classmates in college, and I sold him and Mrs. Abernathy a large floor model Zenith television set. King purchased two table model Emerson TVs."

Inside the store, appliances were stacked up in boxes that lined aisles. Many of them were Admiral TV sets, left inside the manufacturer's boxes, placed so they faced the street. You could see what was for sale before you even entered. Televisions were new in the early '50s. Everybody didn't have one. When there was a popular event scheduled—a boxing match or even the news—Dad and Mr. Singleton would take out some of the TVs and display them side by side in the window so people walking by could stop on the sidewalk out in front of the store to watch.

Dozier's Radio, TV and Appliances Sales and Service on West Jeff Davis Avenue, owned and operated by my father and his former college classmate William Singleton.

"Hey man," Dad must have told Singleton, "I know how we can get some more business in here." It was during that time that Dad also had a part-time job, as an announcer at a local radio station.

"I can get some of the other disc jockeys down at WRMA to come in and spin some records, do some live radio broadcasts from right here inside the shop." Which they did. I later found some black-and-white photographs showing young people hanging out and dancing in the store, while the DJs played the latest tunes.

Maybe he hadn't taken any courses in marketing, but Dad was a master.

Years later, the story about the veterans' protest is one my brothers and I practically had to pry out of my father. I wondered how it was that he had sat on such a remarkable story. I suppose the details of the killing of Hilliard Brooks were considered unsuitable for our young ears. Dad talked a lot about the 1955 bus boycott as I was growing up, but very little about the events leading up to it, the same as he hardly ever mentioned his experiences during World War II in the segregated navy. I am embarrassed it took so long for my two brothers and me to express the appropriate amount of interest in what turned out to be important chapters in our nation's history.

"Time to get out the camcorder." It was a threat from Thomas Jr. that usually made us all roll our eyes.

In the summer of 2004, my husband, Chris Houston (who died in 2006 of pancreatic cancer), and I made a road trip to Montgomery from our home in Silver Spring, Maryland, to visit my parents. My brother Thomas Jr. motored in from Columbus, Ohio. I'm one of the few people he lets call him Tommy. Anyway, he took his darn camcorder everywhere. We thank him now. But back then, the omnipresence of the camera and his incessant videotaping used to just get on our nerves.

That day we were all sitting around in my parents' family room at their house in the Arrowhead area of suburban Montgomery. Tommy whipped out his video camera, plopped Dad in front of it, and told me I should do the interview.

"We need to get some of this history down on tape," said Tommy.

We all listened attentively, except for my mother. "What are you all doing?" she asked as she noticed us gathered around Dad. She was in the early stages of Alzheimer's and, as was her habit, drifted aimlessly around the house, walking from their bedroom to the kitchen, occasionally stopping to sit on the sofa to watch the goings-on.

She often wore her soft salt-and-pepper gray hair in an updo. I glanced at her hands, now wrinkled with age, and thought about how those hands had once labored over patches of material to create beautiful quilts for each of her children. Years earlier, when my parents lived in Cleveland and my brothers and I had gone off to college, Mom had invited girlfriends over for quilting bees, allowing them to carefully cut out simple designs that would become the repeated squares that made up our quilts. Mine was a pattern of soft yellow and green dolls. Tommy, who to this day loves to play chess, has a quilt with squares of chess pieces. Freddie, who passed away in 2018, had from time to time played golf with my father. He was gifted a quilt made up of golf clubs. The quilts were labors of love. I liked mine so much, Mom made me another one. Dolls again, the second one lilac and ivory in color. I still treasure them both.

The day of the interview, I sat in a chair directly in front of Dad in the cozy family room. Tommy was right next to me, his camera atop a tripod, pointed at my father. My husband, Chris, sat on the sofa, soaking it all in. Mom couldn't stay focused. She would listen for a while, then get up and go putz around. She probably walked behind my father into camera range once or twice, seemingly oblivious to what was happening.

Dad went on with his story. You could tell by the smile on his face and from the way he watched the reactions on our faces that he was proud of what they achieved the day of the big veterans' protest.

––––––––––––

"We were able to get hundreds of our people out there," Dad said. "Most of the veterans taking training classes over at St. Jude's participated.

Singleton was going to be one of the leaders. I was going to meet him down there."

He continued, "One of us was going to have to go back over to Dozier's to check on the shop later in the day. We decided it would be me. I left Singleton overseeing the vets during the latter part of the first day."

There was an air of secrecy over the planning. They wanted to catch white people—the police, especially—by surprise. No fliers went up in advance. It was word-of-mouth organizing. Singleton walked across the street to our house the night before the first day of the protest. "Hey, Gray," he said. "We forgot about Mrs. Jimmie Lowe." Mrs. Lowe ran a small school for veterans not too far from their shop on West Jeff Davis Avenue.

"I'll run by there on the way downtown tomorrow, to see if she'll let some of those guys out early so they can participate too," Dad said. Mom, pregnant with me, sitting in a chair in the living room when Singleton came over, was visibly nervous. This could be dangerous. Something bad could happen. My father was not afraid. As was his habit, Dad told her everything. As was her habit, she expressed concern, then stepped back and let him do his thing.

In the sultry heat of an August morning, my father rose from his bed, got dressed, and packed some signs in the back of his car. He grabbed my mother by the waist, gave her a kiss, told her not to worry, and drove off. He headed over to Mrs. Lowe's school, a small building on West Jeff Davis, between Holt and Ewell Streets.

"Mrs. Lowe, have you been keeping up with what happened to Hilliard Brooks? You know, that young Negro the policeman killed by the bus?" Dad asked.

"Uh-huh, I heard a little bit about that," she said in a slow southern drawl.

"Well, we think that white man should go to jail, and we're holding a protest downtown today. Can you let some of your guys out of classes for a few hours to join us?" he asked.

No problem. It didn't take long or much convincing. A few student vets jumped into his car with him. Others made their own way to Dexter Avenue, which is the main street downtown.

In my mind's eye, I can see Dad now. I've gone through boxes of pictures from his younger days, and he was a dapper dresser. Every photo from his college days shows him sporting a suit, except when he was in a football uniform, sitting on the sidelines of Alabama State's stadium with fellow members of the Hornets team.

In those days people dressed up to go out, even in the steamy Alabama heat. The day of the protest Dad was probably wearing a taupe fedora, with the brim turned up in the back, flat front, angled slightly to the right. It was the fashion then. I remember him wearing such hats. Even though it was a hot August day, he no doubt had on a dark jacket, which he could take off and throw over his shoulder if he needed to, and black lace-up Oxfords. Shoes were heavy then too, with chunky, stacked wooden heels. There was still a shortage of leather for civilians right after the war. Walking in them for long periods of time was probably no picnic.

"This was an important protest," Dad told us.

He arrived to a hubbub of activity. The men had agreed to gather on Dexter Avenue, not far from Dexter Avenue Baptist Church. Dozens of veterans were already pouring out of cars. Some had come by bus. Many walked, joining the blocks-long line of protesters. With the magnificent white domed state capitol building as their backdrop, they marched down Dexter Avenue, across Hull and McDonough Streets, and left on Lawrence Street to the county courthouse. They marched from late morning until the courthouse closed at the end of the business day. There were hundreds of them, maybe as many as four hundred, before it was all over.

"The white folks had never really seen anything like it." This, he said, was one of many racially stoked events that preceded the 1955 bus boycott.

"Hey, here's a sign," Singleton was yelling out to vets as they showed up for the demonstration.

"The vets had put together signs over at St. Jude's earlier in the week," Dad told us. They were large white poster board, some glued to wooden sticks, which the demonstrators held in the air. Others they just carried in front of them. Writing in black ink stated BALLOTS WILL STOP BULLETS.

Dad and some of the other protest leaders helped Singleton pass out the signs. They barked out orders like they were still in the military.

"Walk in twos and keep moving. Don't block the sidewalk."

Dad's voice always resonated a deep bass tone that commanded attention.

"If somebody wants to get by, let them pass."

They were walking down a main street downtown and encountered shoppers and people going in and out of city and state government buildings. White people who passed by looked at them. There was an occasional, "What y'all doing?" To which a vet would respond, "Protesting an unfair shooting." Some of the passersby leered at them; most just kept passing by. It would not have been odd to see a robed Ku Klux Klansman in the streets. During the '50s they sometimes made their presence known to discourage Negro citizens from coming downtown.

Singleton, the sleeves on his beige shirt rolled up, wearing neat khaki pants, led the way, up toward the front of the line, on the sidewalk.

I felt like I was in class, being schooled, as Dad went on, "We almost circled that block by the courthouse. We were able to demonstrate, see. We couldn't have done it, unless they all had somewhere to go. Loitering would have gotten us arrested. They were all going to the courthouse to get registered to vote. That was our strategy, to go down to the Board of Registrars in the courthouse, so folks could get registered to vote."

None of the vets seemed to mind the ninety-degree temperature. They walked proudly, backs straight, some wiping beads of perspiration from their brows with the white handkerchiefs every man used to carry in his pocket back then. Those with signs held them up high.

Montgomery's white sheriff apparently didn't like the looks of things and sent a couple of deputies over in a cruiser early in the protest to find out what was up. The sheriff's office was only about a block away from Dexter Avenue on Perry Street.

The marked sheriff's car pulled up near where the vets made the turn to go down Lawrence Street, and one of the deputies got out. He approached Singleton near the front of the marchers and said, "Look, you know, you've got some signs over there, and I'm really interested in your protection. I don't want things to get disorderly out here. If you would just put those signs down."

Singleton politely responded, "I'm not authorized to tell them, as a member of AMVETS, Sheriff, but you can."

It was an unexpected challenge from a colored citizen. Not an out-and-out refusal to a not exactly direct order from a white law enforcement officer. The protesting vets kept walking, but they strained to hear as they passed the two talking.

The deputy, wearing his tan uniform, gun in his holster, shouted back a haughty, "So you won't tell 'em? You refusing to tell 'em?"

"No," Singleton said. "I can't tell them. I don't have the authority."

The deputy retreated to his car across the street to speak to his partner, who was standing by their cruiser.

Singleton was nervous about what might happen next. In the South, Negroes had been killed for less. He went over to the protesting vets, grabbed a sign one of them was holding, and said, "Fellas, I think you're going to have to put those signs down. I don't know if the sheriff's going to send some folks over here or what. But be prepared for it."

My father, cocky and not usually one to cut and run, agreed. "Maybe we should put the signs down, but we're not leaving."

Sure enough, one of the deputies came over and said, "Y'all gonna have to get rid of the signs that ya have." So they put them down in a pile in an area near the sidewalk and didn't bring them back the next day or the next. The protest went on for about a week.

Dad's pretty sure a healthy number of those vets got registered to vote. It's not clear if their message got to the intended audience. But a story in the next day's newspaper quoted the chair of the Montgomery Board of Registrars as saying she had received applications for voter registration from about fifty Negroes. It went on to say reports indicated as many as three hundred Negroes, mostly men, had gone to the courthouse seeking to register. The registrar couldn't explain the reason for the sudden rush. The *Advertiser* story made no mention of the line of protesting veterans outside.

My father, who enlisted in the US Navy during World War II as soon as he turned eighteen, had registered to vote as soon as he was eligible, at age twenty-one. In 1950 only eight hundred or so blacks in Montgomery were on the voter registration rolls. The city's population at the time was just over 105,000. Fewer than a third of the residents were black citizens.

4

UNCLE TEDDY: TO DESTROY EVERYTHING SEGREGATED

AROUND THE TIME OF THE VETERANS' MARCH, my father's youngest brother, Fred, was enrolled in college. Naturally, he was going to the only school of higher learning available at the time to people of our skin color in Montgomery: Alabama State College for Negroes. It was the same college my parents had attended.

On any given day, Fred took the South Jackson–Washington Park bus from his mother's house in west Montgomery, crisscrossing the city to his classes at Alabama State on the east side. It had been his routine since 1947, when he finished Nashville Christian Institute (NCI) in Tennessee. My grandmother had sent him there for Bible training. "You going to be a preacher, boy," she told him. "And you're going to be a good one."

Fred was easygoing as a child and minded his mother. He was never one to look for a fight, except much later, when he took his battles into the courtroom. He was slim, still is. His skin is chestnut brown. The trim mustache above his full lips is always neatly groomed. He has always worn eyeglasses that make him look studious. I remember him standing out from the crowd right down to the way he dressed. Back in the day, he was as fashionable as his meager funds allowed. Just the right skinny tie, a smart suit, shoes polished. It was the best he could afford, purchased most likely from a place called the Classie Clothing Store over on Commerce Street. He liked to shop at Stein's on Dexter Avenue near Court and Perry Streets for his shoes. Both he and my father had a voice and manner of speaking that made people sit up and notice. Dad's voice was deeper.

When he graduated from NCI and moved back home to Montgomery, he applied to Alabama State so he could also study to become a teacher.

"Teaching and preaching were two of the main professions for Negroes back then," he said often—at least the two that were within reach. "I decided to do both." But then the kernel of another idea began to germinate in young Fred as he took those rides on city buses. His plan, which he kept to himself until many years later, was to go to a law school up north that would admit Negroes and return to Alabama to, in his words, "destroy everything segregated I could find." This desire he began to have of wanting to change the system wasn't something he talked about. It was just the deep-seated yearning inside a young man who dreamed of a new South few then dared to imagine.

"Morning. Howdy do?" Fellow passengers who greeted Fred Gray grew accustomed to watching the attractive, well-mannered young man board the bus. He carried books and the attitude of somebody important.

As the bus snaked its way through town on the way to the college, other Negroes got on. Many were domestic help headed for the homes of well-to-do whites in the Cloverdale section of town. It was an area of beautifully manicured gardens, lawns sprinkled with virgin pines, yards full of stately magnolia trees, and open glens dense with clover. Many of Cloverdale's homes were designed by the city's top architects. They remain to this day—Tudor-style houses, cottages, and bungalows nestled between wide streets and scenic parks.

Fred couldn't help but notice the stark contrast between Cloverdale and where he lived in west Montgomery, populated by low-income blacks. Along the way, his bus passed through the middle of town, which housed a small white population. A lot of white people who didn't have cars also needed transportation and often boarded the South Jackson bus. As was the custom, they sat in the front.

Long before emissions controls, exhaust fumes and a lack of air conditioning already made the typical bus ride somewhat uncomfortable. But what left my uncle reeling most days was a common ritual. A scenario that let the white drivers and the white bus riders feel superior. Negroes would climb aboard, pay their dime fare, turn around, and leave from the same front stairs they came in on to exit and head to the side rear door, so they could sit in their assigned space in the back of the bus.

"Hurry up," the driver often yelled out.

Sometimes the driver would pull off before the passenger could get back on. Disgusted and destined to be late for work or school, that person had to wait for another bus and pay another fare.

It was the same revolting scene day in and day out. And my uncle took a lot of buses. He worked his way through school with a newspaper delivery job, a supervisory job overseeing young black boys who delivered the afternoon *Alabama Journal* to Negro neighborhoods. He was a district circulation manager, which meant still more bus rides during the day. "I might have ridden the bus six times a day, seven days a week," he remembers. What he saw on those dusty old buses stuck in his craw. It offended anybody else with a sense of common dignity. However, like most other Negro passengers, he never intervened or commented on the practice.

From my point of view, many moons later, I didn't understand why people of color put up with it. I couldn't imagine ignoring the daily slights, the insults, suffering the humiliation. After all, there were more black than white riders on the buses. Why not revolt? A few did get fed up, yelled back at bus drivers, refused to move for white passengers, in their own individual protests. But in the late 1940s and early '50s, most black citizens in Montgomery had simply adjusted to southern traditions and went along with the status quo.

To get a deeper understanding of the times, and my uncle, I spent a lot of time talking to him about them in the years after I retired. He also graciously allowed me to tag along to many of his speaking engagements around the country, where other audiences were also interested in hearing about the events of Montgomery that launched a movement.

Fred and Thomas Gray overlapped at 'Bama State. Dad graduated in 1950 and played on the college football team. He majored in mathematics, minored in social studies, and managed to find time to become a member and basileus of Omega Psi Phi fraternity. "Come on, Teddy. You may as well pledge," my father had suggested. (No one, including my uncle, can tell me why now, but when he was young his friends nicknamed him Teddy. When my two brothers and I were growing up, we called him Uncle Teddy, which rolled off our tongues easier than Fred or Freddie.) At any rate, Dad's younger brother joined the fraternity, his membership no doubt sealed since his older brother was the chapter president.

Dad was more of a party animal than Fred. It's hard for me to see my uncle hanging out with a bunch of extroverted, hard-drinking, risk-taking frat boys. But he looked up to his brother and went along with the program. My mother, flouncing around in bobby socks and poodle skirts, was probably Dad's biggest distraction in those days. She graduated first. They were married before he got his degree.

In 1950 Harry S. Truman was president. Senator Joseph McCarthy launched his infamous witch hunt for American Communists. The price of gas was eighteen cents a gallon, though most households did not own a car. Families were moving from the city to the suburbs. And Montgomery, Alabama, was on the verge of a crisis it didn't see coming.

5

THE BROTHERS GRAY:
THE EARLY YEARS

By the time I was born in 1951, there was a small store in the front yard of my grandmother's house at 705 West Jeff Davis, years before she moved away to a bungalow near Alabama State. My father bought the store in 1946 after he got out of the navy, to help my grandmother bring in some extra income. They called it the Petite Grocery. While in the service, Dad and his brothers Hugh and Samuel, who both served in the army, all sent money home to assist with household expenses.

"They were good boys. Always thinking about their mother," my grandmother, Nancy Jones Gray Arms, would say. Everybody called her Mom. My brothers and I referred to our own mother as Momma when we were around my grandmother to avoid any confusion.

The street on West Jeff Davis was unpaved. The rare car passing by whipped up dust from the iron-rich Alabama red dirt. The house was wood framed, painted white, and sat on a foundation of concrete blocks. There were four bedrooms, two in the front and two down a long hallway in the back. A concrete sidewalk led up steps to a front porch. In the back was an outhouse.

With no hot water inside the house, bathing was a chilly ritual. Mom would boil vats of water on her gas stove and pour the water into a big tin tub she'd put in the middle of the living room to give her children

My father and his mother, Nancy Jones Gray Arms, at Uncle Teddy's home on West Edgemont in Mobile Heights, circa 1957.

a quick bath. Thankfully, years later, once Dad's radio and TV repair business got off the ground, he was able to afford to have a bathroom built inside Mom's house, with a porcelain toilet, bathtub, and sink with hot and cold running water.

The tiny grocery store was a much-needed gift. Mom could use the money. She attended school only up through sixth grade, staying home to care for younger siblings after her mother died and her father remarried. A widow for much of her adult life, she became a domestic, mostly cooking for well-to-do white families.

I'm not sure where Dad found the odd-looking structure he gave his mother, but it evolved into the neighborhood convenience store long before 7-Elevens. Somehow he convinced his friend Willie Cummings, who was known as Pee Wee, to help him drag the empty building from Dorsey Street up the hill that led to the house on West Jeff Davis. This was long before the luxury of U-Haul trucks. It was a hike. Finally, after huffing and puffing about a mile, they deposited it at the bottom of Mom's front step.

"What is that thing, and where'd you get it?" she asked as they pushed the tiny building into its place.

"Don't you worry your head about any of that," Dad told her. "It's for you. I'm going to help you make it into a small grocery store, and you're going to become a businesswoman."

"You are always up to something!" she replied. "You boys look like you could use some ice-cold lemonade and some fried chicken." Mom loved to feed people. Folks who lived in the neighborhood knew that. If anybody ever knocked on her door asking for food—and plenty of poor people who were hungry did—she would bring out a plate of whatever had been cooking on her stove. There was always enough for one more.

How bad could life be that a barefoot man, wearing clothes that were tattered and torn, would come knocking on a stranger's door, begging for food? I was always just a little frightened and uncomfortable each time I witnessed such a scene as a child, wondering if the man might be dangerous. Mom would not invite the beggar inside the house, but she lived her Christian faith and never turned anyone away. I remember watching in fear and amazement each time a man none of us knew would sit on her front step, devour one of her delicious meals as if he'd never seen food before, then thank her and walk away.

My grandmother's store was an oblong building made of tan fake-brick asphalt shingles. A tin roof came to a peak just above the front door. You had to climb two wooden steps to get inside. Three, maybe four people could fit inside comfortably. There were two small windows that you could barely see in or out of. The Petite Grocery was an odd-looking store.

One window on the front of the store faced the sidewalk leading to Mom's house. The other window looked out on the street, across the dusty road, to an empty red-dirt lot. People came by to purchase deli meats, bread, milk, eggs, and some canned foods. A big clear plastic jar with an aluminum screw-on top contained giant pieces of red-and-white peppermint. Lots of children stopped in to buy penny candy. It was a store on the poor side of town. It attracted kids and adults with little money to spare. Young and old, they would saunter down the street on a warm summer day, dressed in well-worn clothes, often not wearing shoes.

I loved to see my grandmother open the large, white, horizontal freezer in her grocery store. The oversized freezer chest took up much of the room in the store. It could have been five feet long and was just tall enough for me as a small child to peep over into it to discover the much-treasured Popsicles and ice cream bars inside. During the day, the store was padlocked shut until a customer stepped onto Mom's sidewalk and yelled out, "Miz Arms!" When my brothers and I were visiting, sitting on the front porch, which often meant Mom was babysitting, we would race inside to let my grandmother know it was time to open the store. The screen door let out a loud squeak as it swung open and slammed shut. My grandmother moved briskly from the kitchen out through the living room, often in her slippers. If Tommy, Freddie, and I had been good that day, we were rewarded with a piece of candy or maybe an ice cream bar. Rarely did any potential customers have to shout "Miz Arms" twice, whether we were there to announce them or not.

It was a long way for my uncle from that house on the west side of Montgomery to a law office in downtown Montgomery. It was a quicker drive to my father's appliance business at 1002 West Jeff Davis Avenue, way down on the other end of the street, the paved end, across the street from Loveless School, where most of Mom's children had attended elementary through high school. To get there, you had to pass row after row of shotgun houses and ramshackle shanties. As the years went by, I watched them decay. The people who lived inside didn't seem to notice as they sat in beat-up chairs on porches with missing planks, shouting "Howdy" to folks walking by.

Many of those homes don't exist anymore. Like my grandmother's house, they were mowed down by bulldozers in the 1970s, all casualties of urban renewal. Mom used the money the government paid for her house full of memories, with some additional financial assistance from her youngest son, Fred, to buy a new home on the east side of town, in a quiet neighborhood a block away from Alabama State, a mere two blocks away from where the rich white folks lived over in Cloverdale. It was a duplex she would leave to her children when she died; my brother Frederick used to live in one unit, and my brother Tommy and I called the other side of the house our crash pad when we were in town.

Over the years, as he became more successful, my uncle liked to remind people that he grew up in a "part of town that nothing good was supposed to come from." Growing up, Uncle Teddy was the family favorite. No doubt about it, though my grandmother would never admit to that. He was the baby, who got the most attention—from his mother and from his siblings. By the time Fred came along, he probably didn't get spanked. At least, he doesn't remember being on the receiving end of corporal punishment. If Mom had disciplined her other children, she was probably tired of wielding the rod by child number six. One of her earlier children, a girl, had died in infancy. I know my grandmother never took a belt to me or my brothers when we were around. But she had a way of looking at you that made you want to do the right thing.

My grandmother was extremely religious. She was an active member of Holt Street Church of Christ in Montgomery. So was her first husband, Abraham Gray. He was a carpenter who helped build the church. "Not only did he build the church," as Uncle Teddy tells it, "he used to round up the neighborhood kids to take them to Sunday school."

Church was a large part of the Gray children's lives. The siblings had been Sunday school teachers at Holt Street and served as deacons there. Fred preached his first gospel sermon there as a teenager and later served as an assistant minister.

Sadly, the Gray children knew tragedy young. Their father got sick in 1932, took to his bed, and died of pneumonia. The funeral obituary notes that on the Wednesday before he died, Abraham called his wife and children to his bedside for a farewell talk. He also summoned his sister Mary, who lived just down the street, to give her some final advice. Then he sent for the minister.

"Brother Busby," he said, "I want you to preach the word as you have been doing. And live a perfect life as you have been." Then Abraham Gray sang his favorite hymn.

> *God will take care of you,*
> *Through every day, o'er all the way;*
> *He will take care of you,*
> *God will take care of you.*

He died Friday morning, December 23, at 4:30 AM, leaving Nancy Gray at a loss as to how she would care for five children all by herself. Many years later, she would admit that she pondered taking her own life. But she pushed those thoughts aside out of concern about what would happen to her offspring. After all, the country was in the middle of the Great Depression. Everybody was poor. People were standing in lines for food. Somehow, she managed.

Mom became the family's main breadwinner. She filled her days cooking and cleaning for others. She baked and sold cakes and pies. For many years she was a housekeeper for a white woman named Betty Aldridge. I cannot imagine what it must have been like to be a domestic servant for a white person during the Jim Crow era. I did come to realize how black women who worked for very low wages as maids and cooks for white people navigated complicated worlds. Sometimes snubbed in society, many of those black women were still allowed to raise white children and were trusted enough to prepare white people's food. Strangely enough, bonds of friendship often developed between them.

In my grandmother's case, Betty Aldridge helped her name her youngest son. When Mom was pregnant in 1930, one of her own sisters suggested his name should be Fred Lee Gray. For whatever reason, Ms. Aldridge thought his middle name should be David, and according to Uncle Teddy, my grandmother changed the name on his birth certificate to read "Fred David Gray."

Mom walked long distances to get to work. Her other major job several years later was as a cook at a nursery school at Maxwell Field (now Maxwell Air Force Base), five miles away. She prepared meals for those children so she could put food on the table for her own kids, who pitched in at young ages to keep the household going, getting jobs as newspaper and drugstore delivery boys.

As a little boy, Uncle Fred would leave their house to meet his mother at the end of her workday, near the railroad tracks about a mile away. She had already covered several miles, walking through fields and paths, taking shortcuts to meet up with young Fred, who walked her the rest of the way home. "Boy, my feet are tired today," she would complain, then spout one of her favorite sayings, "There's no rest for the weary."

The Gray children certainly came from humble beginnings. The house they were born in was an extremely modest shotgun house on a short street with a great name: Hercules Street. It had a front porch and two rooms directly behind each other, a back porch, and a kitchen. They were called "shotguns" because if you fired one from the front door, the buckshot would travel straight through the rooms and out the back door. The bathroom was an outhouse near a wooden fence in the backyard. The first house the children knew had no running water, no telephone. They had no electricity and used kerosene lamps until after the kids had entered school.

But it was home. There were several red rose bushes, a pomegranate bush, and a chinaberry tree in the front yard. Two fig trees and a pecan tree were as tall as the house. Sweet potatoes, collard greens, turnips, and squash grew in a well-tended garden. There was a fenced-in yard for a small chicken house. And enough space for the kids to play.

There was nothing more fun than racing down to the westerly end of the street, drawn by the high-pitched wail of the whistle and rumblings of an approaching train.

"Hey, guys, it's coming," Dad would yell. They'd all go running, along with a handful of their friends.

The fabled Atlantic Coast Line railroad rolled its Dixie Line trains within earshot of their house. The Louisville and Nashville passenger train came through here too. But what the kids were most excited about were the freight trains. They could almost feel the clickety-clack of the oncoming boxcars, hear the roar of the engine. They sat on the hillside overlooking the tracks, waiting.

"Look, hobos!" somebody would scream when they saw homeless vagabonds sitting on the floor in an open boxcar. During the Depression, many of those who couldn't find work in their hometowns hopped trains, crisscrossing the country to look for work. Every now and then, the Gray boys would see a hobo trying to hitch a ride.

Two years after my grandfather passed away, my grandmother bought their next home, the four-room house at 705 West Jeff Davis Avenue. It was big enough to also house two other families to help pay expenses.

When my brothers and I were growing up, Dad tried to instill in us the value of work. "When I was a boy," he'd tell us, "I used to throw papers for the *Alabama Journal*." He also tossed a weekly newspaper called the *Grit* and the widely distributed black newspapers, the *Pittsburgh Courier* and the *Chicago Defender*. He was about ten or eleven. "We had to work to keep food on the table. I used to ride my bike as a delivery boy for High Street Pharmacy." His siblings also chipped in. Getting a job delivering newspapers or goods from stores was an easy way to scrub up a few nickels and dimes.

———————————

Trust in Him who will not leave you,
Whatsoever years may bring,
If by earthly friends forsaken
Still more closely to Him cling.

It was one of my grandmother's favorite hymns, "Hold to God's Unchanging Hand." I can see her sitting in a pew close to the front of the church, tapping a foot and clapping her hands, passing peppermint candy to the little ones sitting next to her to bribe them to behave. As certain as the sun shines, the Gray family was in church every Sunday morning. As they became old enough, the boys took leadership roles, reading from scripture, saying prayers, passing communion, collecting the offering.

It was at church that the family became acquainted with civil rights activist E. D. Nixon. His wife, Arlette, was a member of the congregation, and she also taught Sunday school classes. She was E.D.'s second wife. His first wife, Alease, the mother of his only son, E. D. Nixon Jr., died in 1934. The Nixon family lived on the west side of town, where lower-income blacks resided, though they had a stately, two-story brick home on Clanton Street. More well-to-do, college-educated blacks lived on the east side of town near Alabama State College.

Like I said, Mom's plan for her youngest child was for him to be a minister. On those days when my brothers and I gathered around my grandmother on her porch, she would regale us with stories about how she sent Fred away to high school at Nashville Christian Institute in Tennessee. NCI was a coed boarding school for black students that was run by members of the Church of Christ. It took money to get and keep Fred there, money largely raised by my grandmother and the ladies at Holt Street Church of Christ in Montgomery. They took a great interest in recruiting students for the school, selling hand-sewn aprons to help with tuition.

I can see Mom now, standing on her front porch wearing one of those aprons. Probably a floral print, with a long pocket along the bottom where you might tuck a small container of spice or a potholder as you worked around the kitchen. "I was the one who collected the money to send to NCI every month, near the first. We were very happy to help. The church took up special collections to help keep my son in NCI," she used to boast.

Mom told those stories about raising money to send Fred and other students to NCI so often that her daughter Pearl tape-recorded some of her oral histories. Aunt Pearl also wrote a book about the family church, *The History of the Holt Street Church of Christ and Its Role in Establishing Churches of Christ among African Americans in Central Alabama, 1928–1997*. It was a very long title, and Aunt Pearl was very proud of her work. She was convinced there was considerable interest in the topic. Whenever she visited a Church of Christ anywhere in the country, she would take along copies to sell and sign.

Marshall Keeble was NCI's dynamic president and a nationally recognized pioneer among black leaders in the Church of Christ. When traveling on school fundraising trips, he thought donors should see the product of their contributions. He saw a lot of promise in young Fred, so he took him and a few other outstanding students with him as "boy preachers" to help raise money for NCI.

Fred's siblings had noticed his interest in the ministry years earlier. Other kids liked to play hide-and-seek or pull wagons. Their little brother seemed obsessed with religious rituals and would practice being a preacher by baptizing dogs and cats.

The oldest of the Gray children, Abraham Samuel, is an intriguing part of my family history. He preferred being called Samuel and, as far as I have learned, he lived much of his life passing for other than

African American, though no one in the family said it out loud. After graduating from high school in 1938 as valedictorian, the only job he could get under President Roosevelt's New Deal programs involved a pick and a shovel, digging ditches. Some young white students got jobs in offices. Offended by the racism, he left Montgomery. He moved in with my grandmother's sister, Aunt Adella, known as Big Sis, in Republic, Pennsylvania, and vowed never to return. Cousin Donna (Dean), who now lives in suburban Maryland outside Washington, DC, remembers being impressed by his intelligence and grasp of history.

Samuel became a Muslim and changed his name to Hassan Ghandhistani, which didn't sit well with my grandmother. She didn't care who heard her say, "I'm not calling him that. I named him Samuel. I'm calling him by the name I gave him." But eventually, she and the rest of the family grew accustomed to referring to him as Hassan.

Hassan Ghandhistani, né Abraham Samuel Gray, kneeling to pray in his apartment in Philadelphia.

Hassan straightened his hair and learned to speak Arabic and, they say, several other languages. He spoke with an accent that sounded almost British. If you met him, you'd assume he was a foreigner. He was a psychologist and private tutor who wrote several books. During his later years he told people he was born in the Maldives. He did eventually return to Alabama, but only briefly to visit his mother and siblings.

My grandmother had high expectations for all her children. Despite her own lack of formal education, she valued it deeply, insisting that each of her children get an education. She instilled in all five of them that they could be anything they wanted if they would do three things: "Keep Christ first. Get a good education. Stay out of trouble." For the most part, they took her advice. Uncle Teddy also added and nurtured a secret promise he kept to himself.

The five Gray siblings, from left to right: Hassan Ghandhistani, Thomas Gray, Pearl Gray Daniels, Hugh Gray, and Fred Gray.

Brothers Thomas and Fred were six years apart and as different as night and day. Older brother Tom was outgoing and fun-loving, though sometimes quick to show a flash of temper. And boy was he a snappy dresser, always sporting the latest trends. (Fred was stylish in his own way, dapper in the more traditional sense of the word.) My father had a penchant for dark-colored, loose-fitting coats with broad shoulders and wide lapels. And loved oversized apple caps. In college many of his best buds called him "Big Apple Tony." I don't know where the "Tony" came from, but his friends did tease him about those caps. He liked to fish, and sometimes after my brother Tommy was old enough, Dad would wake him up in the wee hours of the morning to go to his favorite lake or stream to catch catfish and big mouth bass. Dad also liked to hunt, small game mostly, like rabbits and squirrels, which my grandmother would skin and cook. I can remember they tasted kind of like chicken but with a gamey tang. At some point my mother made Dad get rid of his guns because she thought they weren't safe around young children.

Fred, the baby boy of his siblings, was more serious and spent more of his time as he grew up concentrating on his books. He wore glasses and looked studious, but would soon dream of how he could transform the segregated world he lived in.

6

REDISCOVERING MONTGOMERY

THE FRIENDLY SUPPER CLUB: the name conjures up images of a cozy, dimly lit lounge for late evening dinner and cocktails, with patrons listening to local singers crooning old standards. But the Friendly Supper Club in Montgomery is something else altogether.

When I arrived in my old hometown in July 2014, my cousin Deborah Gray said, "Your timing is perfect. The Friendly Supper Club meets tonight." It just happened to be the first Monday of the month. To learn more about the past, I would take a close look at Montgomery present and connect with people familiar with what had gone on before.

It was fitting that I was meeting up with Deborah. She's my uncle Fred's eldest child and the person I turn to most for help and guidance on Alabama history, to find out what's happening with my Alabama relatives, and to discover where to go and what to do in the hometown I had left behind many years ago.

Deborah is petite like me. She's not as obnoxiously outgoing as I can be, but we're both ambitious in our own ways, and fiercely independent. She is the managing director of the Tuskegee Human and Civil Rights Multicultural Center, also known as the Tuskegee History Center. It was created after my uncle helped convince President Bill Clinton to make a public apology for the Tuskegee Syphilis Study, as a permanent memorial to the victims and to document other lesser-known local civil rights history. The victims' names are etched in stone in a circle on the floor of the museum.

Deborah and I became close friends as adults. When we were young children, we saw each other infrequently because my family moved away to Cleveland after the bus boycott. We saw Uncle Teddy and his family when we visited Montgomery, usually once a year, during the summer. They were in Cleveland on rare occasions.

In that summer of 2014, Deborah picked me up at the house that used to be my grandmother's old duplex on Terrace Avenue. She drove us just around the corner to the faculty dining lounge at Alabama State University. Our destination, the Friendly Supper Club, was not a place. It's a dinner meeting of blacks and whites that began after a racial incident in Montgomery in 1983.

The circumstances of the so-called Todd Road Incident are unclear. One day in late February 1983, two white plainclothes police officers chased a young black man into a house in a black section of town. The family inside, including out-of-town mourners, had gathered after a funeral. Shots were fired. The young man chased into the house may have been struck. A bloody confrontation followed. When it was all over, the two police officers had been beaten, and one of them had been shot. Family members said they thought the plainclothes officers were burglars. One of the policemen said he thought he was chasing a drug suspect. Both sides claimed to be victims. Eleven of the family members were charged with crimes ranging from attempted murder to kidnapping and robbery. Some said they suffered beatings in jail. After a polarizing trial, the white officers were acquitted of any wrongdoing. Charges against seven of the family members were dropped. There was no further attempt to prosecute the remaining four. The racial tension spilled over into the community.

The formation of the Friendly Supper Club in May 1983 was an attempt to improve race relations in town. An anonymous person sent a letter to one hundred Montgomery residents, inviting them all to dinner. The letter was signed "Jack Smith." No one seems quite sure who "Jack Smith" was, though people have theories. Recipients of the mysterious letter were each asked to bring a guest of another race. The intention was to get people together socially, with no agenda except to open lines of communication. The opposite race rule has loosened, but the membership remains interracial. The club still meets. Members, who can be anyone who wants to attend, spend seven dollars each for a cafeteria meal.

"Well, hello. It's great to see you," said Rev. Robert Graetz as we walked inside. He and his wife, Jeannie, exchanged hugs with us.

"I was hoping you would be here. I want to talk to you," I said. They were just the people I needed to consult for insight. They are lifelong civil rights activists and had been close friends over the years with my parents.

As club members gather each first Monday, hot food beckons from the buffet's stainless-steel service counter. You can see the steam rising and smell the fragrant aromas of roasted turkey and baked fish, rice and brown gravy, fresh green beans and corn. I leaned over the person pushing a tray along in front of me and called out to my cousin, "Deborah, save me a seat next to you." She was already heading for a spot near the Graetzes. Before sitting down at tables in the dining hall, we all passed down the line and served ourselves salad, slices of cake or pie, and iced sweet tea.

As I sat down with my tray, Jeannie told me, "I want to know more about your road trip. I really want to hear more about your new boyfriend." Jeannie didn't pull her punches.

The summer of 2014 was not my maiden introduction to the Friendly Supper Club. My parents had taken me to supper club dinners on several occasions. On the fiftieth anniversary of the Montgomery bus boycott, December 5, 2005, I did a news story about the boycott at my TV station in DC. I mentioned that some residents were still concerned about improving Montgomery's racial situation fifty years after the fight to integrate the buses. The story included interviews with my father and NewSouth Books publisher Randall Williams, who I don't believe ever misses a meeting of the Friendly Supper Club. He is a white journalist and civil rights activist who organized the Klan Watch Project for the Southern Poverty Law Center, where he says he watched and wrote about racists.

At other Friendly Supper Club dinners while I was researching my book, I met Alabama trial attorney Julian McPhillips Jr. A white attorney, he's known as a lawyer for the people, a man with a reputation for being an advocate for the underdog and defender of the wrongly accused. The couple of times I saw him, he was late, but he made an entrance with a lot of bluster and strong opinions. When his book *Civil Rights in My Bones* was released in 2016, I was honored to have him autograph it for me at a book signing. He wrote, "What a great heritage and family you have with Thomas Gray as your father and Fred Gray as your uncle."

Dot Moore is another notable Friendly Supper Club diner. Casually stylish with a shock of curly white hair, you always know when she's there. She, too, has strong opinions on many subjects. She is somewhat hard of hearing and speaks very loudly to be heard. Diners like her because they're bound to be amused by her. When I first met her and she learned I was Fred Gray's niece, she announced to the table, "You know, he's not just a famous civil rights attorney, he's also a preacher. A Church of Christ preacher. You know at the Church of Christ, they don't have piano or organ music at the services." Then she looked over at me and said, "Where do you attend church?"

The question was an assumption that comes naturally in the Bible Belt. I could have given a more appropriate answer, but I went for the laugh: "Mattress Baptist," implying no doubt irresponsibly, in the heart of the Bible Belt, that on Sundays I was probably in bed asleep.

But Dot Moore is not one to take lightly. A widely recognized civil rights activist, former teacher, and author, she is immortalized in an oral history conducted by liberal do-gooder Virginia Durr on tape at the Alabama Department of Archives and History. I know that because Dot Moore steered me to that tape collection herself. It was after a book reading at the archives by widely respected archives director emeritus Ed Bridges. I read a lot of books and attended a lot of book events to learn more about Montgomery's civil rights history, and often, selfishly, to learn more about the life of authors because I wanted to one day be one. That day, after members of the audience streamed out into the hallways of the beautiful neoclassical building, Moore and I had a brief chat about the book I was writing. Then, suddenly, she pointed to the end of the hall toward the huge room that is the repository of Alabama's archival records and told me more than once, "You need to go down there and tell them to get you Virginia Durr's oral histories." She was insistent, and it was worth it.

Durr interviewed many local civil rights activists, including Moore. I listened to her oral history on headsets in the archives' research room. Moore moved to Montgomery when she was in high school. Her parents bought the Green Lantern, a roadhouse restaurant and nightclub that was popular with politicians. They sent her off to boarding school. She went to college at Montevallo and met more "liberal people."

After marrying an architect and teaching at Lanier High School, she became an activist with the Democratic Party and developed an interest in women voting. "The League of Women Voters was interesting, but not integrated," she says on tape. "There were some Jewish women in it. Women from Maxwell Field. Their husbands were doctors, lawyers, professional people," according to Dot. The women were very liberal and educated. "We got people to help us register women and work against the poll tax in the early 1950s," says Moore. That's when they got to know Rufus Lewis, the black coach at Alabama State, another voting rights activist. He was the owner of the Citizens Club, the nightclub that required you to be a registered voter to become a member. Durr's oral histories and the memories of the other very interesting people who attend those monthly meetings of the Friendly Supper Club contributed mightily to my quest for knowledge about Montgomery during the bus boycott.

As I finished my meal that first 2014 visit with the Supper Club, Jeannie Graetz said, "What are you doing tomorrow? We want you to go with us to a meeting of One Montgomery."

I had never heard of One Montgomery. Like the Friendly Supper Club, it is a group of concerned citizens formed after the Todd Road Incident. It meets for breakfast at seven o'clock every Tuesday morning across the street from Jackson Hospital, on an upper floor of a rather bland-looking medical building that houses doctors' offices. One Montgomery hosts newsmakers and community leaders for frank conversations. The aim, again, is to promote trust and understanding between people of different racial and ethnic backgrounds. I joined the group to learn more about the city, past and present. Members were eager to help.

Ed Bridges, the director emeritus of the Alabama Department of Archives and History, who has written a book about the state's history (*Alabama: The Making of an American State*), was a rich resource. Tom Clifford, then the executive editor of the *Montgomery Advertiser* newspaper, was the speaker at a One Montgomery breakfast I attended. During a later conversation over lunch, he invited me to become a contributor to the paper's Alabama Voices opinion page column. I wrote about subjects connected to race, about new revelations about the bus boycott, about honors and awards bestowed on my uncle. In the December 21, 2014, edition of the paper, this was my first column:

Churches Rise Once Again to Call for Justice

It was an impressive procession of choir members from the Morning Pilgrim Missionary Baptist Church last Sunday—all dressed in black parading into the front rows at Dexter Avenue King Memorial Baptist Church. This was the 137th anniversary of the church, renamed after its most famous pastor, Martin Luther King, Jr., the slain leader of the nonviolent revolution against segregation. The Rev. James Watts, Morning Pilgrim's pastor, was the guest speaker.

Setting the tone for the afternoon's program, Deacon Sidney Brown urged the church body to "remember our sons slaughtered by police. Maybe we can survive what this church has fought so hard for," he said.

"You all have an impact. We need to help our youth."

Parishioners sang a stirring rendition of the Negro National Anthem, "Lift Every Voice and Sing," which resonated with Dexter Avenue's pastor, Rev. Cromwell Handy. The song, he said, was especially appropriate given the rash of injustices taking place against black men across the nation:

> Lift every voice and sing.
> Till earth and heaven ring,
> Ring with the harmonies of Liberty;
> Let our rejoicing rise,

High as the listening skies,
Let it resound loud as the rolling sea.
Sing a song full of the faith that the dark past has taught us,
Sing a song full of the hope that the present has brought us.
Facing the rising sun of our new day begun,
Let us march on till victory is won.

As part of the proceedings, a video was presented showing how Dexter Avenue Baptist Church, which had its origins as an abandoned slave depot, had been involved in voting rights drives and other NAACP actions.

It pleased me on Sunday to see clergy and church members still active and heeding the call to participate in this week's National Black Solidarity Day, also called Black Lives Matter Sunday. I am a Montgomery native, back after many decades away from the city.

Full disclosure: I have inherited a history of family involvement in the civil rights movement. My uncle, Fred Gray, is the lawyer who represented King and Rosa Parks during the Montgomery Bus Boycott. My father, Thomas Gray, was a founding board member of the Montgomery Improvement Association, which coordinated that social protest.

I was four years old then, too young to remember the mass meetings. But I was reminded Sunday that African American churches are at the forefront of the modern day civil rights movement—as they were at the birth of the boycott.

It was refreshing and uplifting to once again see churches making their voices heard in an outpouring of anger over the recent deaths of two unarmed black men, Michael Brown and Eric Garner, at the hands of white police officers.

"We've been marching a long time for a whole lot of things," said Watts.

"We're starting marching, all over again."

Montgomery has come a long way since Bloody Sunday in March of 1965, when African Americans seeking voting rights were violently attacked by police as they tried to march from Selma to Montgomery.

Yes, the buses and public facilities are integrated, blacks have more education and job opportunities, and we are increasingly elected to political office. But the benefits of progress have been mixed for the black community, he said. As access into the community as a whole opened up many black-owned businesses failed as their clientele flocked to white establishments.

And now as the 50th anniversary of the Selma-to-Montgomery March looms, persistent issues such as questionable police tactics against blacks and restrictive voter ID laws remain as barriers to even more meaningful progress.

"But we survived the march," said Rev. Watts. "We're still in the shadow of the Capitol."

And what of the call for justice in the wake of the police killings? Some have expressed concern about the lack of local outrage from college-aged students to events in Ferguson and New York City. Nobody seems to want to be quoted, but people I have spoken to blame student apathy, a lack of leadership and even fear of retribution by area university authorities.

Much of the world was watching the Selma March almost 50 years ago. Today, with cellphone videos and the growing popularity of body cameras for police officers, the whole world can watch instantaneously.

President Obama announced a plan to fund cameras for 50,000 police officers nationwide. Will body cameras and readily available cellphones result in greater accountability? Advocates believe they will. We can only hope.

I was thrilled to have the opportunity to express my personal opinions in the newspaper. Most of my career had been reporting news stories objectively and not taking sides.

———————————

If I knew one thing growing up it was this: Montgomery and the rest of the Deep South had once been a hate-filled place. It was not a place I thought I wanted to live after my family moved north to Cleveland not long after the boycott. When my brothers and I graduated from college, I didn't understand why my parents opted to return to Alabama. But after I spent a month in Montgomery on that retirement road trip, and on frequent trips afterward, I began to see that my parents felt proud of how the city had changed over time. In their own way, they claimed some responsibility for the transformation. Me, I was just beginning to get reacquainted with the place where I was born.

7

LUNCH WITH ROSA

My uncle Fred returned to Montgomery with a law degree in hand from Western Reserve University in Cleveland. In September 1954, he had passed the Ohio and Alabama bar exams and became Montgomery's second African American attorney, after Charles Langford, who later became his law partner. He became somewhat of a local celebrity as he ventured out to set up a solo practice. My two younger brothers and I were always thrilled when Uncle Teddy came to visit. Six decades later, and probably somewhat to his amusement, I still call him Uncle Teddy.

Whenever he visited our house in Mobile Heights when I was a child, he always made a dramatic entrance. He would walk in the front door, raise his right hand as if he were about to swear to tell the truth on a Bible in court, and, prophetically, exclaim one word: "Peace!"

On a typical autumn day in Montgomery, it was hot, and the fan in the window barely stirred a breeze. Fred Gray sat in his barren new office space downtown on the second floor of 113 Monroe Street. In September 1954 he was twenty-three and a man on a mission.

The offices were in the back, above the Sears, Roebuck and Company auto shop. It was a sublet, fifty dollars a month, courtesy of Dr. Solomon S. Seay Sr. Reverend Seay was the secretary-treasurer of the home mission department of the African Methodist Episcopal Zion Church, and he used the offices in the front. Reverend Seay became Fred's friend and adviser. I don't remember much about the office except that the steps were a steep, difficult climb for a little girl visiting with her parents.

My uncle was broke, living with his mother—my grandmother—in her sizeable but modest house on the west side of town. But soon as he was able, he bought himself a car. The first one, a Ford, he got from my father, who purchased a Plymouth for himself and was happy to let Fred pick up the remaining monthly payments on the Ford. Uncle Teddy had not forgotten about those days when his only transportation choice was city buses.

On most weekdays around noontime, he had lunch with Rosa Parks. He met her when he attended meetings of the NAACP looking to drum up business and to make connections that would help him on his journey to desegregate Alabama. Parks was very connected. She was the secretary of the Montgomery chapter of the NAACP and adviser to its youth council. The organization was then headed up by E. D. Nixon, who in addition to his other political ties had also organized the Alabama Voters League. Nixon trusted and depended on Parks to do most of his secretarial work, and from her position handling the papers and taking phone calls for those organizations, she learned the lay of the land about local politics and racial matters. And, it turned out, unbeknownst to many, she became an all-important field investigator for the NAACP.

As assistant to the tailor at the Montgomery Fair department store, Parks worked about a block and a half away from Fred's downtown office. Montgomery Fair was a white-owned store that got a fair amount of business from black shoppers. Like at most white stores in the city, except the Jewish-owned shops in the Monroe Street corridor, the usual "rules" applied to nonwhite shoppers. The Jewish stores welcomed black business, accepted their checks, and even extended layaway credit to those who could not pay full price at purchase. In other white-owned stores, if there was a line, white customers were served first. Negro ladies were sometimes required to cover their heads before trying on a hat.

My father's preference throughout his life was to shop at black-owned businesses when at all possible. He encouraged his children to do the same. But there weren't enough black businesses in Montgomery to handle all our shopping needs. When the Normandale Shopping Center opened as the city's first mall, we began to shop there, because the stores were more welcoming of Negro clientele—though some white employees and customers still looked at us with disdain.

My strongest shopping memory as a child is going with my mother to Normandale for back-to-school clothes when I was entering second grade. I was appalled in Loveman's department store when Mom shouted at me across an aisle, "Do you need more drawers?" I was totally embarrassed that she didn't refer to them with a more dignified "underwear" or "panties" in front of white people.

Rosa Parks may have worked at Montgomery Fair, but she couldn't bear the thought of eating there. She wrote about the dismal conditions for its black employees later in life—her personal papers reveal a side to Rosa Parks most people are only beginning to discover. The department store had a lunch counter, but Negroes were not served meals there, even though the cooks were black and so were the dishwashers. It was a slight that store employees of color suffered daily—they were forced to eat in a small room next to the restroom. The door between the toilet and that dining room couldn't be closed tightly enough to shut.

But Parks would have had other things on her mind when she climbed the stairs to the second floor of 113 Monroe Street. She would walk down the long hallway to Fred's back office.

"Miz Rosa, how are you doin' today?" Fred greeted her. Like most southern gentlemen, he usually affixed a title of respect to a woman's first or last name. As I grew older, he often called me Ms. Karen.

"I'll be better when I sit down and take a load off my feet," Mrs. Parks responded and smiled softly.

She wore a modest but nicely tailored two-piece suit with a blouse that had a frilly collar tied in the front with a thin ribbon. Her long hair was pulled back and tucked under a hat and, of course, there were sensible shoes. She sported what would become her signature wire-rimmed eyeglasses. She often carried a black pocketbook and a brown bag containing her lunch. Uncle Teddy and Rosa Parks shared some common goals.

Rosa Parks no doubt noticed one day soon after my uncle first opened his office that the wall of books was gone. His fiancée, Bernice Hill, had only procured the books on loan for the office's grand opening. He had to give them back.

Bernice attended the Gail Street Church of Christ. My uncle knew her from his visits there and got to know her a bit when she was in school at Alabama State. One summer when he was home from law school, he really noticed her while he was working as a district manager on his old newspaper job. Bernice lived in the Victor Tulane housing project at 560 Smythe Curve. When he was in her neighborhood, "I recognized her," he told me. "I had seen her around and knew her by name."

He recalled that day she was sitting on her front porch, barefoot. He was out looking for newspaper boys, and she knew somebody who she thought might work out. Somehow, Fred couldn't get Bernice off his mind.

Bernice was a beauty. Skin caramel brown, bright eyes, shapely. She had been homecoming queen at Booker T. Washington High School. She was quick to smile and very independent. Or, as they used to say, she had a mind of her own. Uncle Teddy liked that about her. He used to bring her around to our house in Mobile Heights when they were dating. My brothers and I liked her. She was very friendly, and I guess she liked little kids. It wasn't long before she and Uncle Teddy got engaged.

Like many women of her day, her focus in college had been clerical skills. When Bernice had time, she would sometimes come in and act as Uncle Teddy's secretary, answering the phone and typing up correspondence. Bernice used to kid him about how sparse his office furnishings were. But they were both proud he had an office and was now one of the city's first black attorneys. Still, she knew he needed to make it look as if he were seriously in business. So Bernice called in a favor from the Elmores.

Nesbitt Elmore was a white lawyer in town, a nephew of the prominent Clifford Durr. Durr was also a lawyer, though a southern nonconformist. Born to privilege, he became a Rhodes Scholar, receiving his law degree from England's Oxford University. Durr and his wife, Virginia, were early fighters against racism and intolerance. During the 1940s the couple lived in Washington, DC, where Clifford Durr was a member of the Federal Communications Commission. That is, until he got a little too close to too many left-wing political associates and came under the surveillance of the FBI. When Durr returned to Montgomery, he was one of a handful of white liberals willing to defend African Americans in their struggle for equal rights. He became a mentor to my uncle, who credits Durr's behind-the-scenes assistance with helping make him a good attorney. Elmore was also a beneficiary of his uncle's legal expertise.

As he was preparing for his office's grand opening, Uncle Teddy's fiancée was doing some work for Nesbitt Elmore's wife, Jacqueline. Bernice asked Jackie if she could borrow some of her husband's law books for the upcoming reception. The Elmores were more than willing to assist. The opening was attended by friends, relatives, teachers, church members, and anybody who, by word-of-mouth, might aid my uncle in getting some clients. The reception was a hit, thanks also to family friend E. D. Nixon, whose political tentacles had a far reach. He attended the party, as did, of course, Nixon's NAACP secretary, Rosa Parks.

Books or no books, Rosa still liked to come by Fred's office for lunch. They discussed their similar objectives and aspirations. Both were sick of the white supremacist Jim Crow laws that enforced public segregation, and both wanted to do something about them. When she wasn't working altering clothes, Parks was busy counseling young people in the NAACP's Youth Council to become better adults. But her goal stretched beyond that. The council's stated mission was to train the youth leaders of tomorrow and to promote awareness of problems affecting people of color. The Youth Council was less like the Boy Scouts and more like the Student Nonviolent Coordinating Committee.

One thing that really got under Parks's skin was the fact that black residents were not allowed to check books out of the main branch of the public library downtown. She complained to my uncle that some of the students on her Youth Council stopped by the downtown library to get some books to use at school, but the librarian told them they couldn't take them out.

"She told them the books were for white students!" Parks said. "That just doesn't make any sense. They are just trying to get an education. And the Supreme Court has already ruled the public schools should be integrated. The public libraries should be too. Mr. Nixon and I are thinking we may suggest that they keep going downtown and trying to check out books until the librarian gives in," she said.

"Now don't be surprised if that doesn't happen," my uncle told her. "These practices are pretty entrenched. School officials are still ignoring *Brown v. Board of Education*. We may need more lawsuits to press the issue. And we really need to do something about the situation on the buses."

Speaking between bites of her egg salad sandwich, she agreed. "This bus segregation thing is just vicious. It's been going on too long, and it has got to stop."

He looked over at her, thinking as he often did that her quiet manner and almost schoolmarmish demeanor belied the intensity of her convictions.

"I have to ride the Cleveland Avenue bus downtown every day, and there's one driver who is just plain mean to all the colored people. He put me off the bus one day. It was in the winter. The bus was crowded with Negroes. I got on in the front and walked back through the crowd. When I turned around to look toward the empty seats in the front, the driver told me to get off and walk around to the back to get on. I don't know why I bothered to say anything to him, but I did. I told him I was already on the bus. What was the point in getting off to get back on? Well, he insisted, and when I got off, I decided not to get back on," she said.

"When was that, Mrs. Parks?" Fred asked.

"It was many years ago, but if something like that happens again, I may just refuse to move," she declared.

Fred let that sit while he digested it. He knew Parks was as determined as he was to somehow put an end to segregation. She wasn't just taking notes at NAACP meetings. She was also attending their out-of-town conventions and had even been sent to rural Abbeville, Alabama, in the 1940s to investigate and seek justice for Recy Taylor, a young black woman who was gang-raped at gunpoint by six white men. It was a story featured in the black press. Now she was indicating her willingness to become the face of a legal test case against segregation in Montgomery. He wanted her to know what she might be getting into.

"Now you know, Miz Parks, down in Mobile they have a system on the buses that seems to be working. Negroes are seated from the back toward the front. The whites are seated from the front to the back. And there is no section on the bus that must be kept open for either race. Something like that might work here.

"Also, your boss, Bruh Nixon, has been talking about that boycott they had over in Baton Rouge, Louisiana. He thinks it was an interesting tactic," my uncle said.

"The city council there passed a law saying seating on the buses would be first come, first served. That made the bus drivers mad. One day a Negro passenger refused to give up his seat to a white man. It caused a big ruckus. The colored churches organized a boycott. Told people not to ride the buses. It didn't last. They called it off after about two weeks, when the city came up with a compromise. But the new rules under the compromise still reserved some seats in the front for whites only."

"We must do something," she said emphatically.

"I agree," he said.

Fred and Rosa couldn't single-handedly solve the ugly racial dilemmas troubling the people of Montgomery, but they often discussed what actions they could take over sandwiches and fried chicken at lunch.

8

WHO WAS ROSA, REALLY?

WE ARE FINALLY DISENTANGLING the myth of Rosa Parks. For years, even she herself allowed the world to buy into the narrative of the frail, sweet, subdued seamstress who was just tired that day on the Montgomery bus.

I bought into it too, like everybody else. You've got to admit, it was a pretty good story, one that served the movement well. Over the years, civil rights leaders like Dr. Martin Luther King Jr., Rev. Ralph Abernathy, and other boycott leaders did not dispel the myth. They denied that Parks might have been an activist on her own or a plant by the NAACP to lay the groundwork for a test case of segregation. It wasn't until the 1970s and '80s that the country outside Alabama seemed to even care about Rosa Parks, and it wasn't until 1992 that she herself revealed more of the truth in her own book, *My Story*. Parks may have been soft-spoken and quiet, but her ideas about racial justice were progressive. So why didn't the male leaders of the civil rights movement reveal more to the public about the real Rosa Parks? Pure and simple, they didn't want to give up the spotlight to women.

My uncle added another reason in the 2013 edition of his book *Bus Ride to Justice*. "In part," he wrote, "I was honoring the understanding that developed from the beginning of the bus protest that Mrs. Parks' role should be carefully protected so that she would not be portrayed as some radical."

Now that her role in history is secure, my uncle says he is willing to admit she was a very strong-willed woman who was a dedicated activist. He writes, "She was a willing volunteer to make her place in history rather than as an accidental victim. Mrs. Parks was no more an accidental victim than I accidentally determined to become a lawyer and destroy segregation. We both did what we did with one major intent: to destroy segregation. And both of us have been successful."

In his public speeches, he also speaks more openly now about her role and their relationship. During those weekday lunches in the '50s, they began to talk about how a person should behave if arrested for refusing to give up a seat on a bus to a white person. About what the person's demeanor should be. How it was important not to become angry or belligerent. She knew what to do and was waiting for an opportunity to do it. Just as I had suspected, and before organizers, including my uncle, acknowledged it, there was a lot of planning going on before the boycott, or "protest" as the leaders called it, because boycotts were against the law in Alabama.

It was more than thirty years after the boycott that women like Parks and Jo Ann Robinson finally began to claim credit for their own historic roles, by writing their own stories.

I met Rosa Parks on several occasions as I grew up. Sadly, each time, I was too young and uninformed to have an intelligent conversation with her about her role in civil rights history. She visited my parents in the 1960s when we moved to an apartment in Cleveland. She may have been in town for a speaking engagement.

Many years later, she and her assistant Elaine Steele visited my folks in their home after they had moved back to Montgomery. They also stopped in on my aunt Pearl Gray Daniels on occasion when she lived in Montgomery. Rosa Parks autographed a copy of her book for me. She didn't seem very talkative on the occasions when I was in her presence. But there was a kind of serene calmness about her. She always struck me as a woman at peace with herself and the world around her.

Rosa Parks with Thomas Gray during a visit to the home of my aunt Pearl Gray Daniels on Westwood Drive in Montgomery.

At peace, not tired or exhausted. The impression we all had after she sprang into the national consciousness was that she was elderly and frail. But Parks was only forty-two years old when she ignored that order from bus driver James Blake. In *My Story* she says that, more than anything else, she was just "tired of giving in."

On the evening she was arrested, Fred Gray went to her home in the Cleveland Court Apartments to talk about her case with her and her husband, Raymond. Cleveland Court was a new nice place to live when the Parkses moved there in 1951. It was one of the first affordable housing projects built by the Montgomery Housing Authority (MHA). MHA had bulldozed a blighted section of houses at Cleveland Avenue and Mill Street to make way for the community.

I drove by there one day fifty-nine years later, sad to discover the complex was in a state of decay. It was surrounded by chain-link fencing. A huge billboard announced renovations. Neighbors and others wondered if the work would be completed by December 5, 2016, the sixtieth anniversary of the bus boycott. I got out of my rental car and walked past some parked heavy machinery to look at unit 634. Construction workers had obviously made progress. I wondered if security was tight enough to prevent more thefts. The summer before, the apartment and several others had been desecrated by thieves hunting for copper pipes and tubing. You'd think property associated with a civil rights icon would have been sacrosanct. Then again, I was reminded that some brute broke into Parks's home in Detroit during the summer of 1994 and assaulted and robbed her. Police said the man, reeking of alcohol, struck her in the face and fled with fifty dollars.

It wasn't as if Rosa Parks was a very public figure before her 1955 arrest. Outside of the local branch of the NAACP, few in Montgomery knew about her work to seek justice for a black rape victim in Abbeville, Alabama, which made headlines in the black press in 1944. My understanding is not many Alabamians who knew her were aware of that side of her. They didn't know much about her husband either. Raymond Parks was a barber, a handsome guy. He was very fair-skinned and could pass for white. What Rosa said she really liked about him was he was an activist in his own right, the first real activist she'd ever met.

Raymond Parks had been a longtime member of the NAACP when he met and married Rosa McCauley. He had been secretly involved with efforts to free the Scottsboro Boys in 1931. During the Great Depression, many people hopped the freight trains from towns to cities looking for work. There was a scuffle onboard a freight car traveling in Jackson County, Alabama, between some white teens and nine black teenagers. The black teens were later yanked off the train by police and taken to the nearby town of Scottsboro. They were falsely accused of raping two white women who were on the freight train themselves and trying to avoid arrest for riding without paying.

Raymond Parks apparently knew a thing or two about how dangerous it was to fight for civil rights. He tried to keep his involvement in the efforts to free the Scottsboro boys under wraps to protect his wife. Thanks to a massive justice campaign, the teens avoided execution and were eventually released.

When his wife was arrested, Raymond Parks wasn't too thrilled with the idea that she might become a test case to dismantle busing segregation. But for E. D. Nixon, Rosa's arrest was like a plum falling into his lap.

Nixon had been dreaming about the ideal circumstances to challenge segregation on the buses, and nothing could be more perfect. Rosa Parks was soft-spoken, gracious, had the right temperament and, as others did not know, a steely determination to stamp out segregation. E.D. could barely conceal his delight when he, Clifford Durr, and Durr's wife, Virginia, went to the jail to bail out Parks. In an oral history on record at the Alabama Department of the Archives and History, Virginia Durr says the evening they picked up Parks at the jail, the seamstress expressed an eager willingness to allow herself to be used to help set a legal precedent.

Unbeknownst to me and my little brothers living our quiet lives in Mobile Heights in the early and mid-1950s, everything was finally coming to a head. Something big was about to happen in Montgomery. Oppressed and long-suffering, the city's black population was on the cusp of a life-changing revolution. The problems in Alabama's capital had been

Graduating from kindergarten at Holt Street Baptist Church. I am the fifth student from the left.

brewing for years on the National City Bus Line. The segregated seating. The humiliating rules requiring colored passengers to pay their fare in the front, get off, and re-enter the bus from the back. White bus drivers driving off before Negro passengers could get back on. On top of which, no one had forgotten Hilliard Brooks.

Then in August 1955, teenager Emmett Till was murdered right next door in Mississippi. The black residents of Montgomery had had enough. They were finally poised to protest. They would boycott the bus line.

Jo Ann Robinson's Women's Political Council (WPC) had observed the challenges of segregated transportation in other cities. Council members watched the situation in Baton Rouge, Louisiana, very closely. The boycott there in 1953 lasted only two weeks and ended in a compromise that still left the two front-facing seats on buses for whites only and the long rear seat for Negroes only. The remaining seats were first come, first served. It remained a less than perfect, quasi-segregated arrangement.

E. D. Nixon often talked about the possibility of a boycott in Montgomery after that. "They did it in Baton Rouge, we can do it here," he was known to say. The WPC tossed out the idea in their ongoing meetings with the mayor and other white city officials about the problems on the buses. The conversation came up often between my uncle and Rosa Parks during those lunches in his downtown office. They discussed the hypotheticals, the what-ifs.

What if, for example, a white bus driver did ask her to give up her seat for a white person? Parks rather fancied the idea of refusing to move.

"Fred, I think it would be important for me to sit there quietly and not lose my temper," Parks said on several occasions when they broached the subject. My uncle agreed.

"I think I could be cool as a cucumber. I would just sit there and wait for the police to take me away," Parks would say. "And when they get to my seat, I'll just get up, so they don't have to drag me off." In later years in many speeches, accepting awards and honors for his role in the movement, Uncle Teddy would admit to helping prepare Rosa Parks for the day that made her famous.

By spring of 1955, momentum was building. Teenager Claudette Colvin knew her constitutional rights and had stood up for them. For her, the circumstances just weren't right. Then in October 1955, another young black girl was arrested for refusing to give up her seat to a white passenger. Mary Louise Smith was eighteen. She was convicted of violating segregation law and paid a nine-dollar fine.

There were others, all giving Rosa Parks the moral courage to take her place as the mother of the civil rights movement.

We are learning still more about what made Rosa Parks tick from her personal papers, originally on loan to the Library of Congress in Washington, DC, for ten years, and now a permanent gift. They include handwritten correspondence between Parks and her friends and relatives over the years, as well as her own writings after she left Montgomery. When the boycott ended she could no longer find work in the city, and so she and her husband moved to Detroit.

The personal papers depict more about Rosa Parks than most people ever knew. I used them as the basis for one of my opinion pieces in the *Montgomery Advertiser*:

> **Book Reveals New Aspects of Rosa Parks**
> She said, "I would rather be lynched than live to be mistreated." She felt "oppressed by white supremacy," and "deprived of a proper education." Those quotes are the writings of Rosa Parks, personal notes scribbled on papers that can now be found in an eye-opening collection housed at the Library of Congress in Washington, DC.
>
> Nearly six decades after Parks' quiet but defiant refusal to give up her seat to a white man on a Montgomery city bus, we are now discovering that the seemingly timid and reserved seamstress who became the *Mother of the Modern Civil Rights Movement* was even more of an activist and more radical in her thinking than we knew. She died in Detroit in 2005 at the age of 92. Her niece Sheila McCauley Keys tells me she is thrilled the public can now learn more about a woman Keys believes was "ahead of her time." Ms. Keys says she's also glad "her personal things are housed in a protected place."

The Rosa Parks Collection made its way to the Library of Congress after a bruising estate battle between Parks' relatives and the Rosa and Raymond Parks Institute for Self-Development in Detroit, co-founded by Mrs. Parks' longtime friend, Elaine Steele. It is on loan for 10 years from the Howard G. Buffett Foundation. Buffett paid millions for the personal papers, letters and keepsakes, including her Presidential Medal of Freedom and Congressional Gold Medal and books. The Library of Congress says there are approximately 1,500 items which had been sitting in a New York City auction house for years until a Michigan court authorized their sale as part of the estate settlement.

Keys and about a dozen other nieces and nephews collaborated on a new book, *Our Auntie Rosa*, released in 2015 with a private view into the life of the woman they knew when she moved to Detroit after the bus boycott that made her famous. At a book signing event at the Library of Congress, the family members said they wrote the book to help them grieve her loss.

Their book is a loving portrait of Mrs. Parks, who along with her husband, Raymond, moved in with her brother's family in Detroit when neither was able to find work in Montgomery after the boycott. Mostly it's a family story, which reveals, "Auntie Rosa was a true Southern cook" and includes recipes like her Corn-bread Silver Dollar Griddle Cakes. The story is told with adoration of Parks' place as a civil rights icon, but also touches on specific aspects of her human rights activism. It speaks of her role as more than just a secretary for the NAACP, and recounts how as early as 1944 she was sent by the organization to Abbeville, Alabama, to investigate the case of Recy Taylor, a black woman allegedly raped by six white men. Even after reported confessions, a jury refused to indict. The book says Parks helped "launch a commit-tee to spread the word" which resulted in petitions that went to the governor's office in an unsuccessful attempt to seek justice.

In the collection at the Library of Congress, new and even more surprising details emerge about the extent of Parks' activ-ism in a lifelong crusade for social justice. Her anger about racial segregation and white supremacy is palpable. Keys and her relatives spent some time going through some of the boxes of materials at the Library of Congress. When I interviewed her later she said she was "astonished" and "amazed" to see there was another side of her Auntie Rosie, she'd never seen before. A side Keys saw, for example, in the love letters she wrote to her husband, Raymond, when they were apart. "She called him my darling husband," Keys says. "In her letters she missed him. She liked to hear his voice."

The papers include musings by Parks when she was apparently trying to decide what to put in her autobiography. She wrote, "I wonder if I should write about all the intimacies of the past. What will people think? If I write it all."

Parks writes at length in a firsthand account of a teenager about a near-rape incident at the hands of a white neighbor. Describing what happened Parks pens, "He offered me a drink of whiskey, which I promptly and vehemently refused." "He moved nearer to me and put his hand on my waist." In the narrative Parks refers to the man as "Mr. Charlie." She speaks of feeling "trapped and helpless," "sickened through with anger and disgust," but refuses to give in. In the end she says "Mr. Charlie got the idea that I meant no."

The story is stirring controversy and raising questions about whether this dramatic event prompted Parks' passion for activism. Brooklyn College historian Jeanne Theoharis in her book *The Rebellious Life of Mrs. Rosa Parks*, does acknowledge that "with no clear-cut conclusion to the story, it is not evident what transpired." Theoharis says, "Whether fully or partially true, the piece is a remarkable elucidation of Parks' political philosophy."

Author and Alabama historian Richard Bailey believes Parks "may very well have been writing about something that happened to her," which she didn't report at the time "for fear something might happen to her or her family."

When I asked Keys about the story, she said Parks "didn't write fiction. She wrote truth." But she's conflicted about what might have occurred. "I don't know if my aunt was almost raped," or if she was taking down information about the young women she was investigating as a detective of sorts for the NAACP.

As for Parks' courageous stand that day on a Montgomery city bus, Bailey says many people felt her anger but knew the repercussions if they vented those feelings publicly. He says if it hadn't been her, it would have been someone else. "Segregation was on its deathbed."

So as the debate rages now about the proper place for the Confederate flag and whose face should be on the next $10 bill, it may be a good time to reframe the image of Rosa Parks and acknowledge her as a more complex figure, a lifelong warrior for black freedom and women's rights.

That article ran in the July 19, 2015, edition of the *Advertiser*, four years before the Library of Congress used the collection to create an intimate look at Parks's life in the exhibit *Rosa Parks: In Her Own Words*. The exhibit, which was opened to the public in December 2019, included her account of staying awake nights as a child, keeping vigil with her grandfather as he sat up with a shotgun to protect the family from Ku Klux Klansmen, who rampaged through the countryside burning Negro churches and schools. "I wanted to see him kill a Kluxer," she said. Other highlights from the exhibition included political buttons, brochures, and photographs, including one picture on her seventy-seventh birthday with her Alabama friends Virginia Durr, Johnnie Carr, and Fred Gray.

The new exhibit was launched with a program that included a moving tribute by Georgia congressman John Lewis, who said, "I don't know where we'd be if not for Rosa." He called her "one brave woman." Fred Gray also delivered remarks, saying that Rosa would want us to continue the task of taking affirmative action to destroy racism.

9

THE KKK CHAPTER

"THE KKK IS COMING! THE KKK IS COMING! COMING TO MOBILE HEIGHTS TO GET WINSTON CRAIG!"

I was reading from papers I had lifted from tan legal file folders in a brown metal filing cabinet in what used to be my dad's home office, a cabinet overflowing with legal documents, letters, and old photos. Some had accumulated a layer of dust, just enough to elicit a sneeze. I was going through them one day after he passed away from cancer on April 28, 2011. I settled back and lost myself in his vivid telling of the story. The first two lines were written just like that: typewritten, in all caps. They were part of a prologue to a manuscript he had started. It saddened me that my father never lived to see his story come to life on the pages of a book.

It was early November, either 1954 or 1955. There was word around our neighborhood in Mobile Heights that the Ku Klux Klan intended to pay an unwelcome visit.

The trouble started after E. D. Nixon invited New York congressman Adam Clayton Powell Jr. to Montgomery to help register blacks to vote. Powell, a congressman who happened to be a man of color, didn't hesitate to say yes. A political maverick, a feisty and outspoken civil rights activist, Powell gave a rousing speech about voting rights on the campus of Alabama State College.

But his visit ruffled the feathers of the local Ku Klux Klan, especially after then governor James "Big Jim" Folsom invited Powell to the governor's mansion for drinks. Folsom was a kind of earthy folk hero to some of the people of Alabama. A populist, two-term governor, he was a racial moderate who advocated for voting rights for Negroes. He was elected to a second, nonconsecutive term despite a paternity scandal and a reputation for kissing the ladies at campaign rallies—some called him "Kissin' Jim."

To add to the Klan's rancor, Powell was driven around in a limousine by the governor's black chauffeur, Winston Craig. Big Jim ignored calls from the KKK to fire Craig, who lived in my neighborhood, right around the corner. Somehow word filtered out that the KKK was coming to Mobile Heights one night "to get" Craig.

None of that sat well with my father or Craig's other neighbors. Many of the men living in Mobile Heights were veterans, including Dad's business partner, William Singleton.

One day after the rumor about the KKK coming started to spread, Dad and Singleton were at Dozier's working on some radios in the repair room in the back of the store. Dad looked over and said, "We can't let no Klan come up in our neighborhood and threaten us."

"You're right about that," Singleton replied.

I don't know if the KKK realized it, but many of those black veterans living in Mobile Heights had guns and knew how to use them. They were ready to take on the Klan. My father and many of his friends also hunted small game for sport. And they were not about to let some robed vigilantes encroach on their home turf.

Several of the men decided to form what my uncle Fred calls an "impromptu guard committee" to keep watch. Before any committee members went out on duty, Craig came to their meeting and told everybody the governor was sending highway patrolmen out in an unmarked car to help protect him.

The way Dad saw it, that would mean two "friendly" cars were somewhere out in the neighborhood patrolling, on the lookout for the KKK—one driven by Mobile Heights residents, the other by the highway patrol.

The organized patrols, two men in a car, would drive and watch for four-hour intervals. Other patrolmen would stand guard at likely entrances into Mobile Heights.

Singleton and another neighbor, Marion Smiley, an educator who later became president of the H. Councill Trenholm State Technical

College, were among the first of the patrols, out riding in a dark-green, four-door Mercury sedan. After driving around awhile in the evening, just after dusk, they stopped by Singleton's house to get coffee.

No one could have predicted what happened next. Dad wrote, "Singleton got out of the car, but on his way into the house, a highway patrol cruiser pulled up in front of his walkway."

Singleton and Smiley had not noticed the patrolmen's car following them. But as soon as their car stopped, the cruiser stopped right behind them on Mobile Drive. One of the officers climbed out of the police vehicle, walked into Singleton's yard, and said, "Hey fella, do you mind stepping over here for a minute?" Singleton began to walk over to the officers' car. The officer said, "Ask your buddy to come over too." Well, when the "buddy" opened the car door and the interior dome light came on, the officers could see guns in the car—rifles. Both of the policemen drew their own weapons and lined Singleton and Smiley up outside the house. The officers frisked the two men and discovered Singleton had a .45 handgun in his pocket.

Singleton and Smiley were taken to jail. Years later I talked about the incident with Singleton's oldest son, William III, whom we always called Bimbo. He remembers how frightened his mother was that night. Bimbo was just a tot then, around four years old, but he recalls hearing his mother's harried phone calls. He later found out they were discussing bail for his father.

One of the people Bernice Singleton was talking to was my father. He had been assigned the second drive/watch duty along with Frank "Moon" Taylor, the owner of a Montgomery dry cleaning business who lived just down the street. The loud ringing of the telephone awakened Dad early from his prewatch nap. It was Singleton. "Tom, I want you to come bail me out of jail," he said.

"Jail?" Dad said, abruptly jolted from his slumber.

"Yeah, I've been charged with carrying a concealed weapon," his partner told him.

He wanted Dad to go by the shop and get forty dollars out of the cash register to bail him out, then to pick up Smiley's brother Theodore to get bail money for him as well.

Dad was surprised by the turn of events but tried to be as helpful as possible. He told Singleton, "I'm a property owner. Do you think those birds would let me use a personal bond?" But their conversation was interrupted by a third voice they heard on the line saying, "These birds ain't gonna let you do nothing."

The police were listening in on their conversation. Still, Singleton asked my father to pick up the bail money. Before heading downtown to the jail, Dad called another member of the watch group and suggested that the committee members take their patrol off the streets. They couldn't trust the highway patrol now. He thought they should continue their vigil looking out for the KKK from inside their homes, or outside on their own properties, from posts where the police had no authority to arrest them. Now, they had to be extra careful about their guns.

At the jail, after the bail was paid but before Singleton and Smiley were released, a very tall policeman approached my father. Stopping inches from Dad's face he inquired, "Which one of y'all called us birds?" My father was petrified. Fearing police brutality, he told the officer, "I did, but it was just an expression. I meant no offense by it." The officer bent over, looked my father dead in the eye, shook his finger in his face, and said, "Boy, it's a nasty expression. Don't you ever call us birds again!"

No robed Ku Klux Klansmen ever showed up in Mobile Heights. But the episode reminded everybody of the ongoing and future problems with policing and the black community. The way Dad saw it, "The people who were supposedly trying to protect us were treating us like vigilantes."

Meanwhile, Rep. Adam Clayton Powell had his drinks with Governor Folsom in the governor's mansion. The congressman's next engagement wasn't far away. My uncle Fred, just beginning his career as a lawyer, joined Powell in the ride to Birmingham in the governor's limo, still being squired around by Folsom's loyal driver, Winston Craig.

The ad hoc neighborhood patrol was not disbanded. The vets kept the unit intact during the bus boycott. It became Martin Luther King Jr.'s private bodyguard unit whenever he ventured through town and into Mobile Heights.

The racial climate in Montgomery was tense leading up to the bus boycott, as my father could attest. One day Dad was minding his own business on his way home from work when he had an ugly encounter with a car full of young white men. He was driving down Holt Street, not far from the job, when he saw the car with the three white passengers. "Seemed like they were trying to run me off the street," he would say later. Dad sped up and drove down Fairview Avenue, the main highway heading toward our house. He turned up Mobile Drive.

My father didn't want to telegraph where we lived so he decided not to pull into our yard. Stopping a few doors down, he got out of the car. Dad, though only five foot eight, was always a very strong, athletic kind of guy. To top that off, he was fearless.

"I just happened to have had a lead pipe, about three feet long, that I got from underneath the seat." Negroes might have been oppressed by segregation, but they were not stupid, and they often expected trouble. "When I got out of my car, I got out with that. These guys jumped out of their car." Dad was standing in front of Singleton's house, and he yelled out for him.

"Maybe he wasn't home, but a fellow on the other side of the street heard the commotion, and I saw him open his door. But he wouldn't come out of his house. So I was out there, and I just started advancing on one guy, and he started backing up toward his car. About that time the others, who had gotten out of the car, jumped back in and they all took off. I have no idea why they were chasing me around. I didn't know them. And they had the nerve to come right up into Mobile Heights."

10

CLAUDETTE COLVIN, TEENAGE PIONEER

MARCH 2, 1955, was a turning point for my uncle—and for a fifteen-year-old black girl named Claudette Colvin. She was his first civil rights case. Colvin was arrested nine months before Rosa Parks was taken to jail. They both, in very dramatic ways, refused to surrender their seats on a Montgomery bus to a white passenger. Both were arrested. The outcomes were not the same at all. More than sixty years after the fact, Colvin is demanding what she sees as her rightful place in history.

I'm not sure what I expected the day I went to visit Colvin on the eleventh floor of her apartment building in the Bronx just before spring of 2018. The picture imprinted in my brain was of a girl, looking younger than her fifteen years, smiling through the gap in her front teeth. Walnut-colored skin. Eyes peering out through schoolgirl glasses. Her hair was short and black, probably styled with a straightening comb and hot curlers. I found a few other images of her as an adult by searching her name on the internet. In recent years, stories have begun to emerge remembering this overlooked freedom fighter.

I knew I wanted to also ask her about three other often forgotten bus boycott heroines: Aurelia Browder, Susie McDonald, and Mary Louise Smith. They, too, were arrested on buses in 1955, months before Rosa Parks. Though they were charged with violating the city's segregation

I went to visit Claudette Colvin
in her apartment in the Bronx.

laws and are responsible along with Colvin for a legal case that overturned segregated buses in Montgomery, they have also almost been lost
in the shuffle of history.

Colvin is probably the best known of the four. She has retired from
a job as a nurse's aide at a Catholic nursing home. Her health is failing
her now. The walker she uses to navigate her way around her apartment was parked by her front door. I brought along sugar-free cookies
she craves but is not ambulatory enough to venture out to buy. Two
framed 1950s era pictures of the great-aunt and great-uncle who raised
her decorate a lamp table in her living room.

As one of the first blacks in Montgomery to publicly fight back
and be arrested when ordered to give up a bus seat to a white person, Colvin mostly shied away from the spotlight, rarely speaking
out about what happened to her until late in her life. She collaborated with author Phillip Hoose, who tells her story in detail in a
children's book published in 2009, *Claudette Colvin: Twice Toward*

Justice. A few news stories followed, not enough to make Claudette Colvin a familiar name.

The day we spoke she was casually dressed in loose-fitting, pastel pink trousers and a silky short-sleeved shirt. Gazing through wireless glasses, she seemed immediately relaxed on a floral-print sofa, which, like her, is getting on in age. Colvin seemed comfortable in her brown skin. She was welcoming, almost playful. I had read what was in print, but I wanted to hear the whole story from her.

She giggled as she recalled how her classmates reacted to her arrest. "Oh, some said, 'Claudette, you were very brave, but you was crazy!'" Colvin practically blurted out. "'You could have been killed! You could have been raped! They could have took you out in the woods and left you.'"

She remembered being dragged off a bus by two white police officers and handcuffed as vividly at age seventy-eight as she did when she was arrested. After school she had boarded the Highland Gardens bus with a gaggle of classmates on Dexter Avenue in front of Dexter Avenue Baptist Church. After a few stops, the bus was crowded. A white woman was left standing. "I knew I had a problem," Claudette informed me, "when the bus driver looked in the back and said he needed the seat." He wanted four Negroes sitting on both sides of the aisle to get up.

"It was Jim Crow law," she explained. "A white person couldn't sit in the opposite aisle across from a black person. Colored people had to sit behind white people, to show that white people were superior, and we were inferior."

Three of the students reluctantly got up but Colvin refused to budge. The bus driver hailed a traffic officer.

At some point a pregnant black woman, unaware there had been problems, boarded the bus and sat next to Colvin. Then the traffic officer boarded the bus.

"He came to the back door. You know he wasn't polite. He said, 'Gal, why are you sitting there?' I said, I paid my fare, and it's my constitutional right."

Mrs. Hamilton, the pregnant lady, was still sitting. The officer looked to the back and asked if any of the men would get up so she could sit down. A black man stood up, offered his seat, and suspecting trouble, got off the bus.

Apparently, the traffic officer did not have the authority to make an arrest, so when he got off, the bus moved on. Colvin and her friends, sitting in the section designated for Negroes, thought the matter was over with until the bus arrived at Bibb and Commerce Streets. She figures the traffic cop had called a squad car. Two officers boarded the bus through the back door to ask why she wasn't moving.

"They knocked my books out of my lap. They grabbed me. Dragged me off the bus because I refused to stand up," Colvin recalled. "I repeated, it was my constitutional right. I paid my fare and it's my constitutional right."

Colvin's class at Booker T. Washington High had studied African American history just the previous month, in February. "We had been discussing our heroes and all the discrimination and all the injustice locally and nationally," she said.

"You know, we not only talked about the buses, we talked about not being able to try on clothes in the department store. If you wanted those slick patent leather Baby Doll slippers for Easter, my mother had to draw a background of my foot on a brown paper bag."

All of that was rolling around in her head when the white policemen yanked her from her seat. Her body went limp.

"History had me glued to the seat. My teacher, Mrs. Geraldine Nesbitt, had discussed this so extensively. It felt like Sojourner Truth's hand was pushing me down on one shoulder," she said as she touched one shoulder. "And Harriet Tubman's hand was pushing me down on another shoulder. I was paralyzed to the seat. I couldn't move. I had to do something, because it was my time to respond to this unfairness."

All the accounts I had read indicated that Claudette not only went unwillingly but was also kicking and screaming. But she insisted in our conversation, "I was on my best behavior. I wasn't kicking and scratching like they say I was." She admitted she had long nails back then but said, "I wasn't clawing."

At the jailhouse, Colvin was processed and fingerprinted. When the key was turned and the cell door slammed shut, she cried. "I cried, and I cried. I was beginning to recite the twenty-third Psalms."

She appeared transfixed, as if transported back in time. "I began to pray. I began to say all the Bible verses and poems I had memorized."

Colvin faced charges of assault against a police officer, disorderly conduct, and defying the city's segregation order. Her family contacted E. D. Nixon, who had closely watched the weeklong bus boycott in Mobile the previous summer. Though it did not result in complete integration of the buses in that city, there had been marginal success.

Nixon thought Colvin's would be a good case to test the constitutionality of the segregation ordinances in Montgomery. He called my uncle. Fred Gray, now twenty-four, had been practicing law for about six months when what seemed like the opportunity of a lifetime dropped in his lap. He went to talk with Colvin and her parents at their home in the King Hill area, and he consulted with his mentor, white attorney Clifford Durr.

"I was eager to handle this case," my uncle told me during one of our many talks. "There was no evidence of any delinquency. What they were trying to do was to enforce the segregation laws."

Jo Ann Robinson and her Women's Political Council also saw an opportunity. The well-educated black women in the WPC were fearless activists at a time when some of the political groups headed by black men let their egos get in the way of coalescing over a cause. Robinson, who taught English at Alabama State College, drafted a letter to the mayor, other city officials, and bus company officials to protest what happened to Claudette. They agreed to a meeting with black civil rights leaders, which included Robinson, Fred Gray, and the new pastor in town, Rev. Martin Luther King Jr.

"They all expressed that they were sorry that Claudette had been arrested and indicated it wasn't going to happen again," my uncle says. "During that discussion there was some talk on our part, probably led by Jo Ann Robinson, indicating if something didn't happen, the African Americans would simply have to just stay off the buses until conditions could change."

So now the idea of a boycott was out in the open. Meetings with city officials asking for better treatment for blacks on buses continued, but no action was taken. All of this, of course, was fodder for those daily luncheon conversations Fred was having with Rosa Parks.

When it came time for Colvin's hearing in juvenile court, the judge found Colvin to be a delinquent and placed her on unsupervised probation. For a short time, Montgomery's black community was hopeful and began fundraising efforts to help pay for an appeal.

As I listened to Claudette talk that day in New York, I tried to imagine what I would have done as a teenager in her shoes. I was somewhat shy in my early teens and doubt I would have had the nerve to take such a bold stand. Lucky for me, by the time I was fifteen, a little over a decade later, where I could sit on a bus wasn't an issue. Uncle Fred says to this day he is "still in awe of the courage it took for a fifteen-year-old schoolgirl to defy a white bus driver, white policemen, jailers, and judges."

Fast-forward to the early part of the twenty-first century, and it's often still dangerous for black people, especially men, to stand up to white police on the streets of America.

––––––––––

Rosa Parks worked actively to raise money for Claudette Colvin's appeal. Parks's mother, Leona McCauley, made chocolate chip cookies to sell to help the legal fund. Collections were taken up in churches. "After we got in touch with E. D. Nixon, he told my mom that Rosa Parks had a youth group," Colvin explained. She started attending their meetings.

The NAACP Youth Council met at Trinity Lutheran Church. The church was a black congregation with a white pastor, Bob Graetz, whose family would soon become friends with my parents. Trinity was just down the street from the housing project where Parks lived. The first time they met, Colvin says, "Miz Rosa said, 'When I heard your story, I thought you were an overgrown teenager that likes to sass white people. But when I spoke with your teachers, I found out that you were intellectually mature enough to know your rights and to know right from wrong.'"

According to Colvin, what Parks was teaching the kids in the council was an extension of what she was learning in Mrs. Nesbitt's class at school. "Teaching about why they have to go out of the state to get an education!" she laughs. "Alabama State taught secretarial courses and music courses, but you was a teacher. You still had to get a teacher's degree. You had to be a teacher or a preacher. You could only get a job as a maid in downtown Montgomery. You could not get a job as a cashier. The youth group was talking about all the injustice."

Parks encouraged Colvin to run for Miss NAACP. She won second place. She sometimes spent the night at the apartment Parks shared with her husband and mother, if Friday night's youth meeting ended after the last bus home or she wanted to help sell cookies Saturday mornings.

Two of the charges against Colvin were dropped when Fred Gray filed an appeal of her case in the circuit court of Montgomery County. His efforts to have her completely exonerated were unsuccessful. Claudette was found guilty of assaulting the police officers.

———————

Excitement about the possibility of Claudette Colvin being the case to test the constitutionality of Montgomery's segregation statutes fell by the wayside among some of the city's Negro leaders a few months after her arrest.

Things had gotten complicated. Many of Colvin's classmates shunned her when she went back to school. They made fun of the cornrow braids she was wearing, not considered fashionable in those days. It didn't help when word got out that summer that she was pregnant. E. D. Nixon and others questioned whether a pregnant teenager about to become an unwed mother should be the face of an important push to derail segregated buses.

My uncle, with legal assistance from Clifford Durr, had initially thought Colvin would be a good federal case to test the constitutionality of segregation. When I asked whether her pregnancy changed his thinking, being the true southern gentleman that he is my uncle said, "I don't know anything about Claudette being pregnant at that time or any other lady or female who may or may not have been pregnant. Any pregnancy on the part of Claudette had no bearing on anything that I did in her case. I thought from the time I met her that her case was a very good case to be filed."

What he wanted to do was to file a case in federal court, to keep anything from languishing in the local system. But without the backing of community leaders, knowing they would not support Claudette Colvin, he had to wait. "I expressed to Ms. Parks and expressed to E. D. Nixon and expressed to anybody who would talk about the buses that we needed to be prepared, so whenever the next situation arose, we won't have to get ready."

There were several other cases before Rosa Parks was arrested: Aurelia Browder, Susie McDonald, Jeanetta Reese, and Mary Louise Smith all had similar experiences, just somehow not the perfect set of circumstances, backgrounds, or personalities.

The days ticked by. Uncle Fred was concentrating on what direction to take next. Like Jo Ann Robinson, E. D. Nixon, and a few others, Fred Gray wanted more. His next move was a federal court case demanding full integration of the buses. He and Montgomery's other black attorney, Charles Langford, filed suit against the city's mayor, William Gayle, in *Browder v. Gayle* on February 2, 1956, three days after the bombing of the King parsonage.

Browder v. Gayle asked the court to declare segregation unconstitutional. Aurelia Browder, Claudette Colvin, Susie McDonald, Mary Louise Smith, and Jeanetta Reese were named as plaintiffs. At the young age of twenty-five, Fred was an inexperienced lawyer and knew it. Inexperienced, but smart enough to ask for help. He turned to some big guns for assistance: Thurgood Marshall and Robert Carter, attorneys with the NAACP Legal Defense Fund in New York. The case was responsible for overturning segregated seating on Montgomery buses after making its way to the US Supreme Court.

Rosa Parks's name was never on the lawsuit. Gray opted not to include her. She had been convicted of disorderly conduct in a local court, and her case was on appeal to the circuit court of Montgomery. Gray did not want a challenge of Alabama segregation laws to become bogged down in Alabama courts, so he filed a separate federal case, using other plaintiffs.

Reese was one of the original plaintiffs but dropped out later. My uncle got in some trouble when white authorities alleged he was representing her without her consent. He was indicted by a grand jury in March 1956. He believes the case against him was politically motivated, an attempt by whites to stop the bus boycott. Fred writes in his book that he had received Reese's consent in writing and had tape-recorded conversations to back him up. He also discovered Reese worked in the home of a high-ranking Montgomery official who, along with some other authorities, interrogated Reese about her involvement in the case. Reese had also neglected to inform her husband that she was a plaintiff. After she began receiving harassing phone calls and threats, she wanted out. The criminal prosecution against my uncle went nowhere.

Over time, the four remaining *Browder* plaintiffs were overlooked by some historians. Rosa Parks, who was not a party to the landmark case, has overshadowed them in the narrative about what happened in Montgomery. Parks has been honored with a Presidential Medal of Freedom, statues in downtown Montgomery and the US Capitol's National Statuary Hall, a library and museum in her hometown, and the moniker of "Mother of the Civil Rights Movement." When she died, she was the first woman to lie in state in the US Capitol rotunda. I remember standing in line for hours on a chilly October night with my husband, Chris, to file past the coffin.

It took decades after the boycott for Montgomery and the nation to acknowledge and even embrace the history. A memorial to Dr. Martin Luther King Jr. finally graced a prominent spot on the National Mall in Washington on August 28, 2011. It was the forty-eighth anniversary of his "I Have a Dream" speech and followed twenty years of planning. Fundraising wasn't easy. I covered the unveiling of the memorial when I worked for WTTG-TV and remember reporting six years earlier that Washington Mystics basketball team owner Sheila Johnson planned to personally give $1 million to edge memorial backers closer to their goal of raising $100 million.

A bronze bust of King was unveiled in Montgomery in 2018 outside the renamed Dexter Avenue King Memorial Baptist Church, where he had been the young pastor during the boycott that thrust him into the national spotlight. That bust was embroiled in controversy, however. The original intent was for a life-sized statue, but concerns about the artist's depiction of Dr. King have delayed that project. Troy University built the Rosa Parks Museum, which opened in Montgomery on December 1,

2000, on the anniversary of her famous stand on a bus. A library and street are named after her in Montgomery.

The day I visited with Colvin in New York, she had a specific bone to pick with the Smithsonian's new National Museum of African American History and Culture and its exhibit depicting the bus boycott. "It's incorrect. It's inaccurate and confusing," she insisted. "Change it. Get it right! Because people coming from all over the world sees that. They should change it. Give the four women the credit they're due." Colvin hadn't visited the museum, but a granddaughter informed her that Claudette was mentioned almost as a sidebar.

I support the concept of a museum that attempts to document the history of African American life from being enslaved people to the present. I even became a charter member. Eager to see how the museum portrayed the period of the Montgomery bus boycott, I visited opening day and on several other occasions. In an article I wrote for the Alabama Voices column in the *Montgomery Advertiser* newspaper, I expressed pleasure at the inclusion of pictures and mentions of Fred Gray and Jo Ann Robinson and noted the exhibit included the dress that seamstress Rosa Parks was working on the day of her arrest. I also noted the dearth of artifacts relating to Martin Luther King Jr., and how that was not surprising because of the King children's reputation for demanding a price for use of his name and collectibles.

Rosa Parks looms large in the museum, with a huge picture of her face and a smaller one of her mug shot, the dress, and an explanation of her role. On the right side of the mug shot is this statement: "Rosa Parks—A Test Case. Rosa Parks was not the first black woman arrested for defying segregated bus seating. Claudette Colvin was arrested in March 1955, but she was only 15 years old, and lawyers did not think hers would be the best test case."

That drives Colvin up a wall. "They should change it," she said, words tumbling out of her mouth. "They should have not displayed me with Rosa. Let Rosa be to herself and then have another exhibit for the women in *Browder versus Gayle*, because she was not a part of it! They should have said Rosa was the spokeswoman for the Montgomery bus boycott. But the successful end of Jim Crow law was by the four women, whose case went to the Supreme Court.

"Give the four women the credit that they're due! Because their lives were put on the line too. I'm just saying they should correct that. That doesn't take anything away from Rosa. She'd still be the mother of the civil rights movement. It won't take anything away from her, because of her connection with Dr. King."

Early in 2018, Colvin's sister Gloria Laster launched a Change.org petition asking the Smithsonian to "set the record straight by including Claudette's story." The petition asks, "Did history fail to get it right?" In 2013, Colvin's nephew, Antonio Jenkins, started a Change.org petition asking President Obama to award Claudette the Presidential Medal of Freedom. In that online petition, Jenkins says he didn't get to grow up with his aunt living nearby because "she faced so much discrimination in Alabama after her arrest, she had to move away to New York." His petition says Colvin's "contribution to creating a more fair America for everyone shouldn't be forgotten. It should be celebrated, just like Rosa Parks is."

Colvin has no presidential medal, and at last check the exhibit in the African American museum remained the same, though museums do sometimes rotate their displays.

Colvin is more pleased with the Montgomery bus boycott depiction at the new Legacy Museum and National Memorial for Peace and Justice in Montgomery. The Equal Justice Initiative's stated purpose in creating the museum is to acknowledge the country's legacy of slavery, lynching, racial segregation, and mass incarceration. The memorial, set on six acres, puts context to seven decades of racially motivated lynchings using art and sculpture. At its core, eight hundred hanging steel monuments representing counties where lynchings took place are a dramatic display, containing the names of victims engraved on the columns.

The museum opening was a celebrity-studded, two-day event of panels, concerts, and speeches. Claudette Colvin was flown in from New York and she, Mary Louise Smith, and Fred Gray were honored during a ceremony at the Montgomery Convention Center as the three surviving participants in the landmark *Browder v. Gayle* case. A video exhibit of Gray talking about the boycott and the role of Colvin and the other *Browder* plaintiffs is housed in the museum.

Claudette said for her, being honored with a medal for her contribution to overturning segregation on Montgomery's buses was an "awesome, an amazing thing." But she added, "I'm not seeking notoriety. I just want people to know it wasn't easy. Especially the young people. They don't know the history of what was accomplished by the civil rights movement."

Not as mobile as she'd like to be, Colvin did not try to navigate her way around the powerful lynching memorial. "I didn't want to see the monuments hanging down. I don't want to see the horror. It was too macabre for me to go look at it," she said when we talked a few days later. "I had heard of people who were lynched when I lived in Pine Level [Alabama] as a small child. I was shown trees where it happened. Crosses were burned on people's property. We knew white people had ways of dealing with you and putting you in your place. Things can happen to you for even just talking back to a white man. You had to stay in your place, be humble and submissive. Young people now don't know that."

Most of her young life, Claudette lived in a house on East Dixie Drive. In recent years, her street was renamed Claudette Colvin Drive at the behest of Montgomery city councilman Tracy Larkin, whose sister, Annie, was on the bus when Colvin was arrested. March 2, the day of the arrest, has been proclaimed Claudette Colvin Day by Montgomery mayor Todd Strange and members of the city council. The King Hill Development Corporation announced plans to redevelop the drug-infested, low-income King Hill neighborhood where Colvin grew up. It wants to beautify her run-down childhood home and remake it into the Claudette Colvin Park and Garden. Colvin's response to that: "I don't know how they'll get rid of the drug dealers." But she's happy to finally be honored in some ways for the role she played. "I think it's wonderful," she told me. "I get some recognition, and people will get to know the struggle was really hard, and I couldn't have traveled it by myself."

The baby Colvin was pregnant with as a teenager was raised in Alabama. Raymond went into the army, and as Colvin would say later, "He lost his way. He felt life was really hard and wanted to bail out." He died of a drug overdose. Her second son, Randy, who also grew up in Montgomery, received a doctorate degree in business administration.

His family lives in Texas. A grandson is a medical doctor, whose wife is also a physician. "My offspring has been blessed," she says. "I think God has forgiven me of my sin of fornication."

———————

There are very few tributes to those other three women whose valiant sacrifices led to the dismantling of segregation on Montgomery's buses. Aurelia Browder Coleman died in 1971, but her family is trying to keep her memory alive. At age forty-five, she was the lead plaintiff in the *Browder v. Gayle* lawsuit. I met her sons Curtis and Butler Coleman at an event at Dexter Avenue King Memorial Baptist Church on December 4, 2017, when their mother, my father, Rosa Parks, and others were given posthumous awards for "courage and commitment to the cause of justice" for their roles in the boycott. The awards were given by the National Center for the Study of Civil Rights and African American Culture at Alabama State University, which is trying hard to keep the story of the Montgomery bus boycott in the public eye.

When I told the Coleman brothers I was working on a book, they were eager to discuss their mother's part in integrating Montgomery's buses, especially Butler, a retired postal employee. He's upset his mother and the other *Browder* plaintiffs haven't received more recognition. The way he sees it, Rosa Parks's prominence shows how a "lie has become history." He says it's important to teach the whole story.

Passionate in his efforts, he has set up the Aurelia E. S. Browder Foundation, a website with information about all five plaintiffs, and he has converted his mother's house at 1012 Highland Avenue into a museum with a historic marker out front. The family hosts a celebratory open house there several days each year, including February 1, the day the *Browder* case was filed in federal court, and May 11, the day the four women went to court to testify. Butler has also created a YouTube video telling the lawsuit story and is trying to get the word out online about the *Browder* plaintiffs through a website and magazine, Tolerance.org and *Teaching Tolerance* magazine, products of the Southern Poverty Law Center.

Aurelia Browder worked at many jobs, including midwife, seamstress, and housewife. She was a widow who raised six children, finished high school in her thirties, and later graduated from Alabama State College. A voting rights activist, she was known for helping to register Negroes to vote during the 1950s. Why didn't leaders start a boycott when she was arrested April 19, 1955? Her son Butler doesn't mince any words: "E. D. Nixon didn't want a dark-skinned person in a court fight to end segregation," he told me. "He thought the judges wouldn't respond well to that. E.D. wanted someone mild-mannered and meek. Aurelia was too strong willed."

Colvin also agrees colorism had something to do with Parks getting all the attention. "The organization wanted someone who could impress white people, and Rosa fit the profile. Just like Lena Horne. Just like Dorothy Dandridge."

But Susie McDonald, seventy-seven, one of the other plaintiffs, was also a fair-skinned black woman, so light she was often mistaken for white, which got her in trouble when she rode the bus. According to Colvin, "White people would sit next to her not knowing that she had black blood in her. And the bus driver got angry at Miz Susie McDonald, then they had an altercation."

Mary Louise Smith was eighteen when she didn't get up to make room for a white bus rider on October 21, 1955. After her arrest, her father paid a nine-dollar fine. Age could have been a partial factor in not organizing a boycott around her. But there was also a rumor that her father had a drinking problem, which the family denies. I met her years later, during the celebration of the sixtieth anniversary of the bus boycott. Now Mary Louise Smith Ware, she was in the audience at the Alabama Department of Archives and History for a screening of *More Than a Bus Ride*, a documentary that tells the story of the *Browder v. Gayle* case.

When I introduced myself to Ware after the showing of the documentary, she told me she was proud of her role in the historic lawsuit even though her own case didn't spark fury and outrage. It quietly went away after her father paid the fine. A petite, unassuming woman in her late seventies at the time of the movie screening, she said nobody tried to intimidate her or pressure her to withdraw as a litigant. Years later, hers is not a household name, as Rosa Parks's is.

Unlike Claudette Colvin, Ware is less perturbed about being in Parks's shadow. After receiving the award from the Legacy Museum for her civil rights contribution, Ware said she appreciated it. And she was not upset at the recognition coming so late in her life. She's willing to give credit where credit is due. "Rosa Parks was just more mature than myself," she told me. "Being as young as I was, I might have flown off the handle or said curse words. I have no ill feeling. She was more mature." She also acknowledges what people have come to know about Parks's prompting a boycott. "It was already in the plan for her."

Still, Mary Louise Smith Ware played an important part in events that spelled the last nail in the coffin for segregated buses. She seems content with that.

11

BOYCOTT: DAY ONE

In the predawn hours of December 5, 1955, an aura of excitement and apprehension settled over Montgomery. After late-night phone calls and strategizing sessions, the bus boycott planners tried to catch a few hours of much-needed sleep.

At our house, my parents were awake. Thomas and Juanita Gray were always early risers. When I was a child, the sounds of my parents talking to each other in bed were what interrupted the quiet and roused me from my slumber most days, usually around 5:00 AM.

On this Monday, they were awake even earlier, still under the covers. Dad was gearing up for the part he would play in the protest. My mother was scared to death and admitted it. She had reason to be. Negroes in the city were about to go up against the white establishment at a time when racial oppression was the order of the day.

In some parts of the South, violent and sometimes public lynching spectacles were used to traumatize African Americans. Horrific news of Emmett Till's murder had come out of Mississippi in late August, a mere three months earlier. His mother shocked the world by putting his grotesquely deformed body on display in an open casket during his funeral back at home in Chicago. In September the two white men tried for killing him were acquitted by an all-white jury. It weighed heavily on the minds of the Negroes preparing to boycott in Montgomery.

"Gray, I'm afraid," my mother confided to my father. "That police commissioner guy was on TV last night saying 'Negro goon squads' would be out trying to intimidate the very people you're going to be giving rides to."

"Juanita, don't worry," he said, reaching over to pull her closer. "For one thing," he said, "there are no goon squads. He's making that up. For another, I'm not going to let anything happen to me or any of my passengers."

I was only four at the time. My brother Thomas Jr. was three and brother Freddie was a newborn. We were bratty, fussy little kids, living close together in a tiny house. Freddie was still in a crib in my parents' room. Tommy and I had twin beds in a bedroom that shared a wall with my parents' room. We were close enough to run and jump in their bed if we got scared during a thunderstorm.

Tommy and I always hated to see my father leave the house. We would race to the door and cling to his pant legs. Of course, we were excited every time he came home, fighting each other to be the first one Dad picked up. He would flip our tiny little bodies up, one at a time, and toss our legs into the air so our feet almost touched the ceiling. It was a daily ritual that left us squealing with delight.

Mom still had on her nightgown as she hugged my father at the front door on his way out. Tommy and I did our usual whiny good-bye routine. This time, though, instead of heading to work at Dozier's, Dad hopped into his Plymouth in our driveway, leaving home hours earlier than usual, heading in a different direction. This would be no ordinary day at the office. He went out in search of passengers, anybody who needed a ride to work who normally took the bus.

On the other side of town, Dad's younger brother was also up early. Fred Gray was already swept up by the momentum of events. He had had a very busy and restless night preparing his legal case for Rosa Parks's trial. They were due in the Recorder's Court of the City of Montgomery at 8:30 AM. He had also spent time with Jo Ann Robinson planning boycott strategy. Neither of the two of them talked much publicly about their plotting and scheming until many years later. It wasn't until 1987 that Robinson published her book, *The Montgomery Bus Boycott and the Women Who Started It*. It was also decades later that my uncle wrote about boycott planning, in 1995, when the first edition of his book *Bus Ride to Justice* came out.

But around 5:00 AM that day, Fred had left home, driving his 1954 stick shift Ford all over town to see if people were staying off the buses. My uncle was ecstatic to learn that they were.

The morning of the boycott Rev. Robert Graetz also jumped into his car early. Pastor Graetz and other supportive ministers all over Montgomery had heeded the call from the boycott planners. Sunday, from the pulpit, he asked his parishioners to please stay off the buses on Monday to support Parks and the boycott. Monday morning Graetz drove around himself, checking out bus stops. He picked up any black commuters he saw out walking.

My father had a job as an announcer at a local radio station and often played Bob Graetz's taped Sunday church programs on the air, though the two didn't meet until the boycott. Reverend Graetz was invited to become a member of the board of the Montgomery Improvement Association, which ran the day-to-day activities of the bus boycott, after it became clear the protest would be more than a one-day affair.

Graetz was not included in the MIA at the outset. "One of the problems I had was that they did not dare to trust me, because I was white. So I was not part of the planning ahead of time," he told me during one of the many conversations we had during my research.

Bob and his wife, Jeannie, and their kids became lifelong friends of my family. Their parsonage home was bombed three times because of their activism during the boycott. My father said later that friends eventually convinced them to leave town. "We told them they would probably be killed if they stayed." The Graetzes eventually moved away to Ohio.

Bob Graetz writes about his experiences in *A White Preacher's Message on Race and Reconciliation*. I have in my possession, and treasure, an advance, limited-edition copy of the book, signed for my parents on July 5, 2006. It is inscribed by Bob and Jeannie, "To our long-time best friends, Tom & Juanita. Let us work together to keep the dream alive." My parents' book is number twelve of one hundred copies.

I have never quite been able to figure out the Graetzes, who endured much alienation in the white community for their contact with blacks, but I am grateful for their friendship, which continues even now, with both my parents deceased.

Rev. Martin Luther King Jr., the relatively new pastor at Dexter Avenue Baptist Church, soon to be christened the principle leader of the boycott, and his wife, Coretta, were also awake earlier than usual the first day of the boycott. They lived in the Centennial Hill neighborhood on the east side of town, home of many of the city's prominent and wealthier black residents. The church parsonage was on South Jackson Street, and the South Jackson–Washington Park bus rode right by their house. The buses would take domestic help who lived on the west side of town over to the east side, where well-to-do white people like doctors, lawyers, and judges lived, in areas like Cloverdale.

Richard and Vera Harris, a black couple, lived a few doors down from the King household. Like the Kings, the Harrises also rushed out to the front porch as the first early-morning buses began to roll by. Richard "Doc" Harris was the owner of Dean's Drug Store downtown, which later became a gathering place for many of the boycott protesters. They and their three young children, Valda, Adrian, and Richard III, watched the empty buses ride past about every fifteen minutes or so that morning.

Valda gets excited to this day talking about it. Both her parents have passed away, but one day while her mother was still alive, I went to visit Valda and Vera at the family home on South Jackson Street. Valda pointed down the street from the swing on her front porch. "The Kings were right there. They were on the porch. Everybody that was on this street, including people who lived across the street. Everybody was on the porch looking."

There is a bus stop barely a block away. That morning King watched as two buses passed. Then a third. There were no black riders on the buses. There may have been two white passengers on the third bus. King then left his house and, like my uncle, cruised around town in his car to see if the boycott was a success.

When Fred Gray, Rosa Parks, King, and their contingent arrived at the Recorders Court of the City of Montgomery for Mrs. Parks's trial, there were hundreds of black supporters waiting outside. Inside, the segregated courtroom was filled, whites on one side, Negroes on the other.

The trial was brief. For her singular act of refusing to relinquish her seat on a city bus to a white man, Parks was found guilty of disorderly conduct and fined ten dollars, plus court costs, which added up to fourteen dollars. A bigger fight over segregation would come later. The disorderly conduct case was immediately appealed.

There were planning meetings all day, one at Dexter Avenue Baptist and another at Mt. Zion AME. Rev. L. Roy Bennett, president of the Interdenominational Ministerial Alliance, was pastor at Mt. Zion. The leaders recognized the need for a group to organize and direct the boycott. They called it the Montgomery Improvement Association.

My father, a businessman, was one of those kept in the loop and invited to attend that second meeting, where officials of the new organization were nominated and elected. He mentioned years later in speeches he gave about the boycott that it was Jo Ann Robinson who called him to let him know in advance about the meeting. Dad always said he went to the meeting prepared to toss E. D. Nixon's name out for president, since Nixon was well known as such a mover and shaker in the community. King, on the other hand, was new in town, a relative unknown. That could have been an argument against voting for King, but his newness also meant he had no strong enemies—something Uncle Teddy and Jo Ann Robinson had discussed during their boycott planning the night before.

As Robinson had pointed out, members of her own Dexter Avenue Baptist Church were already in awe of King's oratory skills. The new minister had obviously made enough of an impression on those assembled at the meeting that his nomination was quickly seconded. King was unanimously chosen as the new president. Dad switched his plan and then nominated Nixon for treasurer.

The selection of King as the head of the MIA avoided a clash in deciding between two rival leaders in the black community, Nixon and Rufus Lewis. Lewis, whose wife was owner of the Ross-Clayton Funeral Home, was an early and aggressive advocate of voter registration. He worked to register young students and even had a local nightclub, the Citizens' Club, for registered voters only, a club my parents used to go to. Nixon, as an activist with the Sleeping Car Porters Union, was the logical choice to raise money as treasurer of the MIA. Lewis later became chairman of the MIA transportation committee during the boycott.

Now that the MIA was formed, the first real item of business was to decide what was to follow. The boycott was initially intended to last one day. But if the new leaders wanted to accomplish anything, they probably needed to extend it.

Recently I touched base with the man who became the first recording secretary of the organization, Uriah Fields, who then was a graduate student at Alabama State College and minister of Bell Street Baptist Church. He now lives in Charlottesville, Virginia, and is one of the few surviving original members of the board of the MIA.

Fields remembers the plan being to present the leaders to the community and discuss strategy in the first of many mass meetings at local churches. Holt Street Baptist Church would host the first meeting. Dr. King asked Reverend Abernathy to draft a committee to come up with what amounted to a mission statement. Abernathy named four people to his Resolutions Committee. Fields says one of the four people on that committee was my father.

Meanwhile, all the events of the day gave the protest momentum. Inside the College Hill Barbershop on the corner of South Jackson and Hutchinson Streets, a block away from Alabama State, a few blocks from King's house, the barbers and patrons inside were wondering whether the boycott was really going to work. They had their doubts. As Nelson Malden put it to me many years later, "Black people never stood together before on any program."

Malden, a young college student then, was cutting hair to help pay his way through school. He was working the first day of the boycott. Suddenly, one of the barbershop customers yelled out, "Here come the bus!" Everybody in the shop jumped up and ran to the window. They saw a tall black man standing on the corner at the bus stop. He had on a hat and a trench coat. "We ran to the window to see whether the man was gonna get on the bus," Malden told me. "When the bus came up across the street, in front of the barbershop, we couldn't see the man, whether he got on or not. But then the bus pulled off, the man was still standing. And we hollered so loud, it was like Joe Louis had knocked out Joe Schmeling! That's how loud we were hollering in the barbershop. One man yelled out, 'It worked. It worked. It worked!'"

At the mass meeting that evening at seven at Holt Street Baptist Church to decide on the next steps and to motivate the protesters, a crowd of hundreds packed the church and spilled over onto the street and sidewalk outside an hour before the meeting even got started.

12

RAY WHATLEY

THE STARS WERE OUT ONE CRISP WINTRY EVENING above an unlikely gathering in the basement offices of Dr. Martin Luther King Jr. at Dexter Avenue Baptist Church. It was an interracial group, the only such forum at the time in Montgomery. A dozen or so blacks and whites, mostly laypeople and some ministers, took their seats as the meeting was gaveled to order, likely by Rev. Robert Hughes, a minister of the North Alabama Methodist Conference. He was the white executive director of the statewide Alabama Council on Human Relations, which had an office in Montgomery. Rev. Ray Whatley, the white pastor of St. Mark's Methodist Church, was president of the council and believes Hughes convened that session at Dexter. The bus boycott was just beginning to pick up steam.

"Ladies and gentlemen," Whatley said, "many of you know how I feel. I feel strongly that we should be talking about building some bridges."

Ray Whatley never really endorsed the bus boycott. But when I spoke to him, he told me he felt it was a just cause, that the problems black riders were having on those buses needed to be remedied.

My parents were friendly with a small handful of white people who were allies in the movement. Ray Whatley was not one of them. I bumped into him on my journey to find out what the bus boycott was all about.

Whatley has vivid recollections of behind-the-scene strides Montgomery was making toward fuller citizenship for black residents, as well as of efforts to unhinge any progress in that direction. He was eager to share his thoughts with me when I met him in the fall of 2015. Whatley was living independently in an apartment of a beautiful retirement facility in Asheville, North Carolina, nestled in the western part of the state. The city is in a valley, surrounded by the spectacular Blue Ridge Mountains at the edge of the Appalachian chain. I arrived after an early-morning drive.

The scenery along the way was breathtaking. Thick forests of oak trees, bright red and burnt orange in their autumnal beauty, clustered among regal pines, offering unparalleled views from winding roads. From a distance, the bluffs appear to be blue.

A widower, Ray Whatley had left Alabama many years before. He was now living in the city where his only son, David Whatley, had a thriving stone masonry business. I could see why they had settled there.

Watley was ninety-six then, a gentleman with a quick mind. Despite the hearing aid in his left ear, he's still a little hard of hearing.

Rev. Ray Whatley and I at his apartment in a retirement community in Asheville, North Carolina.

My cousin Deborah had pointed me in his direction after she met him earlier that summer. He and his son, David, and nephew, Joe Whatley, were attending a family reunion in Alabama and stopped by the Tuskegee History Center. Deborah showed them around the museum. Ray gave her some printed material about his own civil rights history. She thought he might be a good person to interview for my book.

Back in the mid-1950s few in Montgomery knew about the meetings of the city's chapter of the Alabama Council on Human Relations. Dr. Martin Luther King Jr., whose church hosted the monthly meetings, was elected vice president.

"Now, I have to say frankly, we were not attacking segregation as such at that point," Whatley told me in the living room of his apartment. He sat on the sofa, next to stacks of books and old documents he wanted to share with me. I faced him from an upholstered chair next to a lamp table. Dressed casually in khaki trousers and a tan print shirt with a background of leaves, he wore the frailty of nine decades, his living facility name tag on a metal chain around his neck. Peering at the stranger in his home through large, thick, wire-rimmed glasses, he seemed eager to get started. So much to talk about, so little time.

"In fact, Dr. King was criticized by some, I understand, because he was in the council, and not attacking segregation," Whatley said. He's right about that. In an article that ran in the *Alabama Journal* a few days after the boycott began, Reverend King said Negroes were not asking for an end to segregation. Introduced as evidence by the defendants in the *Browder v. Gayle* lawsuit, the newspaper story quotes King as saying, "All we are seeking is justice and fair treatment in riding the buses. We don't like the idea of Negroes having to stand when there are vacant seats. We are demanding justice on that point." The white city officials trying to block integration on the buses argued in court that even the black leader of the boycott was not calling for an all-out end to segregated seating.

One of those who spoke out against King's lack of efforts to actually get equal treatment for blacks on buses was, surprisingly, someone working closely with him, Rev. Uriah Fields. The then pastor of Bell Street Baptist Church, Fields was also the first recording secretary of the Montgomery Improvement Association, which directed the bus boycott.

With Uriah Fields at his home in
Charlottesville, Virginia.

When I reached him one day by phone, Fields acknowledged that he became a kind of pariah of the boycott movement. "I said, 'We ought to call for integration,'" he told me. "It was the first time anybody had publicly called for total integration." And that made the other boycott leaders and many blacks in Montgomery very angry. Fields had taken it upon himself to publicly affirm at a mass meeting at a church, in front of reporters, that he thought the MIA should be fighting harder for complete integration and push beyond their strategy of compromise. That ran counter to the MIA negotiations with city officials.

At the outset, the boycott leaders had three proposals. They asked for courteous treatment of blacks by bus drivers. They wanted a first come, first served seating policy in which black passengers were seated from the rear to the front and white passengers from the front to the rear, with no seats reserved for any race. And they wanted black bus drivers hired on buses in predominantly black neighborhoods.

It's clear that not everybody was always on the same page about the desired end goals of the boycott. Fields either resigned or was fired as secretary of the MIA, depending on whom you believe, after he made public allegations that the organization was misusing funds that were flooding in from around the world to support the boycott. He later apologized and said the allegations were not true. Fields has written a book about his experiences, *Inside the Montgomery Bus Boycott*. When I talked to him in the spring of 2017, Fields said he retracted the statement because he strongly supported the boycott and didn't want to do anything to block its progress.

As for Ray Whatley, knocking down segregation was not really at the top of the agenda of his Human Rights Council "because we were simply trying to—at least this is what I understood about the boycott—we were trying to get more justice for African American people. That is not the term we used back then, as you know."

His thin lips pursed in a straight line, his pale cheeks blushing pink, he turned his head to look at me, as if to check my reaction. I'm accustomed to white people wondering how we black people feel about what we are called, how we're described. But I was ready to move on. I tried to make him comfortable by asking if we might have known some people in common. I asked about the one white person I figured he might have run into. "Do you know Robert Graetz?" I asked.

"Robert Graetz. I knew Robert Graetz. You know whether he's still living?" he wanted to know.

"Yes! He and his wife, Jeannie," I said.

Whatley did not know Jeannie but was tickled to learn that at the age of eighty-five she had just received her college degree from, of all places, Alabama State University, an HBCU.

"She was integrating that school!" Whatley said, bursting out laughing. He recalled that her husband was also a member of the Human Relations Council that met at King's church, and that Bob was an active participant in the bus boycott whose parsonage was bombed three times.

"Did you feel in any danger when you were meeting with the council and those black ministers?" I asked.

"No," he said. "I never felt that I was in physical danger. And the resistance that I had at St. Mark's did not even hint at a physical threat. But character assassination is another thing."

Whatley had a gentle, easygoing manner and an almost devilish sense of humor. During our conversation he wanted to sneak in that he had a personal tie to Harper Lee, the reclusive Pulitzer Prize–winning author of *To Kill a Mockingbird*. He tossed out the reference, almost like a fleeting thought, while he mentioned being a pastor at Montgomery's St. Mark's Methodist when he met Martin Luther King Jr. St. Mark's was a Montgomery church with about six hundred members, a block north of the governor's mansion on South Perry Street.

"This is a parenthesis," he said, drawing out his vowels, as many southerners do, speaking in a distinct southern drawl. "I was in Monroeville in 1951 to '53. It happened to be the time of the setting of this recently published book by Harper Lee." Released in July 2015, *Go Set a Watchman* touched off a furor over whether Lee had consented to have the newly discovered manuscript published. What's more, fans of *To Kill a Mockingbird* were shocked to learn that their beloved character Atticus Finch, a white lawyer who defended a black man falsely accused of rape, now had a dark side in the sequel. In the new book, which picks up two decades later, Finch's daughter, Scout, returns home to find her father is a racist, a repugnant defender of segregation.

Whatley acknowledged the book is fiction, but he likes to refer to it as a "historical, autobiographical novel." He said it "obviously reflects Monroeville, at the time I was pastor there." He didn't come right out and say he's the minister in the book, but he did say he notices some parallels between himself and the new pastor of the local Methodist church Lee wrote about. Both were relatively young. "I was thirty-one years old when I went there," Whatley said. He also noted, "The Lee sisters became among my closest friends over the years."

According to Whatley, "The book refers to my being too liberal on race."

"Well, anyway," he said, "they wanted a change in pastors after I had been there two years."

It is true that Harper Lee and her sister, Alice, were both members of the United Methodist Church. In fact, Alice, a prominent Alabama attorney, was also an acclaimed church leader.

For my part, I came to Asheville because I wanted to understand white southerners like Whatley, who put their reputation and even lives on the line to help get more equitable treatment for black people. After a day-long chat that included lunch, plus a look through volumes of letters and papers he had saved over a lifetime, I felt I at least knew Ray Whatley better.

He said he personally felt ending segregation might best come through education and moral persuasion, rather than by court order or legislation. But some of his Methodist church leaders could not be persuaded. They disapproved when they found out he was "meeting with Negroes." There was a complaint when the young minister remarked from the pulpit about the unfairness of the acquittal of two white men in the kidnapping and murder of Emmett Till. Whatley has saved letters and other papers documenting his experiences, including a letter to then mayor W. A. Gayle offering a "fair plan for seating white and Negro passengers on city buses" during the bus boycott era.

In the book *Stride Toward Freedom*, King recalls Whatley "was later shifted to a small backwoods community after his congregation protested his activities in the field of race relations."

Whatley resisted efforts by those in his church who tried to kick him out of his post at St. Mark's. Dr. King's dissertation advisor at Boston University, L. Harold DeWolf, tried to intervene, writing to one of Whatley's superiors asking if Whatley was available to be transferred up north. But Whatley didn't want to leave the South. He eventually wound up in a lesser-paid position with less status in a church in tiny, rural Linden, Alabama. His reputation followed, no thanks to the local White Citizens' Council, which exposed his previous civil rights activities in Montgomery. Whatley, his wife, and son moved again after a letter from his Montgomery church to the officers of the Linden congregation labeled him "everything from an ordinary liar to a dedicated communist."

The way Whatley sees it, he did not deliberately set out to become a crusader for racial equality. He was influenced by a small group of other like-minded ministers and some liberal laypeople. He says he also "came to have a sense of justice for black people" and tried to be faithful to his convictions about the dignity of all people regardless of their racial background.

As for progress, in 2015 the district superintendent of the Alabama–West Florida conference of the United Methodist Church was African American.

I wrote about some of what I learned in one of my opinion pieces in the *Montgomery Advertiser*, in which I concluded that "looking ahead, we'll be making real headway in churches everywhere when 10 o'clock Sunday mornings is not still the most segregated hour in America."

———————

"You ever heard of Mr. Sam Englehardt?" Ray Whatley had asked me during my visit to Asheville.

"Sam Englehardt?" I repeated. "No, I don't believe I have."

"I'm surprised at that," he said, raising his eyebrows in a state of incredulousness.

I scanned my brain hoping to evoke some spark of recollection. Growing impatient with being grilled, I had to confess, "I don't know everything."

Whatley brought up Englehardt's name as he talked about Linden, the small county seat he was transferred to when the Methodists in Montgomery tired of him spouting off from the pulpit about integration. According to Whatley, it was one of the most racist counties in the state.

"Mr. Englehardt was from Shorter. You know where Shorter is?" he quizzed me.

"I do know where Shorter is," I was happy to report. I have cousins who live there.

"Between Tuskegee and Montgomery. In Macon County," he went on. "Mr. Englehardt probably organized more White Citizens' Councils in south Alabama than any other person. I think Marengo County at Linden was the second one he organized. He was the main speaker at one of their rallies. And somebody from the county asked him, 'What about this new pastor, Methodist pastor at Linden?' 'Well, what's his name?' Englehardt wanted to know. 'Whatley.'

"'Good gracious,' Englehardt said. 'You don't want that man in your county. I knew him years ago and thought he was crazy then.'"

"What was it Englehardt was doing with his White Citizens' Councils?" I asked.

He threw me another one of those *you're kidding me* looks. But he answered the question. "They put pressure on people to oppose integration. And influence legislation, you know, and all that. Political pressure. It was, uh, they never promoted violence, you know, like the Ku Klux Klan or some other groups. They were really honorable people, and they were basically good people. Let me emphasize that. There were good folks in Alabama. But they were wrong!" he barked.

I later looked up more background on the White Citizens' Council. I don't recall my parents ever mentioning the name of the group in my presence in all my years growing up. But branches cropped up all over the South after the *Brown v. Board of Education* mandate of 1954 to desegregate public schools. The councils' modus operandi was to target blacks and whites who supported integration. Many council members were supposedly respectable white professionals—teachers, doctors, and businesspeople—who organized boycotts and held rallies to intimidate anyone promoting racial integration. They tried to force white employers to fire black activists and encouraged white merchants to refuse to serve African Americans in stores.

Ray recalled an incident in January 1955 when the White Citizens' Council had a rally at the Montgomery City Auditorium. I dug up more information about the rally. There was talk of school desegregation being a plot to "get the Negro into the white bedroom." One speaker suggested that white businessmen decline to offer credit to blacks who were integration activists or refuse to sell merchandise to them all.

It was at that meeting that Montgomery police commissioner Clyde Sellers jumped up, made his way to the stage to raucous applause, and audaciously and publicly joined the city's White Citizens' Council, proclaiming, "I don't have any Negro customers!".

That really upset Whatley, who had his say at church after the local newspaper ran a story. "I made a statement," Whatley said, "something to the effect, he'd better be concerned about all his people. Well, my pastoral relations committee met, and there were five of 'em on it. They drew up a statement and asked me to agree to it. That I would refrain in the future from referring to anything pertaining to the racial situation in the pulpit."

"What did you do?" I asked.

"I couldn't agree to that," he said. "I said I cannot in advance agree to refrain from any subject that I feel called on to preach about."

"Good for you!" I said.

"Well, then some of them started working on getting me out of the church," said Whatley.

And that's how he landed in Linden. The sad news is that Montgomery's mayor and two other city commissioners also joined the White Citizens' Council.

My cousin Deborah had steered me toward Whatley. So did his nephew, Joe, who I met the summer of 2015. Joe Whatley is a distinguished attorney with a prominent New York City law firm, who had participated many years before with my uncle Fred Gray in a trial involving racial discrimination by the state of Alabama in higher education. That summer Joe was attending a legal conference in New York City where Uncle Fred was a headliner. Joe Whatley told me then his uncle Ray had some things he wanted to get off his chest about how he was treated when he tried to fight racial tensions in the South during the 1950s.

I wrote about the event's civil rights panel discussion and dinner in a column in the *Montgomery Advertiser*. The article was published June 21, 2015. Here's some of what it said:

> Fred D. Gray has been described by some as "a champion of civil rights" and by others as "an unsung jurist." Rep. John Lewis (D-Ga) says he is "a lawyers' lawyer, a man of vision, a national treasure." Gray, Montgomery-born, a resident of Tuskegee, received well deserved recognition this month for his talents, experience and record when he was awarded the prestigious "Pillar of Justice Legacy Award" by the Lawyers' Committee for Civil Rights under Law at its annual A. Leon Higginbotham Corporate Leadership Awards Dinner in New York City.

The Lawyers' Committee is a nonpartisan, nonprofit organization. President John Kennedy ordered it set up in 1963 to secure
the resources and leadership of private lawyers in the fight against
racial discrimination. Its two-day event on June 3rd and 4th, had
an optimistic theme, "The Destiny of Democracy: We Shall Over-
come." Like many groups around the country, the Committee was
commemorating the 50th anniversary of the historic 1965 Voting
Rights Act, which, as dinner speaker Kathleen Kennedy Townsend
noted, "The right wing is fighting to suppress." . . .

This has been a great year for Fred Gray, and it's only half
over. He is crisscrossing the country to accept awards, being
heaped with accolades by legal groups, colleges and others now
acknowledging that it wasn't always just the faces on the front-
lines who were responsible for many of the civil rights successes
of previous decades. Much of the hard work was accomplished
by lawyers and other behind-the-scenes activists and organizers,
who mapped strategy and wrote legal briefs. . . .

Gray has been the headline speaker this year at events sponsored by the American Bar Association and Lipscomb University in Nashville, whose segregation policies he once challenged,
among others.

On February 4th, Rosa Parks' birthday, a historical marker
was unveiled at the corner of Dexter Avenue and Hull in downtown Montgomery. It highlights Gray's accomplishments representing Martin Luther King Jr. and Rosa Parks during the 1955
bus boycott, representing victims and family members in the
infamous Tuskegee Syphilis Experiment, in which hundreds of
black men were used as guinea pigs in a 40-year government
study. It points out a succession of firsts. He was one of the first
African Americans to be elected to the Alabama State Legislature since the Reconstruction era, the first black president of the
Alabama Bar Association. During his distinguished career Gray's
legal cases desegregated transportation, schools, housing, public
accommodations and expanded voting rights.

When President Clinton made a public apology for the notori-
ously unethical Tuskegee Syphilis Study in May of 1997, Gray
co-founded the Tuskegee Human and Civil Rights Multicultural
Center to establish a lasting memorial for its victims.

Fred Gray standing next to a historical marker in downtown Montgomery that documents his life and legal career.

We ascended the long escalator of the New York Marriott Marquis Hotel in our black-tie splendor. I was enjoying all the events of the conference, tagging along once again with Uncle Fred and Aunt Carol, who was celebrating her birthday. Dinner in the hotel ballroom was a glittering affair. Hundreds attended. Huge screens displayed videos during the program showing accomplishments of the honorees, among them David Oyelowo, who starred as Martin Luther King Jr. in the *Selma* movie, though he was not present for the dinner. He was in South Africa, working on a film.

Before *Selma* was released on Christmas Day the previous year, my uncle received an e-mail from the Oprah Winfrey–Brad Pitt production team. It alerted him that Academy Award–winning Cuba Gooding Jr. would play the part of Fred Gray in the film. Our family was thrilled that director Ava DuVernay was acknowledging his part in securing federal protection for marchers who had been beaten back and tear-gassed trying to cross the Edmund Pettus Bridge in 1965. The producers thanked my uncle for the "critical role" he played in the response to that horrendous incident and for his legal and legislative work to destroy segregation and obtain racial justice.

Arrangements were made for a screening of the movie at a Montgomery IMAX theater before the film's official release. It was attended mostly by friends and family. As we were leaving the theater, I asked Uncle Teddy what he thought of the movie.

"I liked it," he said.

"What about Cuba Gooding Jr.?" I wanted to know.

"He was good." But he added, "Maybe one day some movie house will make a film that depicts the role the law, plaintiffs, lawyers, and judges played in the civil rights movement. I suspect it would make a good movie."

The following summer, at the banquet, I admit I stuck out my chest with pride as I sat at a table with a bunch of strangers who applauded as my uncle accepted his award, giving him a standing ovation. I was also thrilled for Eric Holder, the nation's first African American attorney general, who was the recipient of the Lawyers' Committee Robert F. Kennedy Justice Prize. I got to know Holder and cover him as a reporter in Washington, DC, when he became the city's US attorney before moving over to the Department of Justice.

After decades of reporting on political figures and celebrities, I am not normally awed by celebrity and power, but I am proud of Holder's accomplishments. He happens to also be a Columbia University alum. That night I stood in line to congratulate him and have a brief conversation. Both Holder and Gray are lifetime champions of justice. So, too, as I discovered, was Ray Whatley.

13

KING PARSONAGE BOMBING

EARLY IN THE EVENING OF JANUARY 30, 1956, when the bomb went off at Dr. King's house, I was probably tucked under the covers in my twin bed next to my brother's, listening to our mother read to us. Like other children of the era, our parents had wrapped us in a protective cocoon, sheltering us from any of the unpleasantness associated with the bus boycott. My father was out working, repairing somebody's TV set on the other side of town. Turns out it was not too far from the King parsonage on South Jackson Street in the Centennial Hill area.

Dad wrote about that night in some of the many papers he had made us put in boxes marked "Historical." He talked about it in the interview we had taped.

"I heard the explosion," he told us. A veteran of World War II, he knew what bombs sounded like. "The situation with the boycott was getting tense," he said. "The bus company was losing money. City officials were cracking down on black people. Who could predict what the White Citizens' Council might do? My first thought when I heard the explosion was it might have been at Mom's house.

"Your uncle Fred was still living at home," he continued. "As the lawyer, he was the face of the boycott. I thought they might have been going after him. When I found out it was King's house, I rushed right over. A crowd had gathered. There were hostile people in the crowd. Some of them were armed. Making my way through the crowd I noticed the mayor, police commissioner, and a policeman on the porch. Other officers were trying to move people aside, but the people ignored them. Then Martin arrived. He had been at Reverend Abernathy's church, First Baptist, for a mass meeting, a kind of boycott pep rally. The crowd was in an angry mood."

Dr. King raced inside to make sure his wife and baby were OK. When he saw they were unharmed, he returned to the porch and addressed the people gathered at his door. Dad said that King "spoke about Jesus and loving our white brethren. He advised everybody not to panic, and said if anybody had weapons, they should take them home. Only then did the crowd begin an orderly dispersal."

A few doors down, Valda Harris and her siblings, just children then, were home. Their father, Richard Harris, who owned Dean's Drug Store was at work. One summer when I was in Montgomery more than half a century later, I talked to Valda and her mother, Vera, on their front porch. Vera had been next door with some friends when she heard the explosion and all the commotion.

"When the bomb went off," Valda said, "Momma came over here to make sure we were all right." Her mother told the kids to stay inside the house and went over to the parsonage to see what was going on.

Vera said, "Dr. King was busy trying to keep everybody quiet, because you got them coming in there with sticks and bricks and everything else to fight with, you know." She doesn't recall seeing any guns, but Valda believes some people probably had some.

Vera continued, "He was telling them, 'Just be quiet, just be calm, everything is all right. I'm fine. We're all OK. Family is fine.'"

The houses on the street sit close together, and the King parsonage wasn't the only home on the block to suffer damage. "We had a lot of windows that were broken," Valda said. "Glass in shoes and things like that. This window, [she points to a front window] as my sister said at the time, looked like a pregnant window. Because it was altered, like a big bulge. It didn't break, but if you slammed the door hard enough, it looked like it would."

Vera Harris, left, and her daughter Valda Harris Montgomery on the front porch of their house on South Jackson Street.

Their father moved their bedrooms to the back of the house after that. His drugstore was a rallying point for meetings and a place for people waiting for carpool rides to hang out to avoid the police. Valda says he was always afraid his house or drugstore might become targets.

14

THE ARRESTS

THE BOYCOTT HAD ITS FITS AND STARTS. My father, ironically a stickler for law and order, knew he was going to get arrested. It was just a matter of time. There he was—a thirty-two-year-old young black man acting in defiance of white authority. That can get you killed even now.

Days into the protest, the carpool my father was a part of was loose and disorganized. Initially he just picked up any black people he saw walking to work. Then, under the guidance of Rufus Lewis, chair of the MIA Transportation Committee, the carpools assumed some structure. There were dispatch stations in public places in more than forty black neighborhoods where former bus passengers could find a ride in a volunteer driver's private car in the morning.

Dad's station was in front of Bethel Baptist Church on Mill Street at Mobil Road. It became his new routine to stop there each morning in his used 1937 green Plymouth between 6:00 and 9:00 AM.

"Y'all need a lift?" he would ask potential riders. "I can probably fit five or six of you in here if you squeeze in tight."

In the afternoons when workers got off their jobs, they could find rides home in one of the pickup stations in the downtown area, or near the white neighborhoods where they worked. Two black-owned establishments, Dean's Drug Store at 221 Monroe Street and Posey's parking lot, were main pickup points downtown. Black people owned those properties, so police couldn't harass them there. Those who had trouble getting rides at the outset simply walked.

Mom fussed with Dad sometimes about the new routine in his life. "You know the police are watching you," she protested, worrying as any mother at home taking care of two small children would.

From the beginning, December 5, 1955, hardly any black people rode the city buses. Many walked to school and work. Soon, city officials were desperate to end the boycott. Though black passengers were mistreated, the company was financially dependent on them—they made up the bulk of the system's ridership. Montgomery City Lines cut back on the number of buses running and requested permission for a fare increase, which made travel more difficult for white commuters as well. I imagine the white powers that be were furious that Montgomery's black population had brought them to their knees.

Then February 22, 1956, arrived, nearly three months into the Montgomery Bus Boycott. Almost ominously, it was a chilly, gray day. After dropping off all his passengers, Dad was on a service call in Mobile Heights, near our house. It wasn't unusual for him to stop by home if he was in the neighborhood repairing somebody's radio or TV. My mother was usually home taking care of me and my two young brothers. Only this day, as soon as my father opened the door, he found her a bit shaken up, unnerved from a surprise visit.

"Someone from the sheriff's department was here looking for you," she said. "I told him you must be at the shop."

Over the years, Dad told this story often. He wasn't home long that day. As he was leaving, he saw an unmarked police car parked on the street out front. One officer waited in the cruiser. The other sheriff's deputy walked up toward the house. He was a plainclothes officer.

"Are you Thomas Gray?" he asked. "We've got a warrant for your arrest."

There it was, not unexpected. "What for?" Dad asked.

"It's got something to do with violating some boycott law, some antiboycott law we have," the deputy said.

Dad explained he was on a business call in a company van and asked if he could take the vehicle back to the shop and tell his employees what was going on. To his surprise, the white deputies were cooperative. "Yeah, we'll follow you on up there."

My father had known this was coming. One morning a few weeks prior he had been doing his usual passenger pickup outside Bethel Baptist when detectives stopped him, asked him his name, and demanded to see his driver's license. The officer wrote down his information, asked a few questions about why he had so many people in his car, and let him go. Dad must have been frightened. Even today, after an African American was elected to the White House and there was much talk about a postracial America, black men are still fearful of encounters with police, which can quickly turn deadly.

For Dad, this time was different: this time he was going to jail. The deputies followed him to the other side of town, about a mile and a half to Dozier's Radio, TV and Appliances store.

"Funny," Dad would say later, "they weren't hostile at all. They were pretty friendly. I thought, *This is not the usual way Negroes are arrested.* I didn't have any fear at that point. I told the folks at the shop I was about to be arrested. I told them to send somebody down to bail me out of jail. Then I was placed in the back of the sheriff's vehicle."

They didn't handcuff him. It was all very civilized. They drove about a block down West Jeff Davis and stopped in front of Rev. A. W. Wilson's house. He was pastor at Holt Street Baptist Church, the church that had held the first mass meeting after Martin Luther King Jr. had been pressed into service as the leader when the boycott began. One of the deputies got out. Mrs. Wilson came to the door and said her husband was at the church. The officer got back into the car and they proceeded up to Holt Street, which was at the end of the block. Reverend Wilson hadn't quite made it into the church yet. He was walking up the steps to the side entrance.

"Reverend, we got a warrant for your arrest here," one of the deputies yelled out.

"Well, Reverend Wilson knew me and could see me in the car," Dad recalled.

The minister told the officers, "I just got here, and I have a little business I want to attend to. Would you mind if I come on down to the jail on my own?"

"Well, that'll be fine, Reverend," the white officer said. "Come on down to the county jail. We'll expect you and serve you down there. I won't even serve you now. Just come on down." The whole scenario seemed surreal.

When they arrived at the jail, it was a chaotic spectacle like nothing Dad had ever seen. Rev. Ralph Abernathy, King's chief lieutenant, was standing there beckoning to arriving arrestees. A crowd of black residents had gathered outside the front of the jail as the deputies drove Dad around to the rear. He saw curious onlookers and boycott activists just bailed out. Dad got out of the sheriff's car and was taken inside to be processed, fingerprinted, and photographed. When he was marched around to another room, he bumped into D. Caffey, who owned a restaurant and bar called the Silver Moon.

"Here, I'll take this one," Caffey said. Caffey and some other business leaders were there to pay the bonds. Altogether, there were eighty-nine people who were charged. Most were accused of violating the Alabama code that said it was illegal, without just cause, to act in any way that would prevent a corporation from carrying on any lawful business.

Reverend Abernathy and other leading ministers were among the first to be arrested. To their surprise, jail officials provided them with a list of the boycott facilitators they were rounding up to be taken into custody. The ministers notified as many of those people as possible. Learning the news, many went to the jail to turn themselves in. Some of the people who drove cars to keep black commuters from riding the buses were disappointed that they weren't named. The roundup took several days. Among those arrested were Rosa Parks, Frank "Moon" Taylor (who lived down the street from us), Jo Ann Robinson, E. D. Nixon, and Fred Gray.

My uncle was picked up at his law office and placed in a cruiser. Somewhat apprehensive about where he was headed and what would happen, he looked out the back window as the police car drove by Dean's Drug Store, hoping his friends would see him and come down to the jail to post bail. Like most of those who were booked and released on bail that day, my father wore his arrest like a badge of honor.

Eighty-nine people on a court case is an unwieldy number. Only King was put on trial. He was convicted and fined $500. Fred Gray and his legal team, which included Charles Langford and Arthur Shores from Birmingham, appealed the case. In the end, the case was dismissed. No one paid fines or served any jail time.

Dad bragged about his part in this mass arrest all his life. In 2005, he and my mother, my brother Thomas Jr., my late husband Chris, and I went down to the basement of the municipal building that housed criminal records. We found his mug shot and took pictures of a glorious moment.

My brother Tom, my mother, Dad, and I examining the official jail boycott mug shot records.

15

WHITE ALLIES

Rev. Robert and Jeannie Graetz were about the only white people I knew when I was young in Alabama. Since blacks and whites were strictly segregated, we lived worlds apart—most of the time. The Graetzes made no bones about crossing the color line. It nearly cost them their lives.

Though my brothers and I were mostly insulated from the white world, the Graetzes became frequent visitors to our home and began a lifelong friendship with my parents. Bob, then the pastor of the black Trinity Lutheran Church on Cleveland Avenue, recalls meeting my father at a meeting of the Montgomery Improvement Association (MIA). They were both on the board. They both drove their own cars to pick up passengers. Over the course of the boycott, the Graetzes received threatening phone calls, their car was vandalized, and their home was the target of bombs on three separate occasions.

Bob and Jeannie Graetz raised seven children. In 1955, they had two in their home. Why did Pastor Graetz put his and his family's lives on the line by joining forces with the black boycotters to integrate the buses in Montgomery during the 1950s? The Graetzes graciously sat down and shared many an afternoon with me on my trips south. I always came away feeling that if anybody practiced their religion, they did.

They look like they belong together. Bob and Jeannie both have a crowning shock of white hair. Bob's is thinning now. Jeannie's is soft and curly. Both wear wire-rimmed glasses. They usually wear smiles on their faces, and almost invariably when you see them, each has on a necklace with a cross as a sign of commitment to their faith.

"You know, we loved your parents," Bob said as I sat down on a couch in their living room, eager to listen to them reminisce about the time they all spent together. I was especially amused by the cuckoo clock on the wall in their dining room that interrupted the conversation every half hour.

"We really miss them," Jeannie chimed in.

As a child I knew little of the Graetzes' backgrounds, or how it happened that they spent so much time at our house. It must have seemed strange to our neighbors to see a white couple drive up in a 1955 Chevy with two young white kids, Margaret Ellen (she later changed her name to Meta Ellis; Ellis is her mother's maiden name) and Robert III, who played in our backyard with my brother Tom Jr. and me.

"I'm going to guess the neighbors were amused to see you kids, with those young Graetz children, eating watermelon outdoors on the lawn," Dad would tell me much later. Mom insisted watermelon eating was an outdoor activity. She didn't want to have to clean up a mess inside when we all finished.

Bob and Jeannie loved to play cards. My parents said they played a mean game of bridge. From time to time, they also used to enjoy spending a few hours with my folks playing pinochle. That didn't stop, even after my mother developed Alzheimer's. The couples continued a ritual of taking turns eating lunch and playing cards. One week at my parents' house, the next week at the Graetzes'.

Many years after Bob and Jeannie moved to Ohio to avoid violence at the hands of hatemongers in Montgomery, they returned to the South. They were hired as consultants by Alabama State University, goodwill ambassadors of a sort, experts who give lectures on Montgomery's civil rights history. They moved into a house a block away from the college, around the corner from my grandmother's old house.

One day when I happened to be in town at my parents' house in Arrowhead, I hung around to watch them play cards. At the card table under the chandelier in the great room Jeannie turned to my mother and said, "Juanita, play the queen of hearts." She then reached across the table, gently lowered my mother's hand of cards, picked out the queen, and placed it on the table with the rest of the pile of cards.

Mom just grinned and said, "Are you sure that's the right one?"

The Graetzes weren't playing for the love of the game. My mother had lost the ability to understand the rules of pinochle, but her friends didn't care. They just wanted her to know she was still loved. They played after lunch, served in the family dining room. Dad sat at one end of the rectangular table near the window. Mom sat opposite him at the other end, so there was no longer any discussion of who was at the head of the table. I sat across from the Graetzes. We all clasped hands, and Bob said grace.

"Dear Lord, we thank you for this food. We are happy for the opportunity for all of us to commune on this beautiful afternoon." The prayer went on a little longer than I thought necessary for a light, casual lunch. But I peeked up from my bowed head, looked around the room, and thought, *How sweet.*

Bob grew up in West Virginia. Jeannie was from Pennsylvania. They met at Capital University in Columbus, Ohio, which is where Bob says he had "a race-relations awakening." One day at their home, as they sat with me for one of countless talks about the past, Bob told me he was concerned about the plight of African Americans, so he joined the NAACP and organized a race-relations club on campus.

While he was talking, Jeannie interrupted to remind him about demonstrations he organized against the leadership at Capital U. "for their lack of concern about African American people."

"What happened," Bob continued, "I was doing research about discrimination against Jews and almost by accident discovered how poorly African Americans were being treated. I felt compelled to do everything possible to make things better." It was during that time that he "met this young lady, who shared my dreams and my aspirations and everything else." In July 2016 they celebrated their sixty-fifth wedding anniversary. I sent them a personalized, embroidered afghan throw commemorating their years of wedded bliss, which they tossed over the back of a sofa in their living room. I believe it remains there to this day.

Bob and Jeannie Graetz were soul mates who came to Montgomery to serve a black Lutheran congregation at a time when everything was totally segregated. They had worked in black churches before, in Columbus and in Los Angeles. But their experiences at Trinity Lutheran in Alabama were altogether different. In Montgomery the couple wasn't allowed to go to many public places with church members and friends.

The church did, however, give them the opportunity to meet Rosa Parks. The NAACP Youth Council, which Parks chaired and advised, held meetings in their church. Bob says, "We got to know her and to respect her and to admire her for what she was doing."

Bob and Jeannie both agreed Parks was a lot more radical than the public's perception has been for many years. As Bob sees it, "Just being a member of the NAACP was an act of great courage, because in those days that was worse than being a Communist in the eyes of the white leadership."

"And she didn't just talk about civil rights," Jeannie said. "She taught those kids manners, and all kinds of things that she had learned from going to Miss White's school, a kind of finishing school for young ladies."

Everybody called it Miss White's school. The real name was the Montgomery Industrial School for Girls, a private school for young black girls run by two white Christian women, missionaries from the Northeast, Alice White and Margaret Beard. Though they were ostracized by their white peers, their K–8 school had a reputation that exceeded that of any of the public schools black children in the area could attend.

Rosa Parks was born in Tuskegee, but after her father left the family she and her mother moved to rural Pine Level, Alabama, about twenty-five miles southeast of Montgomery. Rosa Parks's mother, impressed with what she heard about Miss White's school, scraped together tuition and sent her daughter there after she completed sixth grade classes at her rural school.

The summer before the bus boycott, Rosa Parks attended the Highlander Folk School near Monteagle, Tennessee. Highlander was a training ground for organized labor activists and early civil rights leaders. Black and white activists there were learning to work together for change. Parks went there for residential workshops on public school desegregation after the historic 1954 *Brown v. Board of Education* Supreme Court ruling.

The school was branded by critics as a "hotbed of communism and anarchy." It was forced to close by the state of Tennessee in 1961 but has since reopened as the Highlander Research and Education Center in New Market. Its stated mission is to be a catalyst for grassroots organizing and to work with people fighting for justice and equality in Appalachia and the South. Highlander was also teaching literacy skills in the 1950s, so black people could get registered to vote. While Parks was there, she was soaking it all up, and she took back everything she learned to be ready to deal with Montgomery's segregationists.

The Graetzes also attended some workshops at Highlander. In fact, Jeannie says, the summer of 1956 Bob was on the staff. That would have been six months or so into the bus boycott, several months after the birth of their third child. "We had taken Mrs. Parks with us and the three children we had then. And while we were there, the last day, we found out that our house had been bombed.

"When we got back, the police had cordoned off our house and things were all broken, broken glass, things like that."

That is still a vivid memory for Meta, who was born in California, moved back to the West Coast for much of her adult life, then moved to Montgomery in 2015. That was the summer she and I became reacquainted. She was divorced and had a daughter. Meta moved into a bungalow on Dunbar Street, across the street from her aging parents, so she could keep a closer eye on them.

Meta, or Margie as she was called as a young child, wasn't quite four years old when the family's home, the parsonage next to Trinity Church, was bombed. She remembers arriving home from Highlander to find their house cordoned off and police officers standing out front. "They took Mom and Dad into the house," Meta recalls.

"There were still one or two more officers outside, not letting anyone else in. I got full of rage, like one of those cartoon characters with heat rising through their body and exploding. I balled up my fist and said, 'You get away from my house, you big, bad policemen!'" She was with her younger brother, Bobbie, who also joined in. "Get away you big, bad policemen! Get away!"

Ask Bob and Jeannie about the same incident, and they'll tell you it was their children's first civil rights protest. Fortunately, nobody had been around when the bomb went off, so no one was hurt. But there was damage—windows, dishes, everything glass was broken.

Jeannie, always high-spirited and fearless, says the bombing made her more angry than scared. "I figured they did it to frighten us. And we got all these calls about our going back north and getting away, not being involved. We wanted to just tell the bombers, 'We're not going anywhere. Leave us alone!'"

"There were three bombs altogether," Jeannie recalls. "That one was in August of 1956. Then in January 1957, after the bus boycott was all over with, in one night the Klan bombed four churches and two houses, including our house. And at our house, they first threw a large bomb, eleven sticks of dynamite and a container of TNT that did not explode. And then they came back by the house with a smaller bomb, hoping to set the big one off. The smaller one did explode, but it still did not set off the big one. It did considerable damage to the house. The authorities told us later, if that other one had exploded, all of us would have been killed, and so would many other people in the neighborhood."

One of the other homes bombed that night belonged to Ralph Abernathy. Abernathy's church, First Baptist, was also bombed, one of the four churches targeted. You would think all that violence would have convinced the Graetzes to leave town, but no. Said Bob, "It convinced us we needed to stay."

Surprisingly, Montgomery police did arrest seven men in connection with the bombings. Bob recalled, "Two of the men were put on trial. And when it came time for the closing arguments, the defense attorney basically said to the jury, a jury of twelve white men, 'If you convict these people, you're telling the colored people in Montgomery they can do what they want. And you don't want to send that kind of message.' And he was right. They didn't want to send that kind of a message. So the verdict was not guilty."

"The police had confessions," Jeannie remembered. "Written confessions. And all the details about it, so they knew [the accused men] were involved and had done it. Those men should have been convicted."

My parents with Rev. Bob and Jeannie Graetz in Columbus, Ohio, where the Graetzes moved and lived for years after the Ku Klux Klan kept bombing their parsonage in Montgomery.

In the days spent at Highlander, Bob and Jeannie and Rosa Parks lived in a universe totally unlike the one in Montgomery. Bob says Parks "liked that there was no discrimination at Highlander. People were people. White and black people sat together in meetings and roomed together. They ate together."

A sense of pride glowed over the Graetzes like a halo as they remembered their involvement with a woman who became a legend. After her first workshop there before the boycott, Bob says, "Mrs. Parks was telling us, she thought about this arrangement and thought this is the way it ought to be everywhere. She decided one of the things she could do when she came back was that she would never give up her seat on the bus."

In his own way, Pastor Graetz was a radical too. "The day before the boycott went on, I urged our congregation to stay off the buses. I told the members I would be driving my car all the next day, driving people to work or wherever they needed to go."

Despite his resolve and devotion to the cause, Graetz wasn't originally a member of the hastily organized Montgomery Improvement Association. But eventually, by the spring of 1956, he was invited to become a member, and like my father took his instructions from the association's transportation committee.

"In the beginning, it was all haphazard. Anybody who had a car just got on the street, drove around looking for people who were walking and picking them up. No organization to it at all. Within a few days, I got a phone call in the middle of the night, saying, 'OK, starting tomorrow morning, you're on from six to nine o'clock in the morning. You're supposed to report in at Dean's Drug Store downtown. You'll be given an assignment for driving people to work.'"

Reverend Graetz and my father were both picking up black passengers and driving them to work. Both were involved with the planning in MIA meetings—how to raise money; where to get cars, station wagons, or funeral hearses; coordinating the pickup of passengers. They became fast friends, as did Jeannie and my mother. Unaware at the outset that they were eyewitnesses to history, they were all proud of how the boycott was evolving.

"First of all," Reverend Graetz explained to me, "Dr. King had studied Gandhi and was impressed by Gandhi's use of nonviolence, of standing steadfast against oppression, yet doing it in a totally nonviolent manner, in such a way as to dare the oppressors to continue with their oppression. And with some of the campaigns in India, where people would march forward and stand in front of the troops and get beaten down, and they would be pulled out of the way and another line would step forward again to be beaten down by the police, by the troops. And they were demonstrating that no matter how much oppression was levied against them, they were not going to turn back. There was that kind of a spirit that Dr. King had assumed for himself as well. And as he began to teach these things, he became truly the spiritual leader of not only Montgomery, but of African Americans wherever they were."

Jeannie jumped in. "And the fact that the world was watching made a big difference. People came from all over the world to see what was happening here, because it was unprecedented. Everywhere else there were protests that tried boycotts, people couldn't get along without working, and they had to have transportation. And they punished them for what they were doing. And so it didn't work anywhere else. This is the first place it ever really worked!"

The Graetzes weren't the only white people in Montgomery lending a hand and a heart to the struggle for civil rights. Liberal do-gooders Clifford Durr and his wife, Virginia, were also the victims of threats and often found themselves shunned by white society. They didn't care and felt they were doing the right thing.

Clifford Durr was the attorney who mentored Uncle Fred. Virginia Durr, an activist in her own right, was also the sister-in-law of Supreme Court justice Hugo Black, who was to some an enigma. Black, the country eventually discovered, was briefly a member of the Ku Klux Klan before becoming a US senator. Ironically, later as an associate justice on the Supreme Court, he established a lengthy record as a liberal advocate of equal rights and racial justice. Many southerners never forgave him for arguing against prayer and segregation in public schools. Many acquaintances of the Durrs never forgot.

Virginia Durr was headstrong, with a mind of her own. She shocked neighbors by inviting an interracial prayer group into her home. She hired Rosa Parks to do some seamstress work for her and became her friend, providing her with a scholarship to attend Highlander Folk School. It was Clifford and Virginia Durr whom E. D. Nixon called on when he learned Parks had been arrested for refusing to give her bus seat to a white man. When her white jailers refused to give Nixon details of the arrest, he asked Durr to call the jail. The Durrs were with Nixon when he went to bail Parks out.

Nixon's niece, Alma Johnson, wants people who don't know to realize that Nixon put his house up for Rosa Parks's bond. "I feel sad over the way they treated Uncle Nick," she told me one day when I visited her home. "As much as he did to get the boycott organized, he was not given credit for what he did."

I don't remember ever meeting the Durrs, though I might have as a child. My parents knew them. In the early 1990s my brother Thomas remembers going with my parents to visit Virginia Durr at her Montgomery home. It was a real treat for him.

Tommy was in town to spend some time with my parents and brought along a pretty young woman, Erica Carpenter. He likes to boast to people outside the family circle about our civil rights history, which I confess I am also guilty of doing. That day Tommy was anxious to introduce his girlfriend to Virginia Durr.

"Let's go on the porch," Durr said when they arrived at her front door one lazy summer afternoon. The visit was a step back in time for my brother and my aging mother and father. Clifford Durr had passed away many years before. Virginia was wearing a casually comfortable soft cotton dress in pastel turquoise. Her white hair was combed back in a kind of pompadour style. She wore big, round, wire-rimmed glasses over dark bushy eyebrows, spoke in a southern drawl, and laughed easily.

Sipping ice-cold drinks on the porch, Durr and my parents took a stroll down memory lane. She looked over at my father, saying matter-of-factly, "I remember how Cliff used to help Fred with Rosa Parks and a lot of his other cases. He used to stop by the office to use Cliff's library."

Smiling as his own mind traveled back, my father noted graciously, "Things could have been a lot different. We appreciate what you guys did to help out, but you put yourselves in jeopardy."

Yes, but Clifford Durr had no fear. He had given Fred plenty of behind-the-scenes legal advice. Virginia Durr recalled, "Cliff and his nephew, Nesbitt [Elmore], were two of the first white lawyers in Montgomery who took cases for blacks, especially ones that involved civil rights issues. They went into practice together and were persecuted for their involvement with black people. Everybody thought they were both being foolish and throwing away brilliant careers. They were just doing what was right."

In her autobiography, *Outside the Magic Circle*, Virginia Durr bemoans the fact that her children were ostracized because of their parents' civil rights activities. Her unabashed candor is also obvious in a series of tape-recorded oral history interviews in libraries at several universities around the country. In most of those, she is interviewed by other people. But in a collection of oral histories now housed at the Alabama Department of the Archives and History, Durr conducts interviews herself with a group of Montgomery civil rights activists she respects. Among those are interviews with voting rights advocate Dot Moore, who I met at the Friendly Supper Club; several ministers, who were social reformers; some who had known Dr. Martin Luther King Jr.; and Johnnie Carr, who was an NAACP leader and a childhood friend of Rosa Parks.

Carr was a good friend of my parents. Her skin a deep brown tone, she wore large wire-rimmed glasses that fit snugly above a broad nose. Her lips were tightly closed whenever she smiled, which was often. Small in stature, her quiet demeanor belied a feisty zest for righting racial wrongs.

I spent a couple of afternoons in the research room of the archives wearing headsets, listening to many of those tapes. If I closed my eyes, I could almost see Virginia leaning in toward her microphone as she questioned Johnnie.

"Were you active in the movement before Dr. King came to town?" she wanted to know.

"Yes," Johnnie almost whispered, as she took a deep breath. "When I did insurance work back around 1941, we were in people's homes, trying to get them registered to vote. Trying to stop police brutality. If there was a rape or a police brutality case, we'd go into court."

Naturally, Virginia knew people would be interested in Carr's relationship with Rosa Parks.

"So many people think Rosa and I started working together when the movement started, but we were working together long before that. I remember Rosa Parks said she saw in the paper I was running for something," Johnnie continued. "Said I wonder if that's the same Johnnie I went to school with. She came to the NAACP meeting that Sunday to see if I was. We got back together. Both of us started going to

NAACP meetings. When they had elections, Rosa would be elected for secretary and vice versa the Youth Council. We were trying to get the youth involved in community and civil rights work."

Virginia already knew much of this, but she wanted listeners to be informed. She asked, "When did you come in contact with white people?"

"The only contact I had," Johnnie confided, "was either when I worked or traded with them. The Human Relations Council was the first interracial group I was involved with, then the League of Women Voters and Church Women United."

Johnnie acknowledged that she and Virginia had become longtime friends. I could imagine her gesturing in her familiar way, hands held apart, as she explained, "I wasn't supposed to come up in your house and talk to you. I was supposed to be a maid, a cook, a washerwoman, or something. People sitting down in cafés to eat with whites was never in nobody's minds back in those days. What we were really fighting for was to keep our people from being lynched and to keep our girls from being raped, and police brutality." She went on, "I've never been afraid to speak up for myself."

As I listened to the tapes I was taken again by how much ordinary black citizens in Montgomery were fearful during the bus boycott. Just about everybody participated, but not without real concern about personal repercussions. Rev. Murray Branch, who became a minister at Dexter Avenue Baptist Church after King left, says in his interview that most of Dexter's upper-crust, middle-class members supported the movement in the background rather than actively participating in demonstrations. "Educators were afraid they might lose their jobs. Few were active in Jo Ann Robinson's Women's Political Council," he says.

During the taped interviews, Durr acknowledges that when her husband assisted Fred Gray with Rosa Parks's lawsuit, "all hell broke loose. People would call late at night and threaten." When the Supreme Court handed down *Brown v. Board of Education*, Durr says her children felt the impact in school from teachers who would tell them, "Just tell them we're not gonna teach no black children, we don't care how many laws you pass." She cleaned up the description of the children to erase the *n*-word on tape. Durr says her own kids would come home "terribly upset. Finally, we had to take them out of school . . . and send them north."

"How do you cope?" Durr said she was often asked. Her reply: "Take each day as it comes."

16

RADIO DAYS

BEFORE, DURING, AND AFTER THE BOYCOTT, my father was on the radio.

"Good afternoon ladies and gentlemen, girls and boys, out of the Southland come the Golden Gate Quartet and other artists with songs of yesterday, today, and tomorrow. Singing only as they can sing them . . ."

Dad's dulcet bass voice was piped over the airwaves from the studios of AM radio station WJJJ. He began working there in 1948 while he was still a student at Alabama State College thanks to the Booker T. Washington Insurance Company and Smith and Gaston Funeral Directors, out of Birmingham, owned by A. G. (Arthur George) Gaston.

Gaston was one of the most successful black entrepreneurs in Alabama. He was said to be the first black millionaire there. His companies had branches in several cities and towns troughout the state, and he was looking for student radio announcers for a sponsored program on WJJJ in Montgomery. Dad auditioned and got a job working Mondays through Saturdays. He alternated weekly with another student, William Johnson. The thirty-minute program they hosted was called *Songs of the Southland*.

Their offices were on Commerce Street downtown. Dad recalled signing off from the *Southland* show, "Until tomorrow when we shall meet again. Same time, same station, from Smith and Gaston and the Booker T. Washington Insurance Company, with locations in Birmingham, phone number 345-8821; Montgomery, 334-2332; and Mobile."

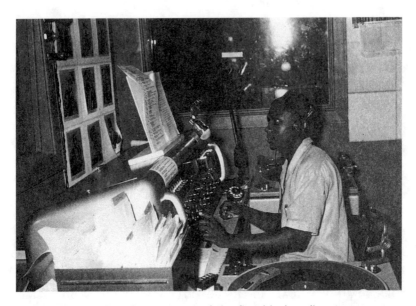

In 1948 Thomas Gray became one of the first black radio announcers in Montgomery.

Dad casually mentioned to us over the years that he had been a radio announcer. He talked about it in more detail when I got a job reporting and anchoring news on the radio myself in Boston in the mid-1970s.

Picking through the papers he had left behind, I learned that one day at work at WJJJ he met a new station announcer, Ralph Allgood, who later started his own radio station, WRMA. Allgood used his initials, Ralph M. Allgood, to form that station's call letters. The studios were on North Lawrence Street, above the Pekin Theater. The Pekin doesn't exist anymore, the victim of a wrecking ball in the late 1990s. It dated back to the vaudeville era and became a movie house for African Americans before it was demolished.

Once Dad's friend Bill Johnson got some experience under his belt, he eventually quit WJJJ, got on board with Allgood at the new radio station, and became the voice of WRMA's commercials. "He became Mr. WRMA," according to my father.

Like Allgood and his friend Johnson, my father also left WJJJ. After five years, Dad resigned in 1953 to teach mathematics and civics at St. Jude Educational Institute and to spend more time with his Dozier's radio/TV business. But some months later, in 1954, the radio bug bit him again, and he took on a new gig over at WRMA on Sundays. He and Allgood worked out a deal where he would get free radio spots for Dozier's in exchange for his work at the station. He would look forward to the time he spent on the air there on Sunday mornings, putting the station on the air by playing the National Anthem. He was on the radio at WRMA for six hours on Sundays. That's a lot of air time, but Dad loved it. When he was there, he did all the announcing, answered phone calls, and played records. The studio was a huge room with a big piano. Gospel singers would come in on Sundays and bring their drums. Sometimes the announcers would go to churches to record rocking, down-home Sunday services. Black churches would send tapes of sermons to be played on Sunday mornings. There were two Sunday morning programs that he particularly liked. One was hosted by a musicologist from Alabama State College, Professor Duncan, who between songs educated his audience about local music history.

I tracked down William Boswell, who worked at WRMA in later years. Boswell was there in the mid-1960s when Tom Joyner arrived; Joyner would eventually become the station's most famous alum. Boswell started on the air when he was a junior in high school and subsequently went on to attend Alabama State College. Boswell is still in radio. He works with another WRMA alum, Tracy Larkin, a member of the Montgomery City Council, on a web-based talk radio station, TLBN, the Tracy Larkin Broadcast Network. "Mouse" is Boswell's air name. It stuck after people teased him about a Mickey Mouse watch he used to wear. What he remembers most about old-time DJs like my Dad is that "people had never heard gentlemen like that, using the king's English and speaking so eloquently." There's a lot of undocumented history out there about black radio in Alabama, Boswell says, and he wants to write about it.

He wants people to remember the part WRMA played during the bus boycott. The way he sees it, "WRMA pulled the bus boycott movement together. Everybody had the radio on in the morning when they were frying their eggs and cooking their bacon. They listened to find out about mass meetings, to find out where Dr. King and Ralph Abernathy were going to be. People got motivated," he said. "They also tuned in to find out where to go to catch a taxi to go to work."

Years later, I found myself similarly educating my community about civil unrest.

The rocks and bottles started to fly as soon as the caravan of buses full of terrified black students began to arrive. They were thrown by white parents and some of their children.

This was not the South. I never dreamed that eighteen years after the bus boycott in Montgomery, I would find myself witness to another bitter battle for racial integration. I was living in Boston. They call it the cradle of liberty. That is not how I would have referred to it in the fall of 1974.

I was a cub reporter then at United Press International's Boston bureau. I had received an unsolicited letter from UPI out of New York asking about my journalistic aspirations now that I had a master's degree from Columbia. I assumed one of my journalism professors had recommended me. Decades later I tracked down my old boss from UPI. Jim Wieck was the Boston bureau chief back then. He told me UPI did have a minority hiring policy in the 1970s. It was run out of the office of the editor in chief, who was then H. L. Stevenson, who grew up in Mississippi. I was surprised to see a young Chinese American woman already reporting at UPI when I arrived there. Janet Wu and I were both eager and determined journalists in the raw, and as kindred spirits we quickly became good friends. We were not expecting we'd be learning our craft against a backdrop of violent rock-throwing and what she calls "venom and racism that were over the top," even for then.

On September 12, the first day of school, the entire city was on edge. Racial tensions were simmering. A desegregation plan for public schools ordered by federal judge W. Arthur Garrity mandated busing black students from all-black schools across town to white schools, and white students from all-white schools to black schools. The intention was to shift a racial imbalance. For the most part, black students were attending schools that were overcrowded and underserved. White critics who didn't want to say they were opposed to having their kids sit next to black children in school said they were against "forced busing."

The black students bused to South Boston High, located in a working-class Irish neighborhood with deep racial prejudices, came from predominantly black Roxbury High. The rioters hurled racial epithets. Police in riot gear tried to keep the peace. The violence that shocked the nation continued for many days. Eventually the National Guard was brought in to maintain order. Call me naive, but as a native of Alabama I was surprised to find such stark racism in a state up so far north.

Fresh out of journalism school, I was a neophyte reporter. I found myself, an African American woman in her early twenties, in a pit of snakes, covering a white school committee openly opposed to integrating public schools. The most public face of racial divisiveness was Louise Day Hicks, the former school committee chairwoman who was elected to the city council. She spoke in code to her white followers: "Neighborhood schools for neighborhood children," Hicks often said. Asked to explain her defiance, instead of using openly racist rhetoric, she spat out her favorite mantra, "You know where I stand."

It had been nearly twenty years since the US Supreme Court struck down segregation in public schools in its historic *Brown v. Board of Education* decision. But the federal judge's attempt to integrate schools there spawned organized resistance, from whites on the streets of the city's ethnic neighborhoods, all the way to the top leadership of the school committee and city hall. Hicks was the brains behind ROAR, Restore Our Alienated Rights, a group of anti-desegregation activists that sponsored angry marches, protests, and sit-ins. Yet despite ROAR's raucous stridency, the group was unable to stop the busing order.

Calls from reporters out in the field were constantly coming into the UPI bureau. As a rookie, my job was a combination of rewrite editor on the midnight-to-eight graveyard shift, which quickly included dayside on-the-street reporting. I recall being indoors the first day of school busing. Just as well. I was still learning to concentrate on taking calls and typing stories on a typewriter instead of writing them in longhand, with the incessant clatter in the background from those noisy Teletype machines. They delivered our news stories via telephone lines to newspapers and radio and TV stations around the country. It was a small bureau of fewer than ten reporters, with several Teletype operators, located conveniently close to the Massachusetts State House.

UPI covered state politics, but while I was there from 1973 to 1975 it seemed we were often preoccupied with busing. I could hardly believe what was happening. As part of its antibusing crusade, ROAR had called for a white boycott of classes at the start of school. In early October, a black man driving into South Boston to pick up his wife was attacked by a white mob. A riot broke out in protest by black students in the Roxbury community. A white student was stabbed by black students at another high school that December.

I was on the street in mid-October when the Massachusetts National Guard was deployed, and I saw up close the name-calling and tension as police escorted black students to school. The unrest continued. I got a new job.

My goal on graduating from Columbia was to work as a TV reporter. Alas, those jobs were hard to find. But I was still sending out résumés and tapes to radio and television stations around the country—and amassing a tall collection of rejection letters. One of them from a news director at a local Boston radio station, WHDH-AM, said while there was no opening, he would keep my résumé on file. A year later Nick Mills called me back saying, "Hey kid, you still looking for work?" It was a great opportunity, as an anchor and reporter. There I was, back covering that horrible busing story.

I rode into Boston on a wave of minority hiring that was sweeping the country. In the late 1960s and early '70s, broadcasters and newspapers were responding to pressure by African Americans over media access. Community groups challenged licenses. The major media groups agreed to cover nonwhite communities. Around the country there were calls for parity in employment, the hiring of nonwhites in proportion to their representation in a community. Young people like me got jobs.

On April 5, 1976, an African American lawyer, Ted Landsmark was attacked outside city hall by a gang of white teenagers, one of them swinging at him with the pointed end of a pole topped by an American flag. A famous newspaper photo called *The Soiling of Old Glory* documented the incident. The white protests were seemingly never ending, ugly, and out of control. At one demonstration on City Hall

Plaza, teenagers, egged on by their mothers, carried signs showing their disgust at Senators Ted Kennedy and Edward Brooke for their support of the desegregation plan. IMPEACH KENNEDY AND BROOKE some said. Then there was TED AND Ed, WISH YOU WERE DEAD. Once, when I was assigned to go to South Boston for a news conference, I tried to hail a taxi. The white driver refused to take me. I got a ride with a white reporter, who stayed close and kept an eye out for my safety.

When I caught up years later with Nick Mills, my news director at WHDH, he acknowledged most radio and TV stations were probably seeking minority hires back then. But he was quick to point out that also included women. "I hired Boston's first flying traffic reporter, Georgia Pappas, and one of the city's first female radio newscasters, Rosemary Frisino." He also hired two black men as newscasters. As for hiring me, he said, "It mattered much less to me that you were black than that you were really smart and sounded great on the air. WHDH was then on its rocket ride to the top of Boston radio ratings, and it was important that the on-air people were the best in town. I did not think I was taking much of a chance when I hired you. I was delighted that you said yes. ABC Radio later shared my judgment."

I was terribly green at my first on-air radio job. Nick was very helpful and encouraging. He was also kind. I'll never forget how he graciously pointed out to me that the *W* in the station's call letters was pronounced "double-you," not "DUB-ya," as I vocalized in a few early news reports, subtle hints of my southern upbringing. A few white staffers let me know in less-than-subtle ways that they thought I wasn't ready for prime time and was probably hired only because I was black. I couldn't have cared less.

In just under a year I received a call at the station from a network executive from the ABC Radio Network. He had been driving through New England during the Christmas holiday season, heard me on the air, and thought I was what he was looking for.

Next stop: New York City, and a career that took me to radio and TV networks and stations, a path unheard of for African Americans before a boycott and lawsuit out of Montgomery, Alabama.

17

THE MOVEMENT
WEDDING

SIX MONTHS INTO THE BUS PROTEST Uncle Teddy and Bernice Hill were married in an event that further galvanized a community coming together for a cause. I was a flower girl in this "Movement Wedding." Some people called it the "Boycott Wedding" or the "Protest Wedding." Whatever they called it, it was big. Everybody wanted to be there. Years later, when I was planning my own wedding, Aunt Bernice tried to convince me to be as inclusive as possible. "I can't invite everybody," I recall complaining. She reminded me that she and my uncle had invited almost everyone they knew to their nuptials. When they ran out of invitations, they circled around and collected invites they had already mailed to many of their friends and relatives and sent them back out to those who had not been invited but wanted to come.

Their wedding was held at Holt Street Baptist Church. There was some construction going on at our church. Besides, it wasn't big enough to accommodate the hundreds of invitees. The turnout was not unlike the droves who descended on the weekly boycott meetings going on at churches all over the city.

I was five years old, one of two flower girls, dizzy from sensory overload. Arriving at the church with my family on the actual wedding day, June 17, 1956, I had only a faint memory of a rehearsal the night before. Standing in the church vestibule with the rest of the wedding party and my mother, I was overwhelmed. "You're going to be fine," she assured me, bending down to hug me.

There were more people seated in the pews than I had ever seen in one place at the same time. My most vivid recollection was of the thick, heavy fragrance of roses, like a cloud hanging over the church. There were flowers everywhere, thanks to my uncle Hugh Gray, one of Fred's older brothers, who owned a florist shop in town. The brides-maids and maid of honor—I think there were five of them—all carried huge bouquets.

Aunt Bernice had on the most beautiful dress. It was delicate silk, ivory, floor-length, in scalloped tiers. She looked like a fairy princess, with a veil that trailed down her back. Uncle Teddy was so handsome, dressed in a smart, white tuxedo jacket with a dark bowtie. My father was the best man. Obie Elie, my uncle's best friend from his days at Nashville Christian Institute, was one of the groomsmen. Obie owned a wrecking company in Cleveland, and before I found a journalism job after graduating from Columbia University, he hired me as a secretary while I looked for work in my chosen field. Rev. Bob Graetz was also a groomsman.

I can still remember walking down the aisle with a basket of flowers, being so mesmerized by the moment that I forgot to toss the petals as I headed toward the altar. I can hear well-meaning church ladies leaning toward the aisle and whispering out loud, "Throw the flowers, baby!"

Obie has since passed on, but his wife, Elsie, remains a dear family friend. In the fall of 2016, I went to visit her at her apartment in a Cleveland retirement community. She still had vivid, fond memories of that wedding. "So many things were going on," Elsie told me. Obie had planned to host a second reception for the young couple in Cleveland with prominent guests, and there was to be a honeymoon in California. So "Obie told Bernice to buy two dresses." Since every bride needs "something borrowed," Bernice got her dress for the ceremony from Dr. Hagalyn Seay Wilson, the daughter of Dr. Solomon S. Seay Sr., the minister of the African Methodist Episcopal Zion Church, who rented out office space to my uncle when he first opened his law practice. According to Elsie, Bernice took Obie's advice and bought a second special dress to wear for the other festivities.

Elsie said, "People from all over the world and newspeople came to the wedding to get Fred's story. Poor Fred, every way he turned, they were taking his picture. Fred was an exciting guy. Everybody wanted to be around him."

There must have been a thousand people at the reception held at Derby Supper Club. To me, as a child, the building seemed cavernous. I got lost in the crowd, sampling delicious food from a series of long tables covered with white tablecloths, sipping the sweet orange sherbet cocktail from glass punch cups.

Obie and Elsie hosted the second reception at Oliver's Sportsman Club in Cleveland. This one, too, was well attended. Uncle Teddy had served as a preacher at a Church of Christ in Cleveland while he was in law school at Western Reserve University. As Elsie remembered, "Everybody who could get here came."

Then came great news for the boycotters—and an exciting wedding present for the newlyweds—the United States District Court for the Middle District of Alabama ruled in favor of the plaintiffs in *Browder v. Gayle*, finding that city ordinances requiring segregation on Montgomery buses were unconstitutional.

Of course, city officials immediately appealed. They were disappointed months later, when the ruling was upheld by the US Supreme Court.

18

MLK AND THE BARBER

THE MONTGOMERY BUS BOYCOTT introduced Martin Luther King Jr., his oratorial skills, and the nonviolent protest philosophy he borrowed from Gandhi to the world. But in early 1954 when King was new in town, few outside of Dexter Avenue Baptist Church knew who he was.

One of the first people King met outside of members and officials at Dexter was Nelson Malden. Malden was a young barber in Montgomery when he became acquainted with Dr. King before he was a household name, before black families kept a framed picture of the civil rights leader hanging on the living room wall or standing up on a coffee table next to a picture of President John F. Kennedy.

Malden got to know King better than a lot of folks—you know, in the way barbers get to know their customers. Born in Monroeville, Alabama, Malden has a ready quip for anybody who asks him if he knows the author of *To Kill a Mockingbird* when they find out the two shared a hometown. "No, I didn't know Harper Lee," he told me, like he tells everybody. "I knew Marva Collins. You know she just died. Her original name was Delores. We grew up together. Her grandmother was my mother's sister."

Malden likes to point out the importance of knowing African American history. I'm glad I knew that Marva Collins was a pioneering educator who opened a school with her own money to teach children in Chicago with learning disabilities. I did not know until I met Nelson that she was born in Monroeville.

As for being a barber, Malden figured he had no choice. His father was a barber, and there were seven sons in the family who all needed their hair cut. When King and Malden met, they were both relatively new to Montgomery.

At the time, Malden considered himself lucky. After graduating from high school in 1952, he was able to get a job cutting hair at a barbershop about a block away from his campus at Alabama State College. He needed the money to help pay his way through school.

In the spring of 1954, King was wrapping up at Boston University, still working on completing his doctoral thesis. He had just recently married Coretta Scott, the attractive young student from Marion, Alabama, he met when she was studying singing at the New England Conservatory of Music. They moved to Montgomery, where King became minister at Dexter Avenue Baptist Church. He was recruited by church deacon Robert Nesbitt, an insurance company executive.

In the winter of 1953, Nesbitt had gone to Atlanta, where Daddy King, Martin Luther King Sr., was pastor of Ebenezer Baptist Church, to convince Martin Jr. to at least consider Dexter Avenue. There were other churches trying to woo King to their pulpits. King agreed to be a guest speaker at Dexter the following January and committed to become the full-time minister by the fall.

Nelson Malden was eighty-one in the summer of 2015, still a barber, working in the Malden Brothers Barbershop, which he and his brothers Marvin and Spurgeon opened in 1958 at 407 South Jackson Street after the boycott was over. It was on the first floor of the building that housed the Ben Moore Hotel, a block down the street from where Dr. King and his family lived at the Dexter Avenue Baptist Church parsonage.

One sunny afternoon my boyfriend, now my husband, and I walked in the door of the barbershop and asked if Nelson Malden was there. A tall, light-skinned black man with a short crown of white hair, dressed in a burgundy barber shirt and khaki pants said, "That's me."

Bob went over, extended his hand for a shake, and said, "Hi, I'm Robert Nesbitt," which made Malden laugh. "I used to know a Robert Nesbitt," he said.

Nelson Malden, Martin Luther King
Jr.'s barber, at the Malden Brothers
Barbershop in Montgomery.

"I know," Bob said, "the guy who brought Martin Luther King to Montgomery from Atlanta. I know all about him. No relation." It was a fun introduction.

Malden had the front chair. His other barber, Steve, was at work clipping someone's hair. The barbershop probably looked pretty much the same as when it opened nearly sixty years earlier, though I'm sure the pictures on the walls have evolved over time.

Prospective customers take a seat in one of the brown wooden chairs lining the wall, where Bob took up a post. The chairs have cushioned seats and arm rests and might have once sat in a school auditorium. The walls are wood paneled and covered with reminiscences of bygone eras as well as reminders of today. Black-and-white photos of Dr. King and his wife, Coretta, hang next to color pictures of President Barack Obama and his wife, Michelle. Nelson Mandela's photo adorns the wall, as does a picture of Montgomery's first black bus driver, hired after the boycott was over. And, of course, an early picture of Nelson Malden himself cutting a young boy's hair. There aren't that many pictures of white people on the wall, though one photograph of a white man figures prominently—that of federal judge Frank Johnson, the architect of many historic rulings that helped desegregate the South.

Signs hanging from a dropped ceiling read COLORED WAITING ROOM and SLAVE CATCHER, prompting the kind of provocative conversations you expect at a black barbershop. Nelson didn't shy away from politics; he ran for the Montgomery County Democratic Executive Committee back in the 1960s, on the advice of white activist Virginia Durr.

No way around it, Malden is a real talker. He's got a lot of stories, and he likes to tell them. That day as he sat in his barber chair, he didn't mind telling them to me, and he wasn't shy about recounting them in front of the video camera I mounted on a tripod in his shop. A small touch of vanity runs through his veins. I think he ran a comb through his hair when I went to retrieve the camera from my car.

Malden was the youngest barber at the first Montgomery shop he worked in back in 1954. As he puts it, "I had a chance to catch all the new customers." He had a ten o'clock class most mornings, so he never liked to take a customer after 9:40 AM—he didn't want to be late for school.

One morning he saw a blue Pontiac pull up in front of the barbershop. "I saw this young man get out," he says. "I looked at his head. I said, 'Oh heck, I can knock him out in ten or fifteen minutes.' When the man entered the shop, I asked him what was his name. He said, 'Martin Luther King.' I said, 'Where you from?' he said, 'Atlanta, Georgia.' I said, 'What are you doing in town?' He said, 'I'm here to preach my trial sermon at Dexter.' I said, 'Oh, that's my church.' He said, 'Good to meet you.' So after I finished cutting his hair, I gave him the mirror, said, 'You like your haircut?' He said, 'Pretty good.' You know, you tell a barber 'pretty good' that's kind of an insult. When he came back two weeks later, I was busy. Another barber chair was vacant, but King waited on me. I remembered that sarcastic statement he had said the first time he sat in my chair, and I said, 'That must have been a pretty good haircut?' He said, 'You're all right.'

"After I cut his hair seven or eight times, I noticed he never gave me a tip. So I decided to use a little psychology on him one day. I said,

'Rev.' I said, 'When you preach a sermon on Sunday and some of the members tell you what a good sermon, doesn't that make you feel good?' He said, 'Yeah.' I said, 'When you go to a restaurant and you have a nice meal and the waitress gave you good service, you give her a tip?' I said, 'Don't you think that makes her feel good?' He said, 'Yeah.' But that's when he turned the tables on me. He said, 'Do you put ten percent of your earnings in church?' I said, 'Rev., I'm a student at Alabama State College. I cannot afford to put ten percent of my earnings in church.' He said, 'Nelson, I'm a pastor at Dexter Avenue Baptist Church, and I can't afford to tip you, either.'"

If he's told that story once, he's told it a million times. I heard him tell it once to a special program at his alma mater, which is still building a collection of oral histories from those who knew King or witnessed the bus boycott firsthand. Malden, by the way, says back in the day his regulars used to tip him twenty-five or fifty cents on a haircut that cost no more than three dollars.

The stories spill out almost in one long run-on sentence, clipped off occasionally by phone calls. "Malden Barbershop," he answers. "Hey! Five o'clock? You coming over? OK. I'll be waiting when you get over. Bye."

Malden picks up right where he left off after answering the phone. His speech is so hurried, twice I had to ask him to slow down.

"I had no idea at the time I'd be cutting the hair of one of the most historical figures of the time," Malden says. "After he got the Nobel Peace Prize, he came by the barbershop. I said, 'Rev., what was the closest call you ever had to death when you was leading the movement?' He said the closest call he ever had was when he had his first book signing in New York, when this deranged lady stabbed him in the chest. He said if he had coughed or sneezed, he probably would have bled to death. He said that's the first time he saw a white light. Closest he ever came to death."

As I continued my interview with Malden, a couple of customers dropped by the barbershop. Each nodded at Malden, then either proceeded to Steve's chair or took a seat to wait and listen in on the barber's ramblings. People are accustomed to seeing Malden holding court and reminiscing about King and the movement. Malden has strong feelings about the bus boycott and why it started. He likes to acknowledge the women responsible for making it happen. He gives Jo Ann Robinson and Dr. Mary Fair Burks credit for distributing fliers that notified people about the boycott after Rosa Parks was arrested. Robinson used the Alabama State mimeograph machine to run off the notices, risking her job at the college.

The flyer they passed out on neighborhood front porches and to churches, with help from students and other activists in the Women's Political Council, said in part, "Another Negro woman has been arrested and thrown in jail because she refused to get up out of her seat on the bus for a white person to sit down. . . . We are, therefore, asking every Negro to stay off the buses Monday in protest of the arrest and trial. Don't ride the buses to work, to town, to school, or anywhere on Monday."

"Who was the Women's Political Council?" Malden asked rhetorically. "Well, all the professional women, doctors' wives, and teachers all joined the organization. They were radical in a sense. But all they were asking for was more humane treatment. See the constitutional question came in much later. Fred Gray, that was much later on."

I knew only three black doctors who worked in Montgomery: Dr. James Caple, Dr. R. T. Adair, and Dr. Moses Jones. They were doctors at a time when physicians made house calls. Fred Gray and Charles Langford were the city's first black lawyers. Truth be told, most of the professional women in Montgomery then were teachers at the college or in public schools in rural areas nearby. But that was just a minor point in Malden's story.

"The main thing, the bus company was losing tons of money because of the boycott, because most of their riders were black. When the supervisor from the parent company came to Montgomery, he said, 'Why do we have this problem with the boycott?' And he figured out it was basically this one bus driver on that one bus line that picked up most of the black passengers. Blake. Mrs. Parks had had a run-in with him several times before.

"City Lines, South Jackson–Washington Park. Large black population on this side of town. White people in the middle. Large black population on the west side of town. I guess Blake was assigned to keep order on that bus," he figures.

Malden was talking about James Blake, who would eventually be named in the *Browder v. Gayle* lawsuit. The city's mayor, W. A. "Tacky" Gayle; the City Board of Commissioners; and the Montgomery City Lines Bus Company were also named as defendants.

How did Malden know so much about what was going on? He was just a young college student at the time. A C student at that, he says. But he had his hands on scissors that cut important people's hair. "I was cutting Martin Luther King's hair. I cut Rev. Vernon Johns's hair before he left. Father Robert DuBose. All these people were in the foundation of the movement. Me being halfway astute, by listening to those people in the shop, that's how I picked up good information. And I had class under Mrs. Burks and Mrs. Robinson. Another thing, what Mrs. Burks did, she had some students ride different bus lines. My assignment was from Court Square to Capitol Heights. I get on the bus and go back to class to report my experience.

"One bus driver, one bus line, where you had the most problems," Malden recalls. "You had less problems on the other bus lines, predominantly white neighborhoods or predominantly black neighborhoods. But South Jackson–Washington Park, where you had white people getting on in the middle of the route, the mixture of east side and west side with a lot of black populations, that's where the problem came in."

Malden remembers details about the bus boycott like it was yesterday. "When the bus boycott first started, the city assigned police escorts. The reason the police escorts were assigned to the buses was because they thought the militant blacks were gonna bother the Uncle Tom blacks. The Uncle Tom blacks thought they might want to ride the bus, but when they saw the police behind the bus, they thought the police might arrest them, so they didn't get on the bus for the most part."

Before Montgomery was really introduced to the King charisma, the highbrow worshippers at Dexter Avenue Baptist Church were about the only residents who had any contact with him. They were the city's upper crust with a reputation of looking down their noses at the lower classes. They had begun to show their displeasure with presiding minister Vernon Johns long before King's arrival. Despite his brilliant sermons from the pulpit, Johns irritated congregants with his lectures about the importance of gaining their own economic independence, with farming as the major tool.

Reverend Johns led by example. He had a garden and sold produce on the street outside the church. My father said many Dexter members were mortified. Others followed Johns's counsel and established a cooperative supermarket in the Mobile Heights neighborhood called Farm and City. My father thought it was a progressive idea, black people producing and selling their own fruits and vegetables. Among his paperwork I found an old yellowing document that showed he bought stock in the company.

The congregation at Dexter Avenue also found Johns to be rather outspoken on matters of race. According to Malden, "Johns used to preach that we should stop going to the back doors of white restaurants to get food and service. Said we have enough eating places in our community to take care of our hunger needs."

The church board eventually took Johns up on one of his threats to resign, and King became the pastor. Lo and behold, says Malden, "King kind of picked up on the same thing, because a lot of the members of Dexter were going to a place called the Green Lantern. It was on Sebring Road, off Norman Bridge Road, near Fairview Avenue. It was a restaurant down there where black people drive around to the back. You blow your horn, and the waitress comes out and takes your order. You wait in your car. It not only was a restaurant, but it was a lover's lane, too, for black people. So then it was very popular," Malden remembers. "When King came to Dexter, he was preaching we should stop."

What stands out in Malden's mind is an incident that happened one Friday night when he was still in college.

"When we got off work my boss man then said, 'Hey, Nelson, let's go over on Fairview and get some of that fried chicken.' So we go over on Fairview Avenue, and you go to the side door. Knock on the door. The waitress comes and takes your order. You pay for it, and you wait on the sidewalk till it's cooked.

"This particular Friday night, we were standing on the sidewalk, waiting for our chicken to be cooked. I looked up, and I saw this blue Pontiac coming. 'Hey, Warren'—my boss man's name's Warren—I said,

'That's Reverend King's car.' He said, 'Shore is!' So I ran and jumped in the car to keep him from seeing us, cuz I know what he had preached about.

"By the time my boss man got ready to come get in the car, to keep the man from seeing us, the lady came out and said, 'Your chicken is ready.' So Warren had to make up his mind whether he was gonna go back and get the chicken, or whether he was gonna be embarrassed. He made up his mind to go back and get the chicken.

"By that time, Reverend King's car was right in front of us. Warren had two chicken boxes in his hand, and he just bowed to Reverend King. Reverend King nodded at him. I said to myself, 'I shore hope Reverend King doesn't come back to the barbershop and say anything before the customers, what he saw us do.'

"Sure enough, the next Saturday night King came in the barbershop. It was full of customers. He came in. He got in the chair. He whispers to me, 'How was the chicken?' I said, 'How'd you know it was chicken?' He said, 'Some of my members gave me some one time. It sure was good.' I said, 'You'd better stop eating those white folks' food. It'll make you sick.' He said, 'I see you're pretty healthy.'"

I'm still trying to understand the inherent contradictions of segregation. White people didn't want to serve Negroes food inside their restaurants, but they let black cooks make food for their families in their homes. It was so odd the way blacks and whites coexisted during the Jim Crow era. They lived in clusters in different parts of town and went to separate churches and schools. They didn't want black children sitting beside white children in school classrooms. But they let black maids nurse their babies. All that aside, it was the segregated situation on the buses that got Montgomery in trouble.

19

THE POLICE CHIEF'S DAUGHTER

STARVED TO KNOW MORE about Alabama's capital and its bus boycott history, whenever I was in town I attended One Montgomery's Tuesday morning breakfast meetings. It's about a ten-minute drive from our duplex on Terrace Avenue.

The crash pad, however, became much more than that. My mother's old piano decorates the front living room. Her guitar rests on the floor beside it. Our place is a block around the corner from the home of Bob and Jeannie Graetz. I sometimes pick them up to go to One Montgomery meetings.

The group meets across the street from Jackson Hospital, on one of the upper floors of a rather bland-looking medical building that houses doctors' offices. Our attendance ritual is like clockwork: drive past the campus of Alabama State University, get off the elevator in the medical building, and enter a big corner room full of tables covered with white tablecloths. Members sign in at the coffee table, grab coffee or tea in Styrofoam cups, and head over to the buffet breakfast for a standard menu of scrambled eggs, grits, bacon, sausage, and toast served on paper plates.

At precisely seven o'clock, when everybody is mostly settled, breakfast plates at our seats, we all stand facing the American flag on the wall in the back of the room. The chair leads the group in the Pledge of Allegiance. Then there's new business. Each meeting there is a special guest speaker, somebody of note in the Montgomery community. At one, the late Mary Ann Neely, a local white historian, came and talked about the evolution of the city's downtown architecture from the 1830s, when decrepit buildings were demolished, to the early 1960s, when malls stole business away from the downtown. Her remarks covered recent history to present times, when the city's minor league baseball team stadium was created out of an old freight train warehouse. Previously the Orlando Rays, the team moved from Florida to Montgomery in 2004 and was renamed the Montgomery Biscuits. One year when my husband Chris was still alive and we were visiting my parents, he found it so amusing that a sports team would call itself the Biscuits that he insisted we go to Riverwalk Stadium to watch a game and buy a team jersey.

At another One Montgomery breakfast, Bill Ford spoke. He's the African American president of the alumni group that fought, albeit unsuccessfully, to keep St. Jude Educational Institute open. St. Jude, a college prep school, opened around 1938 and served the city's black community until the end of the 2013–2014 academic year. Ford discussed the losing battle to block its closure and took issue with claims by the archdiocese of Mobile that the school was no longer financially viable due to low enrollment. He felt young black students would get more support there than on any of the three campuses of Montgomery Catholic Preparatory School, which had largely been the choice of the city's white Catholic students. As with all guests, after a brief talk, he took questions.

I look forward to the meetings. They're informative. Members are congenial. After my brother Frederick died in January 2018, members of the group all signed and sent me a lovely condolence card.

Early on, at the beginning of one meeting I asked if anyone knew anything about the bus boycott era that they thought might be of interest to me. Would they let me know after the meeting? One person eager to chat was Sally Mosher, who happened to be seated at my table that day. Sally is a white woman in her seventies, with fashionably cropped white hair you can't help but notice, chic, rimless eyeglasses, and a vibrant personality.

"You may want to know something about my father," she said confidently.

"Who is your father?" I asked.

"Clyde Sellers," she said.

I knew the name. I couldn't believe my luck. I did want to know more. Everything I'd read or heard about Clyde Sellers had been negative. He was the white police commissioner during the bus boycott, portrayed in history books as a bigot who took a hard-line stance against desegregating city buses. He used his police department to enforce a "get tough" policy instituted by Mayor W. A. Gayle and other city officials to harass black boycott participants to try to force an end to the protest.

Hundreds of black people were stopped and ticketed for trumped-up traffic and loitering violations. My own mother, an extremely careful motorist, was pulled over by a policeman and accused of rolling through a stop sign. My father, who loved to tell the story, says the officer did not give her a ticket. But many of those who were leaders of the boycott were special targets. Martin Luther King Jr. was arrested during the period shortly after the boycott started, charged with speeding. Word is he had just picked up some black folks waiting for a ride at one of the carpool pickup locations. He was charged with driving thirty miles an hour in a twenty-five-mile-per-hour zone.

My uncle references several instances of the "get tough" policy in his book. In one incident, my father drove him to the Montgomery airport so Fred could fly to Boston to give a speech in place of Dr. King, who had a scheduling conflict. The plane was delayed, so Dad and Uncle Teddy took a seat in the waiting room, where they were told to move to the segregated section. My father sensed trouble. When my uncle didn't move, two police officers arrested him. Dad left to go to his car to follow the policemen to be sure they were taking his brother to jail. They did. But once they arrived a bonds man recognized my uncle right away and bailed him out. A newspaper reporter drove Fred back to the airport.

With those stories and others like them dancing around in my head at the One Montgomery breakfast, I exchanged contact information with Sellers's daughter, Sally, and we promised to get together sometime to talk.

Almost before we had time to plan anything, I found a note on my front porch. Sally had driven by and dropped it off. It contained the address of a local eatery in the Cloverdale community, not too far from my house, and suggested I go there for Saturday morning brunch. When I called to ask about the note, she said, "Everybody who's anybody stops through there, the politicos and community leaders." She thought I might find chats with them illuminating. I dropped by the restaurant that very week.

The restaurant is for casual dining and has a hot buffet breakfast of southern specialties. That means you can find fried catfish and grits on the menu with your scrambled eggs. A white man and his son sat down at an empty table where I had left my newspaper. When I returned from the buffet, they welcomed me to join them.

"You're from out of town, aren't you?" the father queried. I get that from most white people I encounter in Montgomery. I guess the lack of a southern accent is one giveaway. Neither of my parents, though both from the South, had strong southern accents either. And they encouraged me and my brothers to always use "the king's English," which made some of our grade school friends ask, "Why do you talk so proper?" more often than I cared for back when I was a child.

That day in the Cloverdale breakfast spot, I told my new dining companions, "I live in the DC area, but I was born here." I told them I was working on a book about life during the 1955 bus boycott. I wondered if the father had any thoughts about the upcoming sixtieth anniversary and plans to commemorate the historic event.

"I don't like the idea of all that hoopla," he ventured. "It's stirring the pot," he said. "Bad for race relations. I was born after the boycott. I didn't have anything to do with all that."

What he essentially wanted to know was "When do the children stop paying for the sins of the fathers?" I didn't have a good answer for him.

Even with the rays of the sun slipping through the sides of the green drapes in my Montgomery bedroom, I was slow to rise. I am not a morning person. It just about killed me when I had to wake up in the wee hours to be at the TV station when I was reporting on Fox *Morning News* in

DC. But this morning I was looking forward to the sit-down interview I had scheduled with Sally Mosher. Coffee and cereal first. Then I checked out my camcorder to be sure it was in order. Sally said she didn't mind if I recorded our chat.

Her townhouse is close by, a lovely tan brick, one-story unit in a small, desirable community. It's tucked away in a tree- and shrub-lined area a few blocks north of Alabama State. After the buses were deseg-regated back in the 1950s, much of the city's housing stock became more integrated as well. Wealthy whites keep moving away, largely to the east, but as soon as they get there, a few blacks move next door. The neighborhood my parents lived in after they moved back from Cleveland is in the eastern part of the city. A handful of their neigh-bors are black. They became friends with most of the whites who lived nearby. I'm not saying racism disappeared, but the desegregation process along with fair housing pressures of the 1960s opened communities that had once been closed to African Americans.

Sally Mosher didn't strike me as the type of white woman who would run away from black neighbors. She's very progressive, down to earth, and easygoing. I liked her immediately. She has a small dog who is very protective of her. She had to put it away in another room so the barking wouldn't disturb our visit.

"Where do you want me to start?" Sally asked. She was as eager as I was to take a walk down Montgomery's memory lane. We began the year of the bus boycott, December 1955. She was thirteen years old, in the eighth grade. The city's black residents were filling the streets, walking on their way to and from work or riding in cabs or in other people's private cars. I'm sure one couldn't help but notice.

"But there was no discussion about it in school," Sally said. "I was trying to think of what we had in the way of history in the eighth grade. I don't remember ever hearing anything in school, until I got in the tenth grade, I believe, or eleventh, whatever year it was we had Alabama history again."

Of course, her teachers did talk about slavery.

"I remember being a little confused by the discussion, because the background that I had, even at that time, was that slavery was protec-tive," Sally said.

"Protective of what?" I wanted to know.

"Of the slaves. They didn't have to be on their own and be responsible for taking care of themselves, according to my teacher," said Sally. "That was the picture I had. I got that in fourth-grade history too."

By the time of the boycott, Sally was living at home with her parents and a younger sister, who was ten years old. An older brother and sister were grown and had already left home. Her father, Clyde Sellers, was the police commissioner, now much maligned in historical references as a bigot. Despite being sworn to protect and serve the city's citizens, he made it clear he was adamantly opposed to looking out for Montgomery's black citizens and to integrating the City Lines buses. He used rabidly racist language, publicly joined the anti-desegregation White Citizens' Council, and threw his police department's weight around to block integration activists at every turn. But when he came home in the evenings, he didn't talk about it with his family.

"He did not," Sally said emphatically. "Now when he was in the legislature, he came home and talked about whatever bill he was involved in, but during the boycott, he did not."

The family wasn't rich, but they lived in a big, comfortable house on Perry Street, between Felder and Clanton Avenues. Sally thought it was a "creaky, wonderful old house," not too far from the then all-white Lanier High School, close to the home of Clifford and Virginia Durr.

"We lived around the corner from the Durrs, where all that activity went on," said Sally. "I did not know then there were things going on. I walked to school, by their house. But I knew nothing."

I suppose some white families were, in the same way as black families, shielding their children as best they could from the ugly truth about segregation and the violence spawned during the boycott. It's hard to imagine, though, that news didn't leak out about the bombings of the houses, parsonages, and black churches. Though I must confess, when we were living through that period, my parents never mentioned anything to me or my brothers about any of that.

Sally does recall threatening phone calls that came into her home. "In my memory," she says, "whether this is because Daddy told me or what I gleaned from the phone calls, was that there were threats to the house. People were gonna bomb our house. I don't know whether it was in response to something. I mean obviously it was in response to the police activity."

Though Martin Luther King Jr. emphasized the importance of non-violence, not everyone bought into it. Certainly, there were some blacks who answered threats with threats. That the racist police commissioner was the target of telephone threats is not a stunning revelation.

"My father was usually soft spoken. But I would hear him yelling, 'Don't ever call here again!' that kind of thing." Sally says her father never mentioned who was making the threats, but Sellers must have figured he needed to defend his family from possible attacks.

"All I remember," Sally said, "is that I was moved to the back. I don't remember if it was before the boycott or after it started or what. But at some point, they moved me from the front bedroom, the only bedroom that could be reached from the street, to Daddy's bedroom, which was in the back." Her father stepped up security around the family home.

"There were policemen under my bedroom window. I was on the second floor, and I could hear the two policemen at night, on the radio, their police radio." She says her mother had a gun and learned to shoot around that time.

"Daddy went out of town one weekend, and my sister and I slept in the bed with Mother," Sally remembers. "The pistol was on the table."

Sally didn't know that during the city's so-called get tough period, her father ordered his police officers to crack down on black residents. Many of those standing around downtown black businesses, like Dean's Drug Store on Monroe Street or the Posey parking lot, waiting for rides home, were charged with loitering. She also was unaware of harassment and ticketing of blacks on trumped-up traffic charges.

Sally did know that her father and Mayor Gayle rushed over to Rev. Martin Luther King Jr.'s house the January evening it was bombed.

"He went over there to be sure everything was OK," Sally said. Sellers and the mayor were booed from the assembled crowd. Despite that, the city officials promised to search for and prosecute wrongdoers.

Through the veil of time, and as she matured, Sally came to view her father not as the man she knew at home but as a more complex figure, like all of us eventually do. Most children grow up thinking their parents are perfect, only to discover their flaws as adults. What do you do when you grow up and find out your father is a racist?

Sally grappled with trying to understand her father and his role in the city's history.

"You would say your father was a racist?" I asked her.

"Oh yeah," she exclaimed, in no uncertain terms. "I don't know how uncommon it was at the time. I don't recall his hating people who were black. I just think he felt, he believed, that they were inferior. Which was apparently very heavily subscribed to in Montgomery. In the South. And maybe in the North," she added matter-of-factly.

"Daddy was very unhappy during the boycott," she says. "He felt overwhelmed with all of the responsibility. He wanted to do what was, in his mind, the right thing."

So Clyde Sellers went to visit his father, who had been the longtime sheriff in a tiny town in Tallapoosa County in central Alabama, looking for advice. Sally says her grandfather told her father his job was to maintain safety in the city.

Of course, what Sellers is known for during the bus boycott is being the strong-arm who enforced Alabama law, banning integration. He spoke loudly and publicly, including when he and the other city commissioners joined the White Citizens' Council.

"My daughter taught freshman English at Auburn [University] one time and heard some of his speeches," Sally told me. "She knew him as her grandfather. He was a nice grandfather. He was old. He was out of politics. And she was so surprised at the racism expressed in his speeches."

Sally speculates that the bus protest might have been shorter and less acrimonious if her father had lost the police commissioner election to his opponent, the incumbent Dave Birmingham, who was more of a liberal populist.

In retrospect, Sally Mosher thinks many of her life choices may have been out of rebellion. For instance, she attended a training program at Tuskegee Institute, a historically black college. "My parents were not happy." Sally says she grew up to be a liberal idealist who hated poverty and wanted to help people. "I felt like racial discrimination was so detrimental," she said.

After attending Vanderbilt University and graduating from Auburn University with a major in sociology, she became a librarian in an all-black elementary school. She worked with the Head Start program and later became an investigator of child sex abuse.

Sally is still trying to make peace with how she feels about her father. She called me back after our first conversation, wondering aloud if her assessment had been too caustic. She thought "racist" might have been too strong a term, venturing that her father was simply a product of his time.

20

THE BUS MANAGER
AND HIS FAMILY

IN THE MAIN SANCTUARY OF THE FIRST BAPTIST CHURCH on South Perry Street, the stage was set for an annual Christmas tradition. It was mid-December 2014. More than 150 choral singers took their places amid the rows of a huge, artificial, twelve-tier Christmas tree decorated with thousands of brightly colored lights with a star on top. Accompanied by a live orchestra, with performances by liturgical dancers, the choir told the story of the nativity. A three-drummer ensemble played a version of "The Little Drummer Boy." At the organ was Sara Jo Bagley. She's been playing the organ for more than sixty-four years.

I had come to the church looking for her. I wanted to find out more about her father-in-law, J. H. Bagley. He had been the manager of the City Lines Bus Company, the bus company targeted for desegregation by Montgomery's black population in the 1950s. Bagley had sat in on meetings with Jo Ann Robinson, Dr. Martin Luther King Jr., Fred Gray, and others as they demanded fair treatment on municipal buses. What I was also extremely curious about was finding out how the white people were living on their side of town during that racially turbulent period in our nation's history.

It turns out people from all over the country wrote letters to the city's then mayor, W. A. Gayle, and to the bus company during the boycott.

After Bagley died, the bus company handed over a box full of that correspondence to his family. Those letters tell an interesting story, which I
wrote about in the April 5, 2015, edition of the *Montgomery Advertiser*'s
Alabama Voices column. Here's some of the article:

> Much has been said about missing voices and how half of the
> story has not been told because those white people who were
> vehemently against the boycott and integrating the buses never
> spoke out.
>
> However, if you want to hear some of those angry voices, now
> you can. It's years after the fact, but they speak in volumes and
> are now available in a treasure trove of letters that were sent to
> the Montgomery City Lines bus company and then Mayor W. A.
> Gayle while the boycott was going on. Mostly they are from the
> Deep South, but some came from as far west as California and as
> far north as Indiana. Surviving family members of J. H. Bagley,
> the man who managed the bus company then, donated the letters
> that are currently housed in boxes at the Alabama Department
> of Archives and History.
>
> Be forewarned, some of the correspondence is oozing with
> hateful vitriol and is unsettling. There are numerous letters from
> people who attached checks for $1, $5 and $10 to help offset
> the bus line's loss of business during the protest as city officials
> fought to continue segregation.
>
> A factory representative from Birmingham enclosed a check
> "as a token from one who is back of you 100% in your fight
> for our Southern way of life and against the forces that would
> destroy this heritage, both the Communists and the NAACP."
>
> A retiree from Alabama City sent money and said, "That Big
> Jim Folsom our Negro loving governor is the cause of all this
> trouble."
>
> One anonymous letter opined that the "non-segregation
> law will lead to vast numbers of inter-marriages in America."
> Another exhorts transportation officials to "keep fighting for
> white supremacy and segregation." A brief note on stationery
> with a Mississippi law firm letterhead and signed by a law firm
> partner said his five dollars was to "help compensate for any loss
> your company is suffering by doing what is right."

There is a strong undercurrent of angst about integration, but the collection also includes a few letters from voices of reason. Many of those were from religious leaders. A Unitarian and Universalists group in Chicago took up a church collection to aid the Montgomery Improvement Association, which coordinated the boycott, "in the aid of the moral and social welfare of the citizens." Many expressed gratitude after the Supreme Court struck down segregation on buses.

Bus manager Bagley responded to all the letters, saying the bus company did not ask for any donations, but that it appreciated any, and all contributions. Mayor Gayle also responded in writing to much of the correspondence. He blamed the city's problems on "outside interference" and said "segregation must be preserved for the mutual welfare of both races."

You won't find explanations for the racism in the collection, but the letters speak loudly of the cultural prejudices of the period. How do those people feel now? If they were so strongly opposed to equal treatment for blacks back then, have they since done an about-face and unlearned hatred based on skin color?

———————

At the end of the beautiful Living Christmas Tree performance, I left my seat in the balcony and walked down to the front of the sanctuary and approached Sara Jo Bagley. I waited for several of her fans in the crowd to fawn over her before introducing myself. I told her I'd been writing some columns in the *Montgomery Advertiser* and asked if I could interview her later. I'm sure she figured I wanted to ask about her career as an organist. I confess I did not bring up the matter of her father-in-law and the letters at the archives until later. Sara Jo agreed to an interview anyway, and I spent a lovely morning a few days before Christmas with her and her husband, James Bagley Jr., at their house made of stone on nearby Lake Martin.

They sat in twin burgundy-colored recliners in a wood-paneled family room. A family picture sat next to a telephone on a credenza. James Jr.'s cane was parked nearby. Recovering from a stroke, he wasn't quite as talkative as his wife. He appeared to struggle to get some of his thoughts straight and his memory in line. When there were doubts, Sara Jo jumped in to try to set the record straight.

Sara Jo, eighty, is a musician who has been playing the organ at churches since high school—Baptist, Methodist, and Presbyterian. First Baptist is her home church now. Before his stroke several years ago, James, eighty-three, attended services at Worldwide Church of God.

"But it's a Living Church of God now," he said. "And it has a black minister in Montgomery. That's where I go."

"Where he *did* go, before he was so handicapped," Sara Jo chimed in, smiling, and not unkindly. They both acknowledge his stroke and its aftereffects, and sometimes joke about it.

James and Sara Jo met when they were in college. He was at Auburn. She was at Montevallo. It was Alabama College, State College for Women, back then. Their first date was a blind date, an introduction through Sara Jo's sister and brother-in-law. The two got married a year later, on December 17, 1955, the same month the bus boycott started. In fact, the boycott almost interfered with their big day at Trinity Presbyterian Church. They were afraid his father wouldn't be able to attend.

"There was a meeting regarding civil rights, the bus boycott, that he was not able to go," said Sara Jo. She thinks it was an organizational meeting, involving the mayor and Dr. Martin Luther King Jr. With a big smile on her face she added, "That was just a meeting that he was not able to attend 'cause family came first."

Which reminded James Jr. of how contentious those times were. "It wasn't Montgomery City Lines that was fighting the boycott, it was the city of Montgomery, Mayor Gayle," he stated emphatically. "Mayor Gayle. He's the one. He told Daddy he'd put them out of business in Montgomery before he'd let immigra . . ." He stumbled on the word, but Sara Jo jumped right in. "Integration."

"Integration is what I'm trying to say," James intoned. "He said, in other words, they'd integrate those buses over his dead body! He was just determined they weren't going to do it."

"Pop was doing his job, following orders from headquarters," Sara Jo insisted. In fact, on more than one occasion the National City Lines parent company had expressed a willingness to allow integration on its buses in Montgomery. But at every turn city officials reminded them that segregation was the law in Alabama's capital, even after the US Supreme Court affirmed an appeals court case outlawing segregation on buses in Columbia, South Carolina.

The South Carolina case was vindication for Sarah Mae Fleming, a maid who refused to give up her seat on the front of a Columbia bus and was arrested in June 1954. It was a case that never gained the clout or notoriety of Rosa Parks's arrest. Bus companies in South Carolina, Texas, and some other southern states began to integrate in late 1956 after that ruling. National City Lines thought they could follow suit in Montgomery, but no.

"The bosses came to town," James Jr. said, "and Mayor Gayle told them, 'You're just not going to do it in Montgomery.' I mean Mobile City Lines, which was the same company, they had already done it down there. And they were wanting to do it in Montgomery, and the mayor said, 'No way!' He wasn't going to do it. So Mayor Gayle just fought 'em tooth and nail."

The lines were drawn. For over a year, Montgomery's blacks stayed off the buses. Getting to work every day was a hassle. I can identify with that, having commuted to jobs in big cities for more than forty years. But I never had to think twice about where I wanted to sit on a bus or subway. The maids and laborers in Montgomery, while loyal to their employers, were also deeply committed to the idea of the boycott for racial justice. Every day they had to decide, *Do I bum a ride with a stranger? Do I walk to a carpool pickup station or just walk?* For my father it meant getting up earlier than normal to drive his car to ferry passengers, which equaled gas expenses, not to mention wear and tear on his personal vehicle. The MIA did eventually gather funds for paying its drivers for gas and expenses. Meanwhile, the bus company lost ridership and money. The city lost tax revenue.

For the manager of the bus company that was caught in the middle of a fight not of its choosing, there was a personal toll. According to his family, James Howard Bagley and his wife had a housekeeper who needed a ride to work.

"They used to have a black lady who worked for them," Sara Jo remembered. "Sylvia. During the bus boycott, instead of not riding the buses, she would ride the bus."

I wasn't sure I had heard Sara Jo correctly and asked her to repeat herself, which she did. And elaborated on it. "For her faithfulness to Bagley, her boss man, she continued to ride the bus during the boycott. She would pay up front, and then walk around to the back door and sit on the floorboard, so nobody could see her riding," according to Sara Jo.

"They threatened to burn her house down," James Jr. claimed.

"Who?" I asked.

"The blacks," said Sara Jo. "The blacks threatened to shoot her. They were aggravated, and the whites were aggravated too."

James and Sara Jo say they believe Sylvia was a woman in her sixties. "She needed the money, and she loved the Bagleys," said Sara Jo.

"They said they were gonna burn her house down if she didn't quit riding the bus," James said. "Well, she rode 'em. She rode 'em the whole time. Now that was dedication, wasn't it? Got off right out there in front of our house. And then Daddy would take her home, if he was out there, but he was so busy back then. She loved Mother and we all loved her. 'Cuz she was a sweet lady."

When asked about the materials the family inherited from the parent company of Montgomery City Lines, James Jr. speculated that "a lot of people would have thrown the letters away." Sara Jo acknowledged to me that a lot of people might resent seeing the material. She said, "Black or white, they might not appreciate that we let the truth be known."

The Bagleys were very open about what life was like when the man they called Pop ran the bus company that the city's black population wanted to desegregate. Pop started out as a streetcar driver for a company owned by Alabama Power. He was promoted to manager, and when buses replaced the streetcars, Bagley became the manager of Montgomery City Lines when National City Lines, based in Minnesota, bought the company from Alabama Power. National City Lines was a big company with bus lines all over the country.

"Here's a picture of him on the wall in there." James pointed to it. He and Sara Jo later showed me family pictures on the walls, on tables, and in scrapbooks.

Sweet guy to the family, target of much vehemence from blacks in Montgomery enraged that the bus company wouldn't give in to demands to treat them with basic dignity. Family members say he received threats, phone calls late at night to their single-family house on the corner of Ryan and Locust, the Capitol Heights area.

"Several different times," James recalled. "They said they were gonna bomb, especially after Dr. King's house got bombed."

One night, James Jr. thought his life was almost over.

"I heard a car drive off. I was worried about it," he said. Then he heard some noises.

"He thought it was somebody throwing some dynamite," said Sara Jo. Turns out it wasn't. It was a stray cat.

"It was up under the house," James said. "We had some loose pipes. You know, water pipes. The cat jumped up and hit those pipes. It made a rattling sound."

"Vibrating," Sara Jo added.

"Vibrating," said James Jr. He didn't realize it was a cat until later. "I grabbed a pillow and put it over my head." He made a gesture like he was pulling something over his head. "I was just ready to go!"

They can both laugh about it now, they say. Like they can look back and be somewhat amused by much of what happened during the boycott. "Like the time we actually—together in the car, two different times I know of—were asked by Montgomery City Lines to go to certain intersections and count passengers," Sara Jo remembered. "Black and white on buses. So they could know at certain bus stops. We—I didn't care where they sat!"

From the day the boycott started to the day it ended, 382 days in all, there were very few passengers of any kind riding on Montgomery buses.

Not surprisingly, James Jr. and Sara Jo Bagley have a musical family: two girls, two boys. Barbara, the eldest, is the principal oboist with the Montgomery Symphony Orchestra. She also plays clarinet and English horn. Diane plays flute and piccolo. Jimmy plays French horn. Tom plays baritone horn. The parents like to joke they birthed an orchestra.

I'm not the only inquisitive daughter of the boycott; their daughter Diane is also searching for answers. She and I had lunch one day after

I met with her parents, and we talk by phone from time to time. She is digging deep into that box of secrets that National City Lines handed over to her family after J. H. Bagley died, trying to make sense of it all.

Her job is no doubt more difficult, because the forces of history are not on her side. Economic pressures probably pushed bus company officials to press for an end to the boycott more than any moral sting of conscience. Diane must reckon with that as she tries to figure out whether the nice man she knew as her grandfather was really a villain.

―――――――――

Sara Jo and James Bagley were very gracious to me during the few hours I spent with them that December morning in 2014. Several organs in their sunroom in their home on Lake Martin attest to the musician that Sara Jo is. Before I left, she played "Silent Night" for me, "Jingle Bells," and "Amazing Grace," her husband's favorite song.

21

ANN CARMICHAEL

Days became weeks, then months. Montgomery's black residents fell into a new routine. Many walked or took advantage of the MIA carpool to get around. My father picked up passengers while my uncle was hard at work on the lawsuit. At our home on Mobile Drive, my mother was busy cooking, cleaning, and caring for three small children.

From the time of slavery, well-off white people were accustomed to having house servants. Young as I was, I had no sense that the white people on the other side of town were panicked when the bus boycott started, because the black women they referred to as "the help" might not be able to get to their jobs. They probably laughed when the mayor told white women to stop picking up their maids and bringing them to work. There's no way to know how many of them sneaked around to make sure they had household help. But one white woman I spoke to who lived in one of the affluent neighborhoods of Montgomery has some thoughts.

When I met Ann Carmichael, she was ninety years old. A gutsy white woman, a widow living alone with a pistol on hand for protection. Ann is a painter and a sculptor. Despite her years, she is very self-sufficient, still driving a car. She recalls that when the buses were boycotted she had to deal with transportation for her housekeeper.

Arriving at Ann's house, I felt as if I had been transported to Japan. It looks like nothing else in the city of Montgomery. A traditional tall, red, wooden torii gate overlooks a curved walkway across a lotus pond leading to her front door. By custom, torii usually mark the entrance to a sacred place. The landscaping—mostly Asian grasses and Japanese maple and bonsai trees—comfortably nestle beside local southern plants and flora, like the magnolia tree growing around a lantern near the end of the walkway.

Opening the door to her Japanese-style house, she was an elderly fashionista, sporting bright-red reading glasses and wearing textured gray leggings with a satiny, hooded gray jacket. Her hair was a luminous bob of silky silver with soft bangs.

"I'm pleased to meet you," I said in greeting.

She said, "I am honored to meet you," lingering on the "honored." I liked her right away.

Ann is proud of her artwork and pointed out a favorite painting hanging on the wall in the entranceway. It was of a blooming lotus, in keeping with the motif of her quiet, Zen-like sanctuary. The rooms were open and airy, full of floor-to-ceiling windows that let the natural light

Ann Carmichael in front of her house in Montgomery, after one of our two meetings.

in. The walls are decorated with her art and family photos. Works of sculpture are scattered throughout.

A small sculpture of a black woman sits on a counter by the sink in the kitchen. Ann shaped and molded it herself. The sculpture was modeled after Ellen, the woman who used to be her husband's nanny when he was a child, when his mother worked outside the home.

"He said she was the long arm of the law," Ann said. "And she still rules over my kitchen."

My introduction to Ann came through Bo Henderson, an art historian, who at the time was cochair of One Montgomery. Bo, a petite ball of energy herself, had attended Ann's ninetieth birthday party, realized Ann had witnessed a lot of history she would be willing to share, and accompanied me on my visit.

The saga of the South postslavery is difficult to understand and explain. Much of the narrative we know is told from the point of view of black victims, formerly enslaved people, ex-sharecroppers, people whose civil rights had been trampled upon. The other side, a white southern heritage or way of life is still held in high regard by some whites. On my returns to visit Alabama I found some whites I encountered were angry at being held responsible for the sins of evil slaveholders, segregationists, and other white supremacists. I suspected some felt guilty about not standing up to protest wrongdoing and wanted to be forgiven. Others, who had turned a blind eye as friends and relatives in the white power structure mistreated blacks, perhaps would rather not be perceived as enablers.

My guess is Ann had her own personal reasons for wanting to be heard. One seemed to be that she wants to shed some light on the unusual relationships that developed between white families and their domestic help.

Seated comfortably in the family room, Ann was eager to begin. She sat on a brick-and-tan striped sofa that backed up to a wood-paneled wall full of framed family photographs and her artwork. She had typed up some notes to jog her memory.

When Rosa Parks refused to give up her seat on that bus, Ann was in her thirties with three children. There were two boys, Bernard Jr. and young son John, plus daughter Antoinette. They were approaching their teenage years at the time.

"I heard about Rosa being removed from the bus. Fred Gray helped get her out of jail," she said emphatically, speaking with a slow southern drawl. (E. D. Nixon and Clifford Durr went to the jail and bailed Parks out. My uncle's involvement came later that evening.) Ann had glowing recollections of Fred Gray, not just as the lawyer representing Parks and Martin Luther King Jr., but also from her husband's dealings with Fred years later. Ann's husband, Bernard Young Carmichael, who was a bombardier during the Aleutian Islands Battle during World War II, was later involved in real estate and did appraisals for some properties my uncle bought.

"I just liked his demeanor," she said about Uncle Teddy. "He was elegant and charming, so calm, positive, so knowledgeable. He was just wonderful. My husband was very fond of him," she recalled.

Ann, who is a tad hard of hearing, did a lot of rambling through some interesting stories, but she wanted me to know up front that she never referred to people of my race as "black."

"I've never called you black. Some people called you colored or Negro, which is the proper term."

"What about the phrase *African American*?" I asked.

"I don't like that," she said, and talked about hearing Whoopi Goldberg discuss a trip she had made to Africa.

"When she came back, she said it was the awfullest place she'd ever been. She said, 'I am not an African American. I am an American.'" Throwing up both arms, Ann nearly shouted, "Yay, Whoopi!"

Then she went on a rant about "those Negro people who give their children those crazy names. I don't understand it."

Talking about race in America can be a sticky wicket. I don't know how often Ann wades into the weeds to have an honest conversation about it, but I surmised we were headed there as we broached the subject of the bus boycott.

"The boycott didn't so much bother me," she said. But it did present the problem of having to figure out how to get her "help" to work. That's how she referred to Christine Calloway: not her cook, nanny, maid, or domestic, but "the help."

Over time, political correctness has swayed behavior even in the Deep South, as I discovered when Ann introduced another touchy subject, the use of the *n*-word, which got me to thinking. How much of what anybody, black or white, remembers now is a revisionist record of past events? Everybody wants to be on the right side of history, especially when we're talking about that dreaded word.

"We didn't use the *n*-word either." The way Ann recalls it now, when she was growing up and her father had a dairy, they called their workers "Negroes."

I will confess to having uttered the word *nigger* in my lifetime. I don't anymore. It feels wrong even just writing it down. I always knew it to be a racial slur. But as a much younger person, I think up into my teens, my black friends and I might use it to refer to each other in a casual, familiar way. It was considered for a time to be acceptable to use in that context, as in "My nigga." Even then, it was a disparaging reference if used by a white person.

We can probably thank the late comedian Richard Pryor for a decline in usage of the word. After a trip to Kenya in the late 1970s, he returned to the United States saying he didn't see any niggers over there. He said black people there had their pride and self-respect. Hearing Pryor say he regretted ever uttering the word and vowing never to use it again no doubt had an impact on the culture. The message is lost on some young people who still use the word as slang. In my opinion, it is one of the most offensive words in the English language.

Before Christine began working for Ann, they had a negotiation, settling their work arrangement up front, agreeing on holidays and pay. Ann said Christine told her that she and her husband, John, had one focus: "a full day's work for a full day's wage."

The prospective housekeeper told Ann, "We don't work for the NAACP, and we won't work for anyone involved with the White Citizens' Council." White Citizens' Council members may not have worn robes and lynched anybody, but they were staunch segregationists who used tactics that involved imposing economic pressure on blacks and whites alike to keep the races apart.

Ann told Christine they were not connected to the council. Everything was fine, until the boycott started. They had to figure out transportation.

The Montgomery Improvement Association had wasted no time setting up carpool arrangements. As the boycott rolled on, money flooded into the MIA from around the country and around the world. Funeral homes provided cars. New money helped provide a fleet of cars for churches, including station wagons, with the church name and the name of its minister emblazoned on the side. Black taxi drivers offered cheap rides, sometimes the same ten-cent fares the buses had charged, sometimes even free rides.

In the face of the success of the protest, there were problems. City officials cracked down, threatening to arrest taxi drivers who did not charge the normal minimum of forty-five cents. Insurance policies on the MIA's fleet of station wagons were temporarily canceled.

Amid all the confusion, Christine, who once depended on the city buses, had to figure out how to get back and forth to work. At the outset, she relied on volunteers in the carpool. Sometimes she took a taxi.

"She came around one or two in the afternoon," Ann said. "That's how she got to work. She stayed through the early evening and cooked a meal. But then she had to be driven home.

"We would take her home. We didn't think it would be proper for my husband, Bernard, to take her into a colored neighborhood at night, so my daughter, Toni, and I would drive her home. Black and white men would have been after Bernard if he took her. Both. The rednecks, the redneck whites would be there with torches. At first, she tried not to concern me about it. She was taking care of it herself."

It was 382 days before the boycott was over. Like the protest leaders, Ann, too, was surprised it lasted so long. She takes issue with the portrayal of some aspects of the boycott in the 1990 major motion picture *The Long Walk Home*. If white women were driving to pick up their maids in the morning to bring them to their houses to clean, she doubts it was happening in her Cloverdale neighborhood. Possible? Maybe, but that was not her experience.

"All in all, the boycott was a big inconvenience," Ann told me. She leaned down, put both hands to her head as if thinking hard, and said,

"Middle-class whites and Negroes were working for the same thing, to give their children advantages they hadn't had. I approved of Dr. King's message of peaceful expression of what was wrong. I agree with the results. It was the path to get there that I questioned. Maybe it was the only way, but all the turmoil bothered me." Turmoil that ended up right inside churches.

"The movement just decided to inundate the churches," Ann said, referring to ministers like Rev. Martin Luther King Jr., who led the boycott and held mass meetings in churches to plot strategy and take up collections to fund the protest.

But then she says they went further than that. Ann says at least one of the white churches locked their doors to keep Negroes out. At her own place of worship, the Episcopal Church of the Ascension, her pastor was more welcoming. Though one incident when blacks attempted to integrate her church stands out. She doesn't remember the number of blacks preparing to attend that Sunday, but there were TV cameras out in front on the church sidewalk.

"Rev. Tom Thrasher was our rector. Tom went out and he said, 'Anybody who wants to worship in this church is welcome. But you're not going to make a circus out of it. Now get those TV cameras away from here, or I'll call the police.'" Ann seems proud about her pastor's handling of the situation. She doesn't think any black people attended services that day but said the church does have some black members now.

"We had a seemingly peaceful world after World War II, and then it was disrupted," said Ann. "But I guess the world has changed for the better. Every citizen should have the right to vote. We shouldn't be importing all these illegal people."

She starts to ramble. The conversation subject shifts to present times. "Obama wants to go over everyone's head using our schools for people who don't pay a dime in taxes. They're not citizens. What about people who do pay their taxes?" Her opinions about immigrants do seem to echo a sentiment Donald Trump tapped into during his 2016 presidential campaign.

I steered Ann back to the 1950s and how people were living at the time. The Carmichael family resided in Cloverdale, not far from downtown, home to well-to-do and rich white people. Residents tended to be older. "We knew there were fire-eaters out there on both sides," she said. "We were not a part of that."

Her new neighborhood in Carriage Hills is a lot different. For one thing, it's integrated.

"I've got wonderful neighbors," Ann says. "One over here [she points to her right] is white. The one over there [she points in the other direction] is black. I've got white ones across the street. I've got a black one on the corner, who's . . . they're just wonderful. She's beautiful. He was formerly a federal marshal. They're high-type people. They are high-type black people.

"We live in harmony, and we love each other," said Ann.

Still, it's not a community without problems. For instance, there's the time she and her husband came home about twenty years ago to discover their house had been burglarized. Teenage black kids on bicycles from the Spring Valley neighborhood broke in and made off with her gun. She says they were picked up days later, on a schoolyard, with a sack full of pistols. They spent some time in a juvenile detention center. She and Bernard had to go down to the police station to identify their gun.

"Well, it was a Smith and Wesson," she says. "An antique, the Lemon Squeezer. What that is, is you can't fire it with just the trigger. You have to squeeze this thing that's on the back of the gun and the trigger at the same time. My father-in-law gave it to me when we were in Idaho. Bernard was an instructor bombardier, flying all kinds of crazy hours back then. His father thought I needed to have protection."

After the break-in, the police chief and some of his deputies showed up at a neighborhood association meeting. Ann says, "The chief told us, 'You've got a wonderful neighborhood. Stay and keep it. Don't leave. You can't run away from something that you perceive as not being the way you want it to be. Stay and keep it safe. Keep it beautiful.' So we did."

22

THE HELP

ANN CARMICHAEL PUT ME IN TOUCH with her former maid. So one day I went to see Christine Calloway. She lives on Virginia Avenue, a community on Montgomery's west side. She moved there in the late 1960s, after the Civil Rights Act passed, outlawing discrimination against blacks. When she moved there, she says, "the whole street was white. I moved when black people had just started moving in." Back during the boycott, she and her family lived on Day Street, also on the west side, a few doors away from Gray's Flower Shop, a popular local business owned and operated by my uncle Hugh Gray.

Christine has some health issues now and walks with a cane. "My feet still worries me today, from all that walking we used to do during the protest," she says. She still has vivid memories from that period. Somehow, despite everything, she believes that for her "it was a kinda peaceful time. I don't remember anything ugly happening in my part of town."

Her current home on Virginia Avenue is a lovely taupe-colored wood house with a gabled roof and white columns enclosing an inviting front porch. It has the charm of an antebellum bungalow, with white-framed windows and shutters. It looks as if it could have been the home of one of those well-to-do people she used to work for. When Christine greeted me there were double doors at the entrance, a wooden door on the inside, and a white wrought-iron barred security door on the outside, the only hint she didn't live on the rich side of town.

Christine was wearing what we used to call a house dress, nice enough to lounge in at home, not really intended for wear outside the house or for company. She apologized for her casual attire, explaining she was dressed for an earlier visit from a nurse who had stopped by to "check my blood." That being the case, she didn't want me to take any pictures of her. She did, however, graciously allow me to take pictures of nicely framed family photographs, pictures showing her late husband and the children she spent a lot of time boasting about. The pictures were placed on lamp tables around the living room and on her piano.

She didn't know me from Adam but welcomed me with a typical dose of southern hospitality. "Sweet tea?" she asked. I declined, not wanting to trouble her, knowing she had squeezed in my visit on a day when she should have been resting. Christine sat in a large upholstered chair with her feet up on an ottoman, in a room that could have come straight out of *Southern Living* magazine.

The colors are all soft pastel and peach. A dramatic candle chandelier hangs from the ceiling. There are opulent window treatments in the living and dining rooms, heavily brocaded drapes with silk panels and gathered swags. They are a wispy coral with lime-green stripes. The living room sofa and armchairs are upholstered in matching colors, work lovingly done by her son John III. "He was a licensed upholsterer," Christine bragged. John also works as a substitute teacher at Carver High School and does some part-time work at a home for the disabled.

Born in rural Snowden, Alabama, Christine is not exactly sure of her age. Could have been somewhere in her eighties, anywhere from eighty to eighty-three, when I stopped by to visit her. "The midwife who delivered me couldn't read or write," she informed me. "I did go downtown one day to check on my birth certificate. They told me the records were destroyed by some flooding."

She was in her late twenties when she went to work for Ann Carmichael in the mid-1950s. She was married to John Calloway. The two of them were high school graduates. He worked for Fannin's, a men's department store downtown. They raised five children, a girl and four boys. "Three of my kids went to college. They earned scholarships. I had good boys, never had any trouble with them. One is a lawyer. I got a lawyer. My third son went to trade school. My daughter finished college. She would have gotten a master's degree in early childhood education if she hadn't died."

Charles, the son who's a lawyer, practices in Montgomery. Larry is a retired music teacher who lives in Dothan, Alabama. Her youngest, Jeffrey, served in the army and lives in Mississippi. Her only daughter, Chrissie Elaine McCoy, tragically died in 1985 of phlebitis. Christine's husband, John, died in 1989. She is convinced he succumbed to grief over the death of their daughter.

I listened patiently while she talked about her family, though I was anxious to hear more about life during the boycott. "I worked for Ann for four years before my last child, Jeffrey, was born," she tells me. "Ann was the sweetest thing." Still, the two women could not have lived more diametrically different lives on opposite sides of town. Their recollections about that boycott era are not entirely the same either.

There was a bus stop right in front of Christine's house on Day Street, near Holt Street. That is where she boarded the bus to get to work at the Carmichaels'. She would get off in the main square downtown on Montgomery Street, near Liggon's Drug Store. Then she would walk over to Perry Street and Dexter Avenue to transfer to the bus that went to Cloverdale Road and Fairview Avenue. The ride took an hour to an hour and a half. "Lots of us would do that," she says, referring to "the help."

Christine and Ann both remember Christine negotiated to get the job. After Christine told Ann she and her husband "don't work for the NAACP, and we won't work for anyone connected to the White Citizens' Council," the deal was sealed.

Before the protest changed everybody's lives, Christine worked from 1:00 to 6:00 PM, arriving late in the day so she could stay and have a meal cooked for dinnertime. Christine needed to be done by six so she could catch one of the last buses home and go tend to her own children. If she was running late, "Mr. Carmichael might drop me off downtown, so I could take the bus home from the square. His office was on Washington and Long Streets. He did appraisal work, and sometimes he'd go back and work at night."

Everything ran smoothly, most of the time. Except every now and then when, as Christine puts it, "devilish children were meddling with me. Devilish white kids would throw eggs at me while I was at the bus stop." She said they were young kids from the nearby all-white Lanier High School, with nothing better to do than to taunt the help.

As for the bus rides themselves? "I don't personally remember any bad treatment from the bus drivers. There was one who used to sit there and wait on us if we were late. They were very familiar with their riders." This may have been the first conversation I had with a bus rider who had nice things to say about a white bus driver.

Christine wasn't a complainer, though there was much to complain about. Like those ten seats in the front set aside for whites. While she didn't complain, she noticed it. "Sometimes the bus would be bone empty, and you still couldn't sit in the front."

During that period, lots of other blacks were complaining to the NAACP and the Women's Political Council about bus drivers who would pull off and leave them after they put their money in the fare box and got off the bus to enter from the back door. Many black passengers resented having to get up and give their seat to white passengers who got on the bus after them. Christine does recall that when the buses drove through white neighborhoods and picked up white passengers, "sometimes the white passengers wouldn't even sit in seats that blacks had been sitting in."

Then came the news about Rosa Parks's arrest. The first mass meeting to pick boycott leaders and map strategy was held at Christine's church, Holt Street Baptist. "I didn't go to any of the meetings, but I still go to the church." She attends services at the new Holt Street Baptist Church near Lanier High School. Regrettably, the original church fell into decay. A historic marker in front of the boarded-up building tells the story of its rich history. In 2018, after two decades of decline, church leaders began a renovation, vowing to convert the old building into a museum and memorial.

As for the mass meetings during the boycott era, "They were so packed you couldn't get in, but they were peaceful and went on a long time. They didn't think we'd stay off the buses that long."

She laments, as I'm sure my father did, that her children didn't know much about the bus boycott. Same for her children's children. "My grandchildren knew nothing about the boycott or what led up to it. They used to laugh when I told them we couldn't drink out of water fountains downtown at retail stores like S. H. Kress or eat at lunch counters. We had to drink water at the colored fountain and take our food at the back door." Kress & Company was a national chain of five-and-dime variety stores that were targeted during lunch counter sit-ins in the 1960s.

S. H. Kress eventually went out of business, but the Kress in Montgomery has been redeveloped as a mixed-use property of retail, residences, and office space. It is not running from its history as a segregated business enterprise and retains slabs of marble marking "white" and "colored" water fountains on display. I'm not sure how I feel about that.

During the boycott, Christine had to deal with how to get to work. Here's where her recollection veers from that of her employer, Ann Carmichael. At first, Christine tried to manage on her own. "We just kept our mouths shut and did what we had to do. We didn't talk about it in front of white people," she said. "They never discussed race around me. It was, 'All right, Chris, we'll see you tomorrow.' Her children were very respectful, sweet as they could be. Never made you feel bad." She did notice that sometimes in caring for other people's children, "white kids would have some new words for you, if they went and spent time with their grandparents." She didn't come right out and say they used the *n*-word, but apparently that's what she meant.

Thankfully, the carpools started up right away at the beginning of the boycott. "A guy lived across the street from my mother's house, Reverend Averhardt," Christine said. "He used to drive a car and would pick me up sometimes." She sighed deeply as she spoke and relaxed into her chair as comfortably as she relaxed into relating her story. "Other people would come pick us up at our home in station wagons. Sometimes we could get a taxi and pay a little of nothing for a ride, fifty cents or a dime. Eventually, the buses stopped when people stopped riding."

The problem for Christine was she worked odd hours. She didn't leave early in the morning like most people going to work. While her boss, Ann Carmichael, says she remembers sometimes driving Christine home because it didn't seem appropriate for her husband to drive a young black woman to a black neighborhood, Christine has a totally different recollection. "Nobody gave the help a ride home," she told me.

"For some folks, if you couldn't get there and back home, you didn't have a job anymore. They never did offer me a ride home. We had to protect ourselves. We made our own rides."

In fact, Christine says, "John and I worked and saved our pennies, so we bought a car before the boycott was over."

Christine says the Carmichaels invited her to bring her children to visit at Christmastime to play with their kids. "They'd like you as one person, don't like you as a whole," as Christine saw it. "Ann was crazy about me and my family. They were nice as they could be. But they didn't go out of their way to let people know they had black friends. They didn't want another white family to know they were being nice to anybody black, wouldn't let a white person know they gave you a ride." Christine says the rides she did get happened before the boycott, and when Mr. Carmichael gave her a ride, he only drove her downtown, so she could catch a bus home.

––––––––––––

Ann and Christine are still in touch. Both have lost their husbands. Ann has visited Christine at her home on Virginia Avenue and says, "Christine has probably one of the finest houses on Virginia Avenue. It was built by a contractor when she got married. She had modern conveniences in her house that I didn't have in mine. She had lights that came on in the closet when the doors opened. My house didn't have that."

Theirs is an interesting relationship, symbolic of an era. Christine remembers that "Ms. Carmichael invited me to her ninetieth birthday party. I couldn't go, couldn't get there, because I walk with a cane now." However, Christine will pick up the phone and call Ann every once in a while. "I called her after she got operated on. I think it was her back."

Looking back, Christine regrets not attending that first mass meeting at her church and missing seeing the charismatic Dr. Martin Luther King Jr. accept his position as boycott leader. "But he did real well. The younger generation doesn't know what we went through to get the freedom we have."

23

WORLD WAR II

WHAT MY FATHER DID EACH DAY OF THE BOYCOTT, driving his car, picking up black passengers in the face of angry white supremacists, took courage, commitment, and chutzpah. Where did he summon the nerve? I surmise the racism he saw during World War II probably helped prod him into action.

The Japanese early-morning surprise attack on Pearl Harbor sent shock waves throughout America. The day after that ferocious assault on December 7, 1941, idealistic young men all over America rushed to enlist, lining up at military recruiting stations to offer their services. My father was just as angry as the rest of the country. He volunteered to join the US Navy in June 1942, three weeks after turning eighteen. He signed up with his uncle Alonzo, his mother's youngest brother, who was close to him in age.

Like many veterans of the Greatest Generation, Dad rarely spoke of events of the war. About the only visual reminders my brothers and I saw and asked about were watercolor pictures Dad painted of the South Pacific and big-gun battleships. He signed the pictures like an artist, but he didn't hang them up until many years later, when he and my mother moved back to Montgomery in 1991 after he took a job as a judge. Then he hung them on the wall in their family room.

"Dad, why didn't you ever tell us about any of this?" my brother Tommy and I asked. He said he wasn't especially proud of what happened and how he was treated. The World War II experiences were among many I found he had put to paper, compiling autobiographical material for his book.

Dad signed up for the navy a year after he had graduated as valedictorian from Loveless High School. He was strapping and strong, ready for action. The bug bit him to join the service while he was working as a waiter at the Officers' Club Bar at what was then Maxwell Field. Alonzo's brother Leon was a veteran cook in the navy. After Pearl Harbor, Leon informed Alonzo when the navy opened its seaman branch to include Negroes. Prior to that, black men could only serve as messmen, stewards, or cooks. My father assumed, wrongly, it would be integrated.

Dad was proud to wear the navy uniform at first, but later said he "resented the duty." There were highs and lows. Early on, he was thrilled to get to see a US president. Franklin D. Roosevelt visited Camp Robert Smalls at Great Lakes, Illinois, where he attended service school. He never dreamed he would see a commander in chief up close, in person.

"I soon found that the practice was not to assign colored seamen to battleships, cruisers, and destroyers, but rather to small boats, doing menial chores," he wrote, "with no regard for the type of work you had been trained for." So since he couldn't seem to get formally assigned to more exciting work on the big ships, he and Alonzo forced the issue by volunteering to serve there.

After training in service school at Great Lakes, Alonzo became a quartermaster. Dad had the title of signalman, second class. He said they were in the same classes, performed similar work. The signalman stood watch on the ship and waved flags, flashed lights, and used Morse code to transmit and receive messages from passing boats and ships. The quartermaster could also serve as a helmsman and perform bridge watch duties. Both men learned navigation and served as aides to the navigator on small ships. On large battleships, they performed only signal work. During their weekend liberties in Chicago, they played bridge with Uncle John and their other Chicago relatives. The rest of the time the sailors were off to the USO for dancing and fun.

Dad also saw duty in Philadelphia, at Cape May in New Jersey, at the Brooklyn Navy Yard, and in New Orleans. Before he left for Hawaii, Dad's tasks were menial assignments. He served aboard a six-hundred-passenger ferry, the *Mohican*, taking war employees back and forth from New Jersey to the Philadelphia Navy Yard. Apparently, there was nothing special about his assignments at any of those locations. Except, as he tells it, he once fell overboard. Whether he had been out and had a little too much to drink beforehand, he never said. It must have been terrifying, though, because even though he joined the navy for long tours on big boats on the ocean, he couldn't swim. He says somebody threw him a life preserver, and they were able to bring him back safely ashore. He was still more concerned about pursuing a career as a navy man.

"I was stationed in Manana Barracks in Hawaii," he wrote. "All the way across the ocean to a camp that was segregated."

My father joined the US Navy during World War II, almost as soon as he turned eighteen.

After arriving at Manana, my father found himself at a naval station where all the enlisted men were black and all the commissioned officers were white. The guards who patrolled along the fences were armed with shotguns. My father and the other black men at Manana Barracks decided the shotguns were designed to keep them on base rather than protect them from the enemy. In their view, this was a war where black sailors faced two enemies, one from within and one from without.

Around that time, my father received word through censored US mail from his mother, long a widow, that she was considering remarrying. She let him know she wanted to marry Bennie Arms, a song leader at her church. She waited until her children were on their own, feeling it wouldn't have been fair to expect another man to care for her five children. I wonder if my grandmother really asked my father for permission.

Eventually, Dad found himself aboard the USS *New Jersey*, 887 feet long, forty-five thousand tons, with legendary sixteen-inch gun turrets, steaming toward the South Pacific. He was assigned to the signal crew with another young African American from New York City. Dad only remembers him as Adams.

"But no duties were required of us, unlike our white colleagues. We were merely being transported," he lamented.

The two sailors were lucky to simply watch the action from aboard the deck of the *New Jersey* as it teamed up with the cruiser USS *Biloxie*, the destroyer USS *Gatlin*, and several other ships that formed a task force that raided Wake Island twice. "The cruiser and destroyer were damaged by Japanese shore fire," he writes in the papers I found in his office files. My father, as was his fashion, grossly understated the fighting that occurred during an amphibious assault in which the navy bombarded highly motivated Japanese forces.

Eventually, at Eniwetok in the Marshall Islands, the two black sailors were put aboard the USS *Edward L. Doheney*, a converted merchant marine tanker, and joined its white signal crew. The *Doheney* was responsible for assigning ships to various tankers for fueling, which required considerable signaling. Dad and Adams were finally allowed to do the job they were assigned and trained to do. My father noted, "I was placed in charge of the *Doheney* signal gang and of other signal

men from other ships in the harbor for duty, on a non-racial segregation basis." My father had a funny way with words.

Dad may have been vague on details, but clearly the racism at home
in Alabama had followed him out to sea. Like integration everywhere,
it did not happen overnight. It wasn't until 1948, two years after Dad
was honorably discharged from the navy, that President Harry S. Truman formally abolished segregation in the military by executive order.
America may have scored a victory over fascism abroad, but black veterans again faced racism at home.

The returning veterans were grateful to the country for the GI Bill.
It allowed my father, who came from a low-income upbringing, to enroll
at Alabama State College. He was not able to save enough while he was
in the navy to finance a four-year college education on his own. He had
also sent some of his earnings home to his mother, like his brothers
Hugh and Samuel, who both did stints in the army.

Their brother Fred never served in the military. He had a 4-D draft
status because he was an assistant minister at Holt Street Church of
Christ when he finished law school. That didn't stop local selective
service officials from reclassifying him to 1-A status after he became
involved with the Montgomery bus boycott, as a lot of other ministers
were. He had to then prepare to be drafted. Alabama officials who really
wanted to chop off the boycott leadership at the head tried to humiliate
him. When my uncle reported to take his physical, they allowed reporters to take a picture of him in his underwear, a picture that wound up
in newspapers and *Jet* magazine.

In his book *Bus Ride to Justice*, Fred recalled presenting evidence to
the local draft board in Montgomery to demonstrate that he was indeed
an active minister. Two elders from Holt Street Church of Christ testi-
fied on his behalf. So did my father, who was the church's secretary.
The draft board refused to reconsider. My uncle appealed all the way to
the top of the Selective Service System. General Lewis B. Hershey, then
the director, overturned the 1-A status, blocking Fred from having to
leave the boycott battle to go into the military.

24

DISPLACED REFUGEES

AS A CHILD OF EIGHT, I wasn't ready to leave Montgomery. But when your parents up and go, you don't have much choice. Life changed at our house once the Supreme Court decision came down desegregating the city's buses. "Hey kids," my father announced to us one day at the dinner table, "We're moving to Cleveland, Ohio, so I can go to school and become a lawyer."

We barely knew what a lawyer was, except that our uncle Fred was one. Unbeknownst to me, Dad, who was then a businessman, had long dreamed of becoming an attorney himself. He had been listening to his friend and mentor E. D. Nixon, who for many years went on about how the South needed black lawyers to fight discrimination.

It was an inconvenient dream for my father. A dream interrupted when he fell in love, married, and had children. Besides, he faced the same obstacle as his brother: black students were not allowed to attend law school in the state of Alabama. Or any other graduate or under-graduate programs in white colleges. It was why Uncle Teddy had gone to Western Reserve University to get his law degree.

Plus, Dad was aware of what happened to Autherine Lucy. She applied to graduate school at the University of Alabama in 1952. School officials rejected her when they found out she was black. She eventually won the battle to attend classes but was faced with an angry, racist mob shouting death threats on her third day. School officials kicked her out, saying it wasn't safe for her to attend classes.

My father got the message. He was a married man with a family to protect.

———————

Getting to Ohio in the first place was dicey. It was going to be expensive to move the whole family to Cleveland. Real estate up north was through the roof compared to what we were used to. My father was able to convince his cousin Joe Thomas to let him move in for a while with him and his wife, Lou Berta, and their kids, Willie Joe and Edward. Joe was a carpenter by trade. His wife was a beautician. She had a throaty voice and spoke in a slow southern drawl. "Thomas, you know we got plenty o' room up here for you." Plenty of space in their four-bedroom home in the working-class Forest Hills neighborhood on Cleveland's east side. The question then was what to do about the rest of our family.

My parents considered leaving Mom and us kids in Montgomery while Dad got some law school time under his belt. Mom had an undergraduate degree from Alabama State College for Negroes and had taught veterans in a special program at St. Jude. Now would seem to be the perfect time to go after a position teaching at a public school, though most of the black woman teachers we knew taught in rural schools outside Montgomery.

Mom made an appointment for an interview. She dropped Dad off at work at Dozier's so she could have the car. She put on one of her nicest dresses and drove downtown for a face-to-face meeting with a school official. I don't know that she ever told us what his name was, but she had a vivid recollection of how she was treated that day.

"Excuse me, I have an appointment," Mom told the receptionist in the lobby of central administration. She took a seat in the waiting room and waited and waited. It seemed like forever before she was ushered into the administrator's office.

He didn't bother to shake her hand, just nodded to the chair in front of his desk. He didn't waste any time with preliminaries. Gazing at her with contempt over the glasses sitting on his nose, he spoke in a deep, southern accent, ice in his voice, and got right to the point. "What relation are you to that lawyer fella, Gray?" He was obviously referring to my troublemaking uncle Fred, the very visible bus boycott leader. Fred Gray was also giving white people grief filing other lawsuits desegregating schools, juries, housing, and anything else that needed desegregating.

It looked like the timing just wasn't ripe for Mom to try to wrestle a job out of the city's white school officials. Two years or so after the bus boycott, they were still feeling the sting of the bitter defeat, even the ones who never rode a municipal bus.

My mother squirmed nervously in her seat. "He's my husband's brother," she replied meekly.

Speaking in a tone that could only be described as sneering, the school official said, "That would have to go before the board." He looked at her dismissively and said he'd be back in touch.

Juanita Gray never got that job. It was time to punt. She had received a letter from one of her sisters and had an idea. "Gray, why don't the kids and I go live with Kat for a while?" she asked. They agreed it made sense.

Fortunately for us, my mother's sister, married with two young sons, one a newborn, needed some child care help. Mom took me and my two brothers on a train ride to live with my aunt Katheryn; her husband, Kenneth Lawson; and their two boys, Kenneth Jr. and Billy, in Albuquerque, New Mexico.

I will always remember that trip. We left late one evening, suitcases packed into the trunk of the Plymouth, destination Union Station in downtown Montgomery. We got there in just enough time to make our train, so we didn't have to sit in the "colored" waiting room. I could see the yellow light streaming out of the station, a monstrous redbrick building, as we walked by. But there was no way around the "colored" car we would be segregated in on the train, the one right next to the train's engine. With a little assistance carrying our luggage from a friendly Pullman Porter, Dad herded us into a section near the door.

"You guys sit here," he instructed me and Tommy. He pressed some extra dollars into Mom's hand. "Use this when you need the Pullman Porters to help you with your luggage on and off when you change trains. Make sure you tip them," he said.

Mom and Freddie sat in the seats directly behind us. Freddie squeezed in by the window, as I watched a sight I will always remember. My father and mother were seated side by side, locked in a tight embrace, kissing, tentatively at first and then passionately, holding each other close, a kiss that to a child seemed never-ending. Kissing like they didn't know when they'd ever see each other again. I recall feeling embarrassed that they had such an intimate moment out in public, where so many people could see, not sensing as deeply as they did how long we were all about to be separated.

Finally, after all the good-byes were said, Dad got off the train. Mom stared out the window and sadly watched him walk away.

"All aboard!" the conductor yelled out. Loud blasts from the horn signaled the locomotive pulling the train was leaving the station. As it slowly chugged along, our adventure began. It was exciting for us. When we woke up in the morning and pulled the window curtains aside, we had already passed the pine forests of Alabama. Speeding across the Mississippi Delta, we crossed over fertile plains and bridges above muddy river waters. Mom had packed lunches for us, since for most of the miles of our journey we were not allowed to go into the dining car. White people, however, could take their formal meals there on tables covered with white tablecloths.

At some point on our trip that all changed. I don't remember if it was in Texas or somewhere in New Mexico. We crossed some state line where the laws of segregated seating didn't apply anymore. A nice Pullman Porter had alerted us that at the next stop, he would help us with our luggage, and we could feel free to move to any other car on the train.

I loved the porters. These black men were always immaculately attired in beautiful navy-colored uniforms, decked out in brass buttons and caps. They were extremely courteous, and friendly to young children.

My mother, social animal that she was, struck up conversations along the way with white passengers on the train. At some point, she took us to the dining car for a meal. Nothing extravagant—simple BLT sandwiches and Cokes. But it felt like something really special because, up to that point, eating in the white section had been verboten.

Back at our seats in the train car we had integrated, the passing terrain was changing. Cypress swamps in East Texas had given way to prairies full of cattle ranches. We counted cows until the unfamiliar sight of oil fields with those strange-looking pumps caught our attention. The arid desert land of New Mexico was completely new to us. It spawned plants we'd never seen, prickly cactus and sticklike shrubs and grasses. We were antsy and anxious, wondering what was ahead of us in our temporary new life about to unfold at the foothills of the majestic Sandia Mountains.

Katheryn Emanuel Lawson was unlike any other black woman I had ever known. She was the middle sister in Momma's family. My mother was the youngest. Her sister Doretha, the nurse, was the oldest. Then there were the two brothers: Leon, the mail carrier, and Walter, the barber.

Katheryn was a chemist working at Sandia National Laboratory on Kirtland Air Force Base, involved in nuclear weapons research. She had a top security clearance and worked for the crystal physics research division of Sandia Corporation, an ordnance engineering laboratory under contract to the Atomic Energy Commission. Her area of interest was spectroscopy. She wrote an enterprising book on the subject, *Infrared Absorption of Inorganic Substances* (Reinhold, 1961). I found it more than fifty years later, still for sale in hardcover and paperback on Amazon.

I thought about her when the movie *Hidden Figures* was released, revealing the story of those female African American mathematicians who played a vital role in NASA during the early years of the US space program. Katheryn was a hidden figure.

Young and ignorant, I had no idea then what her book was all about, and I still don't understand it, but Sandia's mission was to develop, engineer, and test nonnuclear components of nuclear weapons. Aunt Kat had a big brain. My brothers and I called her, and Mom's other sister, "Tee."

Ebony magazine once did a big profile piece on Kat and her husband, Kenneth. He had studied biology and as a chemist-bacteriologist became a superintendent of Bernalillo County's sewage division. In 1965 it was an exciting issue of the magazine. The Supremes, then at the

My mom's sister Katheryn Lawson, the chemist, seen here on the far left, next to sister Doretha Abney, the nurse. Juanita Gray, the schoolteacher, is on the far right.

height of their Motown stardom, graced the cover, which also boasted a story on "Eligible Bachelors: A Public Service for Single Girls." You gotta love it. The article, which acknowledges that her work is hard to explain, noted that the couple was in constant demand for speaking engagements because they were so successful and because of the scarcity of Negro professionals in Albuquerque. The story contains a dozen pictures of them at work and at home, lounging with sons, Kenny and Billy, and the two family dogs, Feathers and Grindell.

When the kids were young, she never really told them much about what she was doing at work. She just said something generic like "materials testing." When they were old enough to understand, she said she worked on the weapons of mass destruction of her time. She also told them it would ruin her and jeopardize her security clearance if they ever got caught doing anything bad.

Kat and Mom were very close, so close that they both decided to attend the same college, Dillard University in New Orleans. The campus is beautiful. Dillard is a private HBCU situated on fifty-five acres with stately, white academic buildings of neoclassical architecture. When Aunt Kat graduated, she went to Tuskegee Institute in Alabama to work on her master's degree. My mother transferred to Alabama State College in Montgomery so they'd be close to each other. Mom met Dad. Kat moved on to do some graduate work at the University of Wisconsin and later received her PhD in radio chemistry at the University of New Mexico. My grandmother, whom we called Little Mamma, used to tell Kat as she moved from school to school, "You know, a rolling stone gathers no moss." It was a not-so-subtle hint that it was time for Katheryn to settle down.

Eventually she did. Kat and Kenneth Lawson met and married when she was a chemistry instructor at Central State College in Wilberforce, Ohio. He was in graduate school, but when Katheryn got a chance to work on her doctorate at the University of New Mexico, they left for the desert city of Albuquerque to build a new life.

Albuquerque was like a foreign country to me: flat land surrounded by mountains. Geographically, the elevation is one of the highest of any major city in the United States. Little brother Freddie, a toddler, had a hard time coping with the high altitude and climate. Every time you turned around he had a nosebleed.

Arid air and blustery winds whipped tumbleweeds along the road as I walked to the first integrated school I had ever attended. I was the only black student in my fourth-grade class. There may have been a handful of other black kids at my elementary school. Being from out of town, and colored on top of that, I didn't make many friends. I remember feeling lonely and alienated. I don't think the white kids knew what to make of me. There weren't that many Negroes in Albuquerque in the first place. Somehow, whenever the teacher went out of the room and left a student in charge of taking down the names of anybody talking while she was gone, my name ended up on the list.

Thankfully, I had my brothers and young cousins at home to keep me company. Mom basically became the household nanny. She didn't mind though. She loved her sister, and it had been years since they had had time to laugh, cook meals, play cards, and generally just enjoy each other.

"Girl, I'm starting on that diet next week," either Mom or Kat was liable to say after one or the other of them dished up a delicious meal, with dessert of yummy cake to boot. In their thirties now, both of their shapely bodies were beginning to show a little weight gain. Not enough, though, to make them take the talk of dieting seriously.

As for my parents, they communicated mostly by letter. Long-distance phone calls were an expensive luxury. Mom used to read us Dad's letters . . . or the parts that were meant for our tiny little ears. When he wrote to her, he called Mom his "Big legged baby," which made us laugh. We missed him terribly and anxiously awaited his visit at Christmas. We all enjoyed the first snow we had ever seen—just a few inches, but magical to young ones who'd spent their early years in Alabama.

What happened the night Dad was returning to Cleveland clinched the decision for us to leave Albuquerque sooner than the end of the school year. Mom piled us all into Kat's car and drove us downtown to the Atchison, Topeka & Santa Fe Railway passenger depot.

"Come on, now. You all stop that crying," my father said as he picked up his luggage before heading for the train. I was sobbing, my brothers were crying. Tears fell down my mother's cheeks. Freddie, who was barely walking, somehow got away from my mother and made a beeline across train tracks to try to go with my father. Fortunately, no train was coming. Freddie caught up with Dad, latching onto his pants leg, refusing to let go.

"Frederick, now you go back with your mother," my father pleaded.

"No, no, I want to go with you," Freddie cried. Dad knew then he had to get his brood back together, sooner rather than later.

Not long after classes resumed for the spring semester, my mother, my brothers, and I were on a train back to Montgomery. Mom headed up to Ohio to be with my father in Cleveland, where she had no trouble finding work as a public school teacher. My parents set out to find an apartment for the whole family to live in while Dad continued his law classes. Tommy, Freddie, and I were handed off to my grandmother, who was to place us in school in Montgomery and look after us until the end of the school year.

Dad, who had done some teaching himself in Cleveland, knew school officials tended to assume black children from the South had inferior educations. He wanted to make sure they didn't put us back a grade if we arrived in the middle of a school year, so he thought it best for us to complete the academic year at a school in Montgomery where he knew the teachers. Tom Jr. and I were enrolled in the Loveless School, where my dad had graduated years before as valedictorian. The school was across the street from the Dozier's Radio, TV and Appliances store he used to co-own, now run by his old partner, William Singleton.

At the end of the school year it was time for another adventure. My grandmother packed up my brothers and me and made the train trip to Cleveland to reunite us with our parents.

25

CLEVELAND

CLEVELAND WAS ONLY SUPPOSED to be a temporary stop. We understood the game plan, the same as Uncle Fred's: law school, then return to Montgomery to practice civil rights law. The 1960s were a tumultuous time. A sit-in by four African American college students at a Woolworth's lunch counter that served only whites in Greensboro, North Carolina, touched off a series of similar protests in other states, leading to the formation of the Student Nonviolent Coordinating Committee (SNCC).

My parents' hunt for an apartment up north in Cleveland was a reminder that we couldn't run from racism and discrimination. Unfamiliar with the neighborhoods in this new and much bigger urban area, they sought the help of a realtor. "Do you believe the first place that woman took us to was a housing project?" Dad said every time he told that story. We were the victims of the same kind of racial steering he battled later in fair housing lawsuits. Eventually, we ended up in an apartment building on Lee Avenue off 105th Street. It wasn't the nicest area in the inner city, but it wasn't the worst. Back then, it was the best we could afford; much of Dad's money from his day jobs at the post office or substitute teaching went to law school tuition.

In the summer of 2014, I went back to check out my old stomping grounds. Our old apartment at 10703 Lee Avenue in the Glenville area is still standing. It is one of two dark-brick low-rise buildings right next to each other, squeezed in the middle of a block full of aging single-family houses. I almost expected to see the hopscotch squares where we used to play, chalk-lined on the front sidewalk. "Do not go across the street or down the street," I could hear my mother's warning. She was nervous about the Cleveland ghetto and what might lie in store for her young children. She didn't know the neighbors, most of whom were unlike her college-educated friends from Mobile Heights. There were more single mothers struggling to raise children alone. Less parental guidance for the children we were playing with. My brothers and I were allowed to play kickball, or games like Red Light / Green Light, on the concrete parking area in the back of our apartment building—no straying farther than Mom could see us from the windows of our second-floor apartment.

We were latchkey kids. Mom got home from teaching, deeper in the inner city at Wade Park Elementary School, about an hour after my brothers and I left Doan Elementary around the corner and a few blocks down 105th Street. We were under strict instructions not to let anybody into the apartment or to play any farther than the front or back of our building. Homework was on the menu every evening after dinner, with parental guidance when necessary.

I was in the fifth grade at the height of the Cuban Missile Crisis in October 1962. Ellen Miles was my teacher. She had attended Alabama State College and was friends with my parents. She kept an eagle-eyed watch over me. She called my mother at home one day complaining, "The principal stopped by my classroom today, and Karen was a little chatterbox. She would not stop talking with her little classmate buddies the entire time the principal was there. You need to talk to her."

Mrs. Miles was a very tall woman with an imposing presence. Most of my classmates were a tad afraid of her. I, on the other hand, was the teacher's pet. A good student, but when I began developing some bad habits, Mrs. Miles would get right back on the phone and call my parents. "She's starting to speak like some of those little hoodlum kids in my class," she told Mom. "You know the ones who couldn't conjugate verbs if their lives depended on it. Or the ones who say 'ax' instead of 'ask.' You need to nip that in the bud." Of course, Mom didn't waste any time correcting me and telling me how important it was to speak proper English all the time.

The Cuban Missile Crisis was a spooky period that I barely understood. My parents kept saying we were on the brink of nuclear war. All I knew was that we were afraid the Soviet Union was going to bomb us with missiles they had deployed in Cuba, a hop, skip, and a jump from the American shoreline.

"Children! Line up at the door," Mrs. Miles would shout out. "We're going down into the basement." Each school day during that tense thirteen-day October standoff, students in classes all over America practiced "duck-and-cover." It was what we were supposed to do in the event of a nuclear explosion. Our classroom at Doan was on the third floor. Students spilled out of the school's classrooms and filed downstairs to the basement, where we would get down on our knees, bend over, and cover our heads. I couldn't figure out how that was going to help us survive an atomic attack. Fortunately, Soviet Premier Nikita Khrushchev agreed to pull his missiles out of Cuba. President John Kennedy promised not to invade Cuba and agreed to take US missiles out of Turkey.

My mother couldn't wait to move away from Lee Avenue. Our apartment had a problem she was unaccustomed to: roaches. Plus, she liked living in a single-family house, not quite so close to the neighbors. Our stay in Cleveland, meant to be brief, stretched almost into a lifetime. You know what they say about best laid plans.

The bug about law school bit Dad even before his brother Fred went off to Western Reserve. My grandmother had boasted about their uncle John Jones, who graduated from law school at the University of Chicago. When Dad was in the navy and at Naval Station Great Lakes in Illinois, he would visit John in Chicago, where his uncle had a law office on the south side of town.

As I grew up, my father also expressed a desire for me to go to law school, so he, Uncle Teddy, and I could work together. I was reminded of that as I rifled through Dad's files and came across an application for the Alabama Bar exam. It was one he never filled out. Thousands of miles away, the long arm of white prejudice had reached out to block his path to a Montgomery law office. The way I heard Uncle Fred tell it once during a speech he gave during an event at his alma mater, now Case Western Reserve University Law School, "Alabama wouldn't let him pass after I desegregated all those places."

Dad took the exam twice but was informed he did not pass either time. The application I found was attached to a two-page memo to bar applicants from the admissions secretary. Bearing the Alabama state seal, it has a telephone number for the Alabama State Bar and its address on Dexter Avenue. The memo informs bar exam applicants who had taken an earlier examination and failed that there are new rules governing admission to the Alabama State Bar. Former rules relating to the ethics examination had been amended. The rule change was effective October 1, 1980. What a shock! Twenty years after he had moved away from Montgomery, my father had not given up on his dream of practicing law in Alabama. I can't believe he even considered taking that state's bar a third time.

In 1961, with a year of law school from Western Reserve University under his belt, Dad transferred to Cleveland-Marshall Law School (now affiliated with Cleveland State University). He could take night classes there while he worked as a US postal clerk and as a substitute teacher. I'm sure my brothers and I had no real understanding of the hardship involved in going to law school while working a job and trying to support a family. I do remember my mother's constant admonitions to us to "be quiet, and take that noise outside—can't you see your father's trying to study?" I don't know how he did it.

As for my brothers and me, we didn't exactly escape segregated schools by moving north. The public schools in Cleveland's inner city were also segregated, enforced not by law as we had known in Alabama, but by housing patterns, reinforced by redlining. The fight for equality wasn't limited to the South.

When Dad didn't pass the bar in Alabama the first time, he hung out his shingle in Cleveland in a private practice. Many of his friends were black lawyers who, like him, also waited until they were married with families before going to law school. Men like Clarence Holmes, who became a close friend and worked with him in an office at One Public Square downtown. That was early on when, Holmes says, "we were blessed if anybody walked through the door." They took in some real estate business, probate affairs, some criminal cases. Dad always said he really preferred not to represent criminals. Holmes told me once that he found it odd that Dad could pass the Ohio bar exam but not the one in Alabama.

As kids in Cleveland public schools, Tommy, Freddie, and I felt we were just biding time. "We're not going to be here long," we told all our new classmates. We were just there until our father finished law school. Then we were going back to Alabama, so our father could practice law with our famous uncle.

Fred Gray was very busy litigating the desegregation of colleges in the South, such as the University of Alabama, where in 1963 Governor George Wallace famously stood in the schoolhouse door to block the entrance of Vivian Malone and James Hood, and Florence State College, where Wendell Gunn sought admission. Fred had a string of successes in high-profile cases he filed, such as the landmark *Times v. Sullivan*, which made it to the US Supreme Court, involving three Montgomery city commissioners who accused a group of southern ministers of libel. The Committee to Defend Martin Luther King and the Struggle for Freedom in the South paid for a full-page ad in the *New York Times*. Some of the information in the ad involving police actions against civil rights protesters was not correct. In that 1964 case, the high court established the standard for actual malice, ruling that the First Amendment protects newspapers from libel even when they print false statements, as long as they are not acting with malice.

My uncle also acted on behalf of students protesting at lunch counters. One of those cases, *St. John Dixon v. Alabama State Board of Education*, involved Alabama State College students and faculty leaders who sat at a lunch counter at the Montgomery County courthouse to try to be served in February 1960. Local officials did not arrest them but had them expelled or suspended depending on whether they were state residents or nonresidents. L. D. Reddick, a history professor, was fired from his job. The actions were ordered by then governor John Patterson, who by virtue of being governor was also chairman of the Alabama State College board of trustees. Fred Gray lost that case.

I was surprised to learn fifty-eight years later during a visit to Montgomery that the state of Alabama acted to expunge the files of twenty-nine students disciplined for their actions at the segregated cafeteria. As one of his final acts as interim state superintendent of education, Ed Richardson also expunged the records of four faculty members who participated in the sit-in. Uncle Teddy, a man of few words in his briefs and e-mail communications, called it "good news," in a memo he wrote to Derryn Moten, the chair of ASU's history and political science department. He thanked Moten for informing him of the expungements saying, "It is a step in the right direction. Thanks also to Dr. Richardson for taking that action. Most people do not know the importance of the Dixon case."

My father was itching to get back to Alabama. His brother was becoming a local legend. My father was probably his biggest champion. Even though Fred's achievements, like the settlement for victims of the Tuskegee Syphilis Study, were high profile and seemed to outshine my father's, there was never any jealousy or animosity between the two. Dad even saved a lot of his brother's old campaign literature from a run for the state legislature. One newsletter, yellowing with age, calls Fred "The Most Qualified Man." The back contains two messages, one for white voters ("Don't vote against me just because I'm black") and one for black voters ("Don't vote for me just because I'm black").

By the time I was finishing at Harry E. Davis Junior High School in Cleveland, we moved. Even though Dad was already beginning to view his law plans in Montgomery as a dream deferred, my mother was insisting on better schools than the inner city had to offer and nicer living surroundings.

In early 1965 they bought a new house in the suburbs on Cleveland's east side, a three-bedroom, part brick colonial on Ashwood Road in the Ludlow neighborhood. A paved driveway led to a two-car garage. Eventually, we had two cars. Nothing fancy, but a big move up to an area that straddled Cleveland and the affluent suburb of Shaker Heights. Mom planted red geraniums in the front yard every spring and a small vegetable garden in the back. We lived in Cleveland to humor Dad, who thought he might want to run for political office in the city one day. But our house was in the Shaker Heights school district, known nationally for its outstanding quality of education. My parents thought my brothers and I would thrive there academically.

Ludlow was an experiment in racial integration that gained national attention. It was eventually home to blacks and whites, with a homeowners' association that worked aggressively to try to make the neighborhood a stable biracial community. A struggle had begun after black families began to move into what had been an all-white neighborhood. A bomb was tossed into a black family's home while it was under construction. When whites rushed to sell their homes, a core group of both races worked together to prevent massive white flight. The Ludlow Community Association raised money and solicited grants to encourage white families to move into the neighborhood with offers of help to finance their homes. It was a controversial maneuver—down payment money for whites to move in, but not blacks.

It was an interesting period for us at school and for Dad at work. He began a remarkable twenty-eight-year legal career in Cleveland. Civil rights and fair housing were his calling. He was dealing with near-in suburbs that favored what were called "benign housing quotas." Officials said they were for integration but didn't want a sudden influx of blacks to trigger white flight. For the most part, it was the exact same thing that was going on in our Ludlow community.

Now it was obvious—discrimination did not stop at the Ohio state line. The greater Cleveland area was and remains an area where the inner city and close suburbs are racially segregated. Maybe less so now, but there are still issues.

Efforts to open predominantly white suburban enclaves to black people kept my father busy through the 1990s. He was director of the Cleveland chapter of Lawyers' Committee for Civil Rights Under Law. It's a national organization formed in 1963 at the request of President John F. Kennedy, aimed at enlisting help from private attorneys to fight racial discrimination. Dad was also director of a group called Lawyers for Housing, a joint pilot project of the American Bar Association and the Cleveland Bar Association. Dad hired two young attorneys at Lawyers for Housing, one black, Gerald Jackson, one white, Avery Friedman. They were at the forefront of a campaign that opened segregated housing to blacks. They pushed the envelope to encourage community development organizations to build more low- and moderate-income housing. Both are still actively practicing law. Friedman is a nationally known fair housing advocate and a legal consultant for CNN.

Parma, a suburb on the west side of Cleveland's Cuyahoga River, was especially resistant to integration. Under Dad's direction, Lawyers for Housing filed a lawsuit against Parma in the early 1970s. The US Department of Justice got involved and determined there was a pattern and practice of discrimination. Parma was found guilty of violating the Fair Housing Act by a federal judge as late as 1980. Jackson says Parma now has more black residents and is more integrated than ever before. But like close-in suburbs all over the country, segregated housing patterns persist.

I was proud to hear Gerald Jackson say, "Your Dad softened the ground on integration into the housing market and increased housing opportunities for black people in northeast Ohio." According to Jackson, my father was "a really good diplomat. One of his big achievements was getting white people to the table. He was a great negotiator who didn't beat people up. But he let those who were excluding blacks know that filing lawsuits was an option. Hardliners ended up in federal court."

Dad mostly worked in offices downtown. Other legal organizations my father directed included Law in Urban Affairs and the Legal Aid Society of Cleveland. Most of those positions and a stint as general counsel for the Cuyahoga Metropolitan Housing Authority involved fighting discrimination and promoting better housing opportunities for the poor. He dodged blatant Jim Crow prejudice in the South only to encounter more subtle discrimination tactics, like steering, redlining, restrictive covenants, and problems getting mortgages, in the North. The passage of the Civil Rights Act in 1964 and the federal Fair Housing Act in 1968 helped, but as we know, the struggle for equal rights continues.

Outside the racial milieu, Dad also took on jobs as assistant general counsel and chief assistant general counsel of the Greater Cleveland Regional Transit Authority. He served as a trustee or president for a long list of associations, legal and otherwise.

Chester K. Gillespie was a well-known name among African American lawyers in Cleveland. Dad was an associate of his, along with John Bustamante. Dad also worked with one prominent group of well-respected black lawyers that shared office space downtown. The group included John Kellogg, Clarence Holmes, Charles Fleming (who later became a municipal court judge), Everett Tyler, James B. Taylor, and Ramon Basie. Attorney Elliott Kelley became a close family friend. So did Don Haley, a tax attorney for Standard Oil of Ohio. In addition, Dad worked with Louis Stokes, who later became an esteemed congressman from Ohio.

Stokes, who died in August 2015, was a revered and popular Democratic member of the US House of Representatives. Powerful committee assignments included chairing the House Intelligence Committee and the select committee that investigated the assassinations of President John F. Kennedy and Martin Luther King Jr.

My father was proud of his friendship with the Stokes brothers, both leading lawyers and towering political figures. When Carl Stokes, was elected mayor of Cleveland in November 1967, he became the first black mayor of a major US city. He sent some of his campaign aides to Alabama to help my uncle Fred during his first try at becoming elected to the Alabama state legislature. Despite the help, Fred lost that race, but he was elected in 1970.

Decades later, after Dad passed away, I found a letter to him from Congressman Stokes. In it he thanked my father for a letter he wrote to Rudolph Janata, then president of the Ohio State Bar Association. Like Stokes, Dad found it outrageous that the State Bar Association, which included many black members, was sponsoring a trip to South Africa. My father's letter to Janata supported the congressman's position that the scheduled Bar Association trip was out of order. In the letter Stokes also acknowledged support from attorney Russell Adrine, who Dad worked with later at the Regional Transit Authority. It was the congressman's conviction "that tourism in South Africa not only lends financial support to apartheid, but credibility as well."

He wrote Dad, "I do think you should utilize the media for expression in this matter. This is the kind of issue on which the black lawyer must stand tall." My friend Shelley Stokes, who is one of Lou's daughters and was a college roommate of mine, found that letter, some others, and a newspaper article about the South Africa trip protest and gave them to me. She is working on a book about her family history. A newspaper article dated May 11, 1973, from the Press State Service quoted the president of the Ohio Bar Association as saying "U.S. Cong. Louis Stokes' criticism of plans to tour South Africa is 'frankly slanderous.'" With his collaborator David Chanoff, Stokes penned *The Gentleman from Ohio*, an autobiography of his remarkable life and career, but passed away shortly before it was released.

"OK, kids. Anybody who wants a ride with me better be ready to leave in five minutes," Mom yelled out from the bottom of the stairway in the living room. Usually we didn't mind the walk to school. It was just under a mile to the high school and the junior high school. Ludlow Elementary was closer and a much shorter walk for Frederick. But on mornings it rained, we had to get ready fast to catch a ride with Mom on her way to her teaching job on the other side of town.

Shaker schools were ranked close to the top in national ratings, but they were a challenge and an acquired taste for my brothers and me. While we formed many lasting friendships there, to our dismay, we discovered black students going into the Shaker schools were almost automatically excluded from programs geared toward the academically talented. African American students were crowded into the classes for lower-achieving students, while the advanced placement courses were predominantly white. I had been an honors student in Cleveland public schools, but my parents had to struggle to make sure my brothers and I were placed in the right classes in Shaker.

As we entered our adolescent years, they also let us in on their progressive ideas about dating. "We know we're putting you in an integrated situation," my father told Tommy and me, "and we want you to know, it's OK if you want to go out with classmates who are white." I was stunned to hear that coming from my father, mostly because I was a late bloomer, not giving dating much thought. One white classmate did give me a ride home once on the back of his motor scooter.

At noon in the cafeteria, whites mostly sat at their tables and blacks, for the most part, sat at theirs. But many overcame prejudices and made interracial friendships. My brother Freddie played on school basketball and football teams. Tom Jr. excelled at the position of pitcher when he attended Woodbury Junior High School. "But they only chose two blacks to be on the baseball team," he says, still pained by that oversight. In 1969 he became the first black captain of the school's chess club, which competed across the city and the state.

As a kid, I knew Dad and many of his friends were lawyers. It wasn't anything he bragged about. I'm embarrassed to admit I can only remember going to court to watch him in action once. It was some minor matter. "It won't take long," he had told me and my mother. We were instructed to take a seat in the spectator section while he argued his case. He had a commanding voice in that deep baritone of his. People seemed to hang on to his every word.

When he finished, we were going to meet another one of Dad's lawyer friends for lunch, Elliott Kelley, who worked with him downtown at the Terminal Tower, the landmark skyscraper on Cleveland Public Square. I was a teenager then. As I watched the proceedings, it was as if I were at a movie. I remember thinking, *So this is what he does every day. This is my father, who comes home from work, grabs a beer with next-door neighbor Merv Garden or our other neighbor Richmond Jones, jokes around with my mother, makes my brothers and me do our homework.* What was unfolding in the courtroom seemed so far removed from our regular life. Not as if I didn't know what lawyers did. I even loved watching *Perry Mason*, one of Dad's favorite TV programs. But it was special seeing my father perform as one up close.

I'll never forget the evening of April 4, 1968. Both my parents were home when I climbed the few stairs to our front door and walked in, late from after-school activities. My father, who is not usually very demonstrative emotionally, looked upset. He said only, "Martin Luther King was shot."

Dad was head of a neighborhood Legal Aid Society office then. Earlier, he was attending a human relations meeting on Cleveland's predominantly white west side at a large church when someone announced that King had been killed. Many years later, Dad spoke at Faulkner University in Montgomery for a Martin Luther King Jr. birthday event, and said, "I don't recall having done so for any other nonrelative or relative for that matter, but there, I wept."

At home that night the news was blaring over the TV in our family room. My mother was crying. My brother Tommy remembers hearing my mother sobbing from my parents' bedroom throughout the evening. For the next few days, we talked constantly about Dr. King.

When my father started law school in Cleveland, he received a letter from King, informing him that he was moving back to Atlanta, "where the civil rights struggle could be continued with less oppression from the opposition."

The Kings kept in touch with my family after the boycott.
Coretta is shown here with my father sometime during the 1990s.

I think my father regretted his decision not to drive our family to DC for the 1963 March on Washington. There were rumblings there might be violence, and Dad had just graduated from law school and wanted to celebrate. He drove us to Niagara Falls for a much-needed vacation, not realizing that we would miss King making his famous "I Have a Dream" speech.

Beep! Beep! It was the sound of that dreaded car horn. You could count on it every Sunday morning. Mom, the boys, and I were always a little lackadaisical about getting ready for services at Mount Pleasant Church of Christ. Old habits die hard.

Growing up in Montgomery, Dad obeyed my grandmother, and like her, my father insisted on punctuality. He was ready before any of the rest of us. Before leaving the house, he would threaten to go to church without us. Invariably, he would get into the car, back out of the garage, and sit waiting in front of the house, blaring the horn. Begrudgingly, my brothers and I piled in. My mother just smiled at the weekly ritual.

Church was important to Dad. I noticed on one of his old résumés, under the personal section, he listed his birth date and place, residence, marriage, and children. Next, he noted membership at his first church, the Holt Street Church of Christ, before his impressive legal credentials and life membership in the NAACP and Omega Psi Phi Fraternity.

One day I discovered a folder full of prayers he was prepared to give on any occasion. I paid closer attention to them than I ever had when he was praying them. The following is an excerpt from one of them:

> We thank thee for this great and unique nation of which we are a part. May the leaders thereof remember that they are servants of its people and not owners of its assets.
>
> We pray to thee: Thou whose eyes have seen the holocaust of the African Atlantic slave trade, which lasted more than 200 years longer than the Nazi Holocaust of Jews; Thou, whose awareness abides of overcrowded American prisons, more than any other Western nation on the face of the Earth.

Dad was deeply concerned about injustice, racial or otherwise.

In a folder of speeches, wedding toasts, and jokes, I learned more than I wanted to about my father's adult sense of humor. Some of the jokes he told in front of his frat brothers are so off-color, I choose not to share them here. He told me once that Dr. King also enjoyed telling jokes and often shared risqué stories when he was with the guys. My father fancied himself somewhat of a comedian. At the birthday of one of his frat brothers, Dad told this one: "How's the marriage going?" a newly married man was asked. "Well, my wife and I have a partnership. She takes care of and decides on all the small things, and I take care of and decide on all the big things." "How are you doing?" he was asked. "So far, no big things have come up."

I don't know how my father did it all. Over the years, he was always on the board of something, including Southwestern Christian College in Terrell, Texas; the Alabama State University Foundation; and the Montgomery Improvement Association. He was a past member of the Council of Delegates and of the Legal Reform and Judicial Administration Committee of the Ohio State Bar Association, president of the Cleveland-Marshall Law Alumni Association, and past president of the Norman S. Minor Bar Association. I could list more.

As I look back, it amazes me because he made time for dinner out with the family almost every Friday night, church on Sundays (whether we wanted to go or not), cards, and board games like Scrabble and, of course, chess. We went bowling. My brothers and parents played golf. But Dad ran a tight ship at our household and meted out tough love, including paid rides for all his children to college.

We grew to love Cleveland. I took piano lessons, went bike riding with friends, learned to swim. My brothers joined sports teams. The city, dubbed the "Mistake on the Lake" one year after the Cuyahoga River caught fire, was also growing on my mother, who had to be convinced years before to leave Alabama and her way of life there. I recall overhearing a conversation in our car one day when Uncle Teddy told Mom, "It'll be for the best. Tom wants to be a lawyer. And when he's through with school, you'll be back."

But now Ohio was our new way of life. My parents made more friends, attended more parties. We all attended plays at the Karamu House theater, which nurtured black actors, visited the art museum, went sledding down the banks of the hill on East Boulevard when it snowed. One day out of the clear blue sky, my mother bought a guitar and took lessons. She liked popular music. If she heard a song she liked on the radio, she would buy the music, practice it, and play it for our friends and serenade my father at night in bed.

Montgomery, the city where Tommy, Freddie, and I were all born, was losing its appeal in our eyes. The idea of going back there became less and less attractive. Dad, we thought, had finally resigned himself to a legal career in Ohio. Then in May 1991, in a highly ironic twist of fate, he and my mother moved back to Montgomery. Dad had received an appointment as a federal administrative law judge in the Social Security Administration at the appellate level. He became a judge in the same state that would not open its law school doors to him in the 1950s, because of the color of his skin. The appointment was especially sweet, since he had run for a municipal judge seat in Cleveland during the 1970s and lost the election. I took time off from my job with UPI in Boston to help campaign and was crushed when he didn't win.

Campaign flyer for my dad's unsuccessful race for Cleveland municipal court judge.

Family photo for the Gray-for-judge campaign.

26

JUSTICE DELAYED

To MY MIND, A ROAD TRIP south to Montgomery from our home in Cleveland the year I turned thirteen was probably the most memorable trip my family ever made. It was in the summer of 1964, after passage of the Civil Rights Act. The ink was barely dry on the legislation President Lyndon Johnson signed July 2, 1964, when my father decided he had to test it. Dad had passed the Ohio bar the year before and was a lawyer in private practice.

The new federal law, my father thought, had promise. It prohibited discrimination on the basis of race, color, sex, religion, or national origin. It was sweeping in its scope, banning unequal treatment in schools, at the workplace, or in public accommodations. But Dad had his doubts about whether it would turn back the clock on decades of entrenched segregation. As he put it, "We're gonna see."

I wish they would stop singing and turn on the radio—that's what I was thinking in the backseat of the family car. It was as if my parents had transported themselves to another world where there were only the two of them. They'd probably forgotten Tommy, Freddie, and I were even there. That deep bass of Dad's voice may have seemed mellifluous to my mother as the two of them sang those college-era love songs over and over, but to me it was an irritant.

They had been college sweethearts. To this day my favorite picture of them is a black-and-white photo showing them standing outside Mom's dormitory at Alabama State. She's wearing a very fashionable two-piece suit, a long full dark skirt with a tailored light jacket, buttoned down the front with a smart collar tight around her neck and puffy sleeves. It looks expensive and may have been a hand-me-down from the rich white people Big Mama, her grandmother, worked for back in Louisiana.

In the picture Dad looks like he just stepped out of *GQ* magazine in his light taupe suit, full pants, wide lapel jacket, and snazzy tie. He's casually holding a pipe in his right hand, wearing sunglasses and a sporty trilby hat. They're standing very close, smiling and looking so happy. About five years and three children later, the spark was still there. Some of their favorite songs were show tunes. They knew all the words to "Bewitched, Bothered and Bewildered," a popular song from the 1940 Rodgers and Hart musical *Pal Joey*.

They just kept singing, and it was grating on our nerves. My two brothers and I were packed into the back of that 1962 beige Plymouth like canned sardines. Dad loved Chrysler cars and had a soft spot for Plymouths. We called this car the Brown Bomber. Bucket seats were becoming popular, but this one didn't have buckets in the front. It had a full front seat, sofa-like, and Mom moved over and was sitting close to my father as he drove on down the road. Love birds, despite us.

Ignoring our incessant begging from the back, they continued singing in the front, about jambalaya, filé gumbo, and all things Creole. Mom's Louisiana roots were showing. She loved country music, and that "Jambalaya (On the Bayou)" song by Hank Williams was one of her favorites. The weather was hot. She was wearing shorts. My father reached over and placed a hand on her left thigh.

It was a totally different world in the back seat. There was never enough room with fidgety Freddie in the middle and big-headed Tommy, who never stopped talking about the cars passing by. We played the usual road trip games, including twenty questions, but did we really have to count the yellow cars or read all those roadside Burma Shave ads? How close were the Williamses in the car behind us?

We weren't on the road trip alone. Earl Williams; his wife, Frances; and their three boys, Earl Jr., Reginald, and Eric, were driving to

Alabama with us. They were riding in their family Buick. Earl and Frances were Montgomery natives who often made an annual trek down south. Mrs. Williams had attended the same high school as my father.

Frances and Earl moved away from Montgomery in 1950, years before the bus boycott. They were a popular couple, with lots of friends. Earl Sr. was tall and thin, very handsome. He majored in sociology when he was in college and was an urban renewal director in Cleveland in the 1960s. He later served as director of community relations for four Cleveland mayors, including Carl Stokes.

Even though we were all living in Cleveland, like many blacks who had migrated north, most summers our family and the Williams family headed back south to visit relatives. Usually our family made the journey alone. This summer of '64, the Grays and the Williamses traveled together. Tommy and I were teenagers, close in age to the Williams kids. During our twelve-hour drive south, my brothers and I were as anxious as my parents to discover whether white merchants in southern states would serve us.

"Neet," Dad said, which is what he called my mother, "I can't imagine those white people are going to just stop what they were doing and obey the law." Before we left home, we talked about whether white restaurant and store owners would serve us at stops along the way.

The two cars cruised along the roadways of Ohio and Kentucky at the nascence of the interstate highway system. We left Cleveland as Route 1 was becoming the new Interstate 71. Along the way the roads were sometimes new four-lane highways, but there were still gaps in the system. Sometimes we had to navigate old two-lane highways, crossing dotted yellow lines to pass slow-moving vehicles.

After leaving Cleveland's outer suburban areas, we passed rolling farmlands and hit flat plains outside Columbus. We began making our way south through Kentucky. The Bluegrass State was one of those where life became tricky during our trips south. It was a border slave state during the Civil War, where brothers had fought against brothers—a legacy not easy to shake. We couldn't be sure how we'd be treated as we passed through. Black people might be permitted in restaurants; then again, they might not.

Most trips we took our own food—fried chicken and sandwiches, potato chips and fruit—so being rejected from southern restaurants wouldn't be an issue. We'd buy ice-cold Coca-Colas and orange or grape Nehi from gas station soda machines. As we motored past the rolling meadows of northern Kentucky, on through the heavily forested mountains close to its southern border, we looked for state-financed roadside rest stops to use public bathrooms. The toilets were cleaner, and we didn't have to worry about being steered to "colored only" toilets at gas stations and white restaurants.

It was stiflingly hot. Neither car had air conditioning. In those days that was an option our parents couldn't afford. We were riding with the windows down, but the hot air did not cool us. Throw in the humidity, and our little legs were either sliding off the seat or sticking to it.

The boys in the Williamses' car were nearly suffocating. "Would you please roll that window back up?" Mrs. Williams asked, turning to her youngsters in the back seat. They looked at each other, shrugged, and obeyed her. Frances was always prim and proper, neatly dressed, her hair perfectly coiffed without a strand out of place. She wanted to keep it that way and insisted on having the windows rolled up, almost to the top. The way the boys saw it, it was a small price to pay. They loved her, and she always looked beautiful.

I recall we pulled into the parking lot of a small eatery somewhere off the highway in Tennessee. That's the way I remember it, but when I talked to Frances Williams about the incident years later, when she was eighty-eight years old, she remembered it as somewhere in northern Alabama. Everybody wanted ice cream as we pulled into the parking lot of a roadside restaurant. The advertising on the exterior walls was enticing, but who knew what lay ahead? Frothy milkshakes beckoned from colorful displays alongside giant scoops of ice cream in waffle cones, with pictures of beefy burgers and thick-cut French fries. I noticed from the car that the only customers walking up to a window in the front to order were white.

"You guys stay in the car," my father told us, as he exchanged a nervous glance with my mother. My stomach did a flip-flop as I tried to decide what kind of ice cream cone—vanilla, chocolate, or strawberry? I held my breath, wondering what was about to happen. Frances Williams says it was a tense moment. She felt a little afraid. The white woman at the window glared out at us. White people coming in drove by slowly and gawked at us, as if we weren't supposed to be there. Yet, there we were—two carloads of Negroes sticking out like a sore thumb. My father and Earl Williams walked up to the window to order.

The next thing my brothers and I knew, my mother was looking out the front window of the car and saying, "Here they come."

Dad and Williams were both walking fast and looking angry. The woman at the store had told them in a crass-sounding southern accent, "I'll serve y'all, if you go around to the back."

Our fathers weren't having any of that. They backed their cars out of the parking lot in a big huff, peeling rubber as we left.

Justice in the United States was a long time coming, and it wasn't served up in a dish overnight.

27

THE WAKE

I LEARNED LIFE LESSONS FROM MY FATHER, even though, as I entered early adulthood, we often butted heads, mostly because I am hardheaded and stubborn. Dad called me high-strung and willful. My mother used to tell me, "You've got a lot of your father in you."

Like Dad, I was ambitious and wanted to carve out my own career path. He wanted me to follow in his footsteps and become a lawyer. He was willing to pay for my schooling but had little interest in my desire to forge ahead with a calling in journalism. "You're too young to run off alone in a big city like Boston," he said, or New York, or Washington, DC, in pursuit of jobs in a profession he frowned upon. He came to eventually admire my accomplishments. And I, his.

One day I stumbled onto a letter to me from my mother dated August 23, 1982. She and my father were still living in Cleveland. I was working for NBC News, covering the Reagan White House. She wrote, "We saw you on TV Sunday morning. Daddy taped the program. We have been turning on the *Today Show* and the *Early Today* program looking for you." So Dad had finally come around. For years he let me know he felt the law was a nobler profession, more intellectually challenging and potentially financially rewarding. We joked about the pros and cons of journalism versus the law. But Dad really didn't like how some reporters covered political news and court stories. He thought too often they had their knives out on the attack, unnecessarily revealed too much information, and—this used to make me smile—made the jobs of lawyers harder. Eventually, he decided that his own daughter did a respectable job of fairly informing and educating the public, and I could tell that he was proud of the work I did.

In April 2011, my father, now living in Montgomery, was sick with cancer. And unbeknownst to me, probably wondering what would happen to his life's collection of writings, documents, and old newspapers. Prostate cancer was eating away at him. It was a slow-growing cancer. He and his doctors had opted for "watchful waiting" as they called it. In other words, because of his advanced age, they would keep an eye on it, but not treat it with surgery, chemotherapy, radiation, or other aggressive measures.

He was eighty-six then. My mother, Juanita Emanuel Gray, eighty-four, was in an assisted living facility, suffering from Alzheimer's. Placing her there had been an agonizing decision. In-home caretaking helped, but when Mom repeatedly strayed from the house, sometimes in the middle of the night, despite watchful eyes, there was no other choice.

Theirs was a close union after sixty years together. I can't imagine his thought process. So very like Dad not to share it with the family. My father had also decided he, too, would move to Elmcroft of Halcyon, the assisted living facility nearby, to be with her. It's a beautiful two-story brick building with imposing, white Greek-revival-style columns on a front porch with welcoming white wood rocking chairs for residents and guests.

The week before the move, my brother Thomas Jr., his girlfriend Betty Meade, and I, along with two close family friends, Joyce Wilkerson, my best friend from high school, and Toni Ashford, who used to live next door to Mom and Dad, were packing up all my parents' belongings. Dad intended to sell the house in suburban Arrowhead that he and my mother had lived in during their later years.

Dad directed us, from a chair in the middle of the family room. "Mark that box 'Historical material,'" he said, as he instructed us on what should be put inside and saved, and what could be tossed. "Hold on to that file cabinet." No serious guidance on what do with what we were saving. Just, "Don't throw that away."

I'm so happy we didn't.

―――――――

"We spend our years as a tale that is told . . ."

The day of Dad's wake, the chaplain of the Sigma Phi chapter of Omega Psi Phi was holding a Bible, reading scripture from the Psalms. Like the rest of his fraternity brothers, he was dressed in a dark suit and wearing white gloves as he led them into the funeral home chapel. They filed in one by one.

"The days of our years are threescore years and ten; and if by reason of strength they be fourscore years, yet is their strength, labour, and sorrow; for it is soon cut off, and we fly away."

The members of the graduate chapter of the historically black college fraternity ranged in age but were mostly middle-aged to elderly. Their faces solemn, their gait formal and slow as they walked the aisles along the walls of the room to the front, forming a circle, enclosing those seated in the chapel pews. When they stopped beside one of the two giant pictures of my father that were set upon easels, they left one space, signifying that their chain was broken. There was no casket. Dad had always insisted he wanted to be cremated. We were left to stare at the bronze urn on the altar that contained his ashes.

"So teach us to number our days, that we may apply our hearts unto wisdom . . ."

I could barely focus on the scripture. I was seated in the front row, fixated on the two photographs of Dad staring back at the rows of mourners. They were two of my favorite pictures of him. He looked handsome. One had been taken on my wedding day, nineteen years earlier. He is wearing a very fashionable black tuxedo and a familiar scowl, his brow furrowed, wide-rimmed glasses atop his nose. His skin a deep, dark chocolate, his hair a distinguished salt-and-pepper gray. It made me think of one of his favorite sayings, "I've been Gray all my life." He always thought that was so funny.

The tuxedo is fancier than anything he would have normally worn, if left to his own devices. But I had reminded him he was giving me away in front of company that day, and he would be representing the family. He laughed and let me have my way.

In the other picture, he's smiling with just a slight hint of teeth showing. Even though Dad liked to get other people grinning when posing for pictures, he wasn't a big grinner himself.

"Say whiskey," he said almost every single time he snapped a shot. "Whiskey is finer than cheese." So corny, but that was my father.

In the second picture, he has on a navy business suit. I would say it was fashionable without being overly stylish, if that's possible. Dad retired as a judge, and he looked like one. He wore a smaller-rimmed pair of glasses in this photo. You could see his dark-brown eyes. There is almost a glimmer of a twinkle. His mustache has traces of whitish-gray hair, as did that tiny tuft of hair just below his lower lip.

I felt myself being yanked back to reality. This was a memorial service. Our family watched it through a haze of grief, each in his or her own way. My mother was seated between me and Tommy. Freddie sat to our left, on the end of the pew.

Alzheimer's had robbed Mom of her memory. The dementia had disrupted her ability to reason and think clearly. For years she, too, had talked of committing her life's story to paper. I found a few pages of scribblings under her bed after Dad died. She had barely collected her thoughts past "I've lived an interesting life . . ."

The day of the wake, I'm not sure she even really understood that we were memorializing her husband of nearly sixty-one years.

"Uncle Gray liked to play golf. And he often took Aunt Juanita with him . . ."

I heard my cousin Fred Gray Jr. speaking from the podium about Dad's life, the fun stuff and the parts that read like a very impressive résumé. From his service in the navy during World War II to going to law school in Cleveland.

"He had a private practice, worked as chief assistant general counsel for the Greater Cleveland Regional Transit Authority, was general counsel for the Cuyahoga Metropolitan Housing Authority, moved back to Montgomery as a federal administrative law judge . . ."

Seated on the pew behind us was Uncle Fred and his second wife, Carol. Bernice had died tragically years before, after what should have been a minor procedure. His other three children, Deborah, Stanley, and Vanessa, and the children's families were there, along with an outstanding collection of friends, neighbors, and acquaintances Dad had made along the way. Many were there to acknowledge his importance during the bus boycott years before. Some were people who turned up at Montgomery events just to be in the presence of my uncle. The revered "Lawyer Gray" was a celebrity of sorts in the state of Alabama. He and his sons, Stanley and Fred Jr., both partners in his law practice, left the room to file in with their frat brothers when the Omega memorial ritual began toward the end of the program.

It was an emotional ceremony. You could hear sobs from the pews. I was glad I thought to bring tissues to blot occasional tears. From time to time Aunt Carol reached over the pew to give me and Mom comforting pats on the shoulder. I squeezed Mom's hand, still uncertain if she even remembered why we were there.

My mind kept racing back to days before. I was home alone with Dad. Mom was nearby at Elmcroft. Tommy and his girlfriend were out to dinner that evening. Dusk was beginning to settle over the city, just before we thought to start turning on the indoor lights.

"Karen, come here. I want to show you something," Dad said. He was standing there in what had become his typical weekday uniform, a casual Tommy Bahama–style polo shirt, comfortable, roomy khaki pants, and fleece-lined slippers. He picked up a piece of paper on the big wooden desk in the family room, next to the cozy recliner he liked to sit in, and handed it to me.

"This is who I want to funeralize me."

The paper had the name Phillips-Riley Funeral Home on it, with the business address and phone number. I almost collapsed from shock. I turned, folded my arms around him, and started to cry uncontrollably.

"This is why I hesitated to tell you. I knew you would be the one to take it the hardest," he said calmly.

Dad had obviously made peace with the fact that he was dying. That he might be gone soon. I, on the other hand, was in denial. I had practice with that. Even after my husband, Chris, had been diagnosed in 2005 with pancreatic cancer and the doctor told us he had three to six months to live, I somehow figured the chemotherapy and cancer treatments would keep him alive. He managed to survive nine months.

Now, six years later, I had rushed to Montgomery because Dad was in the hospital, again. He suffered from prostate cancer for many years, as well as high blood pressure and gout, but none of his ailments seemed life-threatening. He always managed to get into the hospital and get out. This time, however, was different.

"I've had a good, long life," he went on. "There, there now."

I couldn't stop sobbing. He gave me one more big hug, looked at his watch, and said, "It's time to watch Bill Maher." It cracked me up that Dad loved that TV talk show. All my life I had viewed my father as somewhat conservative and rather square. And Bill Maher, well, his sociopolitical views lean way to the left. He believes in, among other liberal ideas, legalizing marijuana. But Dad liked comedy, and I guess he didn't find the right wing funny. So I stood there practically apoplectic that my father had announced he was about to die and was OK with it.

I could hardly think straight as he turned on the television and switched the channels until he got to the station he wanted. We both watched Bill Maher until the show went off. And we talked. Soul-searching, this-may-be-the-last-chance-we-ever-get kind of conversation. He told me some things I never knew about him. I shared some stories about me.

"Do you think I should ever get married again?" I ventured to ask.

"You know, you don't have to get married," he said. "But if you want to, you should do it sooner, rather than later." We both laughed.

This is what I was thinking about, as the frat brothers marched out, as we were all saying our final good-byes. It was then that I had the epiphany. Dad left behind an unfinished task: a book about life leading up to the Montgomery bus boycott and his civil rights–filled law career afterward. He threw down the gauntlet. It became my task to pick it up. Suddenly, I was engulfed with a sense of urgency to write myself.

A few months after my father died, when I was visiting Montgomery, I was summoned to the downtown courtroom of Judge Johnny Hardwick of Alabama's Fifteenth Judicial Circuit. He's a popular African American judge who has been returned to his post by the voters in each election since 2002. I watched the proceedings in his courtroom. When they ended and the courtroom was empty, he called me to the bench and said he had a presentation he wanted to make.

I followed the judge into his chambers and sat across from him at his desk. "Your father was a great man," he said. "But I'm sure you know that.

Judge Hardwick handed me a letter addressed to my mother. He explained it informed her and our family that he had taken the liberty of submitting Dad's name to the National Bar Association's Judicial Council for recognition at its Annual Memorial Service in Baltimore that July honoring deceased judges. The NBA is the nation's largest and oldest network of African American lawyers and judges. Judge Hardwick gave me a lapel pin, commemorating the organization's fortieth anniversary. He also gave me the memorial service official program, which included a picture of Dad and a brief bio of his life.

The letter to my mother offered condolences from the council and said, "We can only hope that our lives will measure up to his example, and that we will make a difference as he did with the short time he had here on Earth."

28

LASTING LEGACY

AFTER DAD DIED, I looked back on his life of service. As I saw it, both he and Uncle Teddy put their lives on hold to pursue justice for others. Black Lives Matter wasn't the name of a movement when my father protested the killing of his friend Hilliard Brooks at the hands of a white police officer. But that's exactly what he was saying when he and Ronald Young wrote a letter of complaint to top city officials and organized a veterans' protest.

The shooting of unarmed African Americans by white cops is still a deeply alarming national problem. When I visited Mobile Heights the summer of 2016, the signs on neighborhood lawns were a stark reminder. The naked anger of neighborhood residents over the shooting of fifty-eight-year-old Gregory Gunn was in full view. He was gunned down in the wee hours of the morning on February 25 by a white police officer—chased, tased, beaten, then shot. As I drove down McElvy Street months later, small, bright orange-yellow poster board signs written in red ink dotted people's front yards, protesting the shooting of a man they knew. The text on the signs read JUSTICE 4 GREG GUNN.

This was sixty-six years after the Hilliard Brooks incident. It made me wonder what had changed. Brooks was trying to get a ride on a bus downtown when he was shot. This time, Gregory Gunn was shot while walking along a street in his own neighborhood. He was on his way home after playing cards with friends.

Time and the climate in the city had changed. Montgomery was now a different place. The city's police chief, Ernest Finley, was an African American. This time there was more accountability at the beginning of the investigation. The white officer, Aaron Smith, twenty-three, was actually arrested and charged with murder. In the wake of strong protests from the community, the national spotlight shone on a fatal shooting the police department couldn't sweep under the rug. A trial was scheduled. But not surprisingly, the wheels of justice turned slowly.

More than three years later, I was shocked to discover no trial had occurred. By May 2019, eight judges, two of them African American, had either recused themselves or been found unfit to rule in the case by the state supreme court. Lawyers for the officer argued Smith could not receive a fair trial in Montgomery, claiming he was a victim of racial prejudice. In a victory for the defense, the Alabama Supreme Court granted a change of venue.

Then on Friday, November 22, a mostly white jury in the rural southeast Alabama town of Ozark found Officer Smith guilty on the lesser charge of manslaughter. The defense had argued that the officer, who was on watch after a rash of robberies, acted in self-defense because Gunn had grabbed a painter's pole as a weapon. Prosecutors described Smith as a "bully with a badge." Gunn's family thanked the jurors. The officer resigned from the department and faced up to twenty years in prison.

Police use of deadly force in the United States has been called into question in so many instances the British newspaper the *Guardian* started keeping track, documenting 1,146 people killed by police in 2015, and 1,093 in 2016. How do you explain it? The correct statistics are hard to come by and often disputed. At least somebody's watching.

There remains a certain level of distrust when it comes to matters of race. A lack of cultural awareness still results in worse-case scenarios, where racial profiling by police too many times leads to violent outcomes. Many black parents feel the need to instruct their teenage sons on how to behave at traffic stops, so the wrong move, or look, or comment won't get them arrested, beaten, or shot.

But the racial profiling is intransigent. One day I invited a few of my former childhood neighbors from Mobile Heights to my house on

Terrace for a wine sip. I wanted to reminisce about old times and try to understand with their insight why some things won't change. It occurred to me we were all members of a declining population, people who had experienced legally sanctioned segregation.

Going back to my college days at Ohio University, I recalled how upset my father was to learn that in 1968 some of my African American friends and I were planning to move into an all-black floor section in one of the new dormitories. He was aghast. "Do you know how hard we had to fight for integration? Now you guys want to resegregate yourselves?" I was young. It was another time. We were all about black power, fighting to get African American studies classes on campus, and protesting the Vietnam War.

In his day, Dad was grappling with King's ideas on how best to achieve desegregation. Dad often described during speeches how he congratulated King early in the bus protest about remarks he made that were quoted in the *Montgomery Advertiser*. In the article King embraced Mahatma Gandhi's philosophy of nonviolence and turning the other cheek to white aggressors. My father says he told King it was a brilliant ploy. But King replied, "No, no, Brother Gray, no ploy. This must be a nonviolent protest."

Leaders seeking equality didn't always agree on strategy, then or now. In 1955, my uncle Fred was determined to stop segregation wherever it raised its ugly head. He was successful to a large degree using the law as a weapon. Despite the view of some whites, mixing the races was never the main goal. The goal in desegregating transportation was equal treatment, pure and simple. The goal in desegregating schools was to get equal funding and equal opportunity for black students, where black schools previously had second-class status, receiving fewer funds and substandard materials, and lacking needed repairs. In public school systems around the country, state-sanctioned segregation remains against the law, but to get around integration whites have moved to suburbs or opened private academies, leaving most public schools overwhelmingly black and still underfunded.

It means the struggle for equal justice that started with the end of slavery continues. Fred Gray stresses that in all the speeches he makes, as he finds more and more people are interested in hearing about the bus boycott that launched the civil rights movement. As Martin Luther King Jr.'s first civil rights attorney, he is frequently called upon to make remarks on King's birthday. In fact, he is so overwhelmed with requests for interviews for newspaper and magazine articles, radio and television documentaries and films, that he has needed help managing them. He has allowed me to step in as his assistant.

One year I tagged along as he gave a speech that struck me as wildly ironic. He was the King breakfast keynote speaker in January 2017 at the Fort Meade, Maryland, headquarters of the National Security Agency (NSA), an agency that—can you just imagine—had spied on Dr. King. For years we have known King was spied on by the Federal Bureau of Investigation, which tried to prove ties to the Communist Party to discredit his name and reputation. Under director J. Edgar Hoover, and at the behest of attorney general Robert Kennedy, the FBI succeeded instead in uncovering embarrassing personal information about extramarital affairs. The bureau then sent an anonymous letter and tape recording to King suggesting that he commit suicide.

It turns out, the FBI was not alone. By the fall of 2013, newly declassified documents revealed the NSA had also snooped on the civil rights icon. During the late 1960s the NSA launched a spy campaign on Vietnam War opponents, targeting King, boxing legend Muhammad Ali, and National Urban League executive director Whitney Young, among others. We found that out thanks to a Freedom of Information Act request by researchers at the independent National Security Archive at George Washington University.

It was the NSA's equal employment opportunity and diversity (EEOD) division that invited Fred Gray to speak. Members had met him a couple of summers before during a training course organized by the Federal Executive Institute. The course was titled "Leading Through Difficult Changes: Lessons of the Civil Rights Movement." The training was a case study to help government leaders develop the skills necessary to lead change even in the face of massive resistance. It included tours of various civil rights sites in the South, including Martin Luther King Jr.'s parsonage in Montgomery and the Edmund Pettus Bridge in Selma.

My uncle and I were invited to a brief meeting with then NSA director Michael Rogers, admiral, US Navy; commander, US Cyber

Command; also chief of the Central Security Service. "Call me Mike," he said warmly as we entered his office and took a seat at the conference table. I was slightly taken aback at the air of informality. I wondered what he was thinking. Rogers was a child when Martin Luther King Jr. was on the watch list of the agency he now headed. I was dying to find out if he would address the past surveillance campaign in any way.

Everyone in our small group, including breakfast organizers, took seats around the table. "Mike" sat at the head of the table. The conversation from then on out was mostly centered between him and my uncle. The director immediately established that the two of them had an Alabama connection. Admiral Rogers, though born in Chicago, attended college at Auburn University in Alabama. The bio on the agency's website says he graduated in 1981.

Turning to face Uncle Fred, who sat next to him, Rogers said, "I want to thank you for all your selfless efforts in the civil rights movement, representing Rosa Parks and Martin Luther King." He continued, "King was a great man, and we are fortunate to have a man like you, who has done everything you did to help make our country a better place."

At the breakfast in a banquet room a short time later, Admiral Rogers addressed the crowd of a few hundred NSA employees, a racially integrated group seated at tables around the room. His brief remarks at the podium were like ones he made in the private meeting with my uncle. He spoke of what a great man King was, saying, "The fight for diversity can't stop. The fight is not over. The color of our skin doesn't define us. We are blessed to have people like Fred Gray."

Trained in the manner of true, old-time southern preachers, my uncle is a charismatic speaker. Those assembled appeared to hang on to his every word. "It was the Montgomery bus boycott that introduced Martin Luther King Jr. to the country as the chief spokesman for the nonviolent movement to end racial segregation," he said. He talked about what a special gift King was to the cause and continued, "The boycott didn't just happen. We planned it."

I marveled as I listened to my uncle's speeches evolve in the years as he aged. A man in his mid-eighties, he seemed to have finally become more comfortable divulging that the boycott didn't just spring from Rosa Parks refusing to budge from her seat that one day in December 1955.

Fred Gray revealed, as he does in *Bus Ride to Justice*, that Montgomery's bus problem started in the early 1940s. He mentioned that as a young college student he made a promise to himself to leave Alabama to attend law school in a state up north where blacks were welcome and return to "destroy everything segregated I could find."

As he had done so many times before, he laid out the long history of African American leaders trying to convince city officials and the Montgomery City Lines bus company to provide more courteous treatment of black passengers. He spoke of working with Jo Ann Robinson, president of the Women's Political Council, to map out strategy. He admitted he didn't discuss his role in planning the boycott at the time because "I would have been disbarred for stirring up discontent."

And, as always, he gave credit to fifteen-year-old Claudette Colvin for her courage.

"We have $130,000, will you bid $140? At $130,000, are we all through? Are you sure? At $130, going once. $130, going twice." The bidding was lively for an album of African Americana, photographs including two of abolitionist Harriet Tubman, which eventually went for $161,000. I found myself at the Swann Auction Galleries on the Lower East Side of Manhattan in March 2017 to discover there is still interest in the 1955 bus boycott.

My reason for being there was to check out who wanted to bid on a large collection of papers and financial records from the Montgomery Improvement Association. Swann was auctioning off binders full of material, including checks (nearly six hundred) from the early days of the boycott. The papers also included the MIA's constitution and bylaws and numerous other papers, such as a handwritten list of members of the original executive board, on which my father sat. One piece of lined notebook paper named twenty of the board members, with what seemed to be payouts for their service. Rev. M. L. King's name topped the list with fifty dollars by his name. Rev. Ralph Abernathy's was on the paper, with thirty-five dollars. E. D. Nixon's name was there too—no dollar amount given. Rufus Lewis, who was in charge of transportation, had ten dollars by his name. My father was on the list as "Thos Gray." No dollar amount. No explanation on the page about what they were paid for, nor why Nixon and my father were not paid. But beginning early in the boycott, those who drove their own cars to pick up passengers were paid for gas.

Some actual canceled checks, signed by King, Abernathy, and Erna Dungee, the MIA's financial secretary, showed $100 payments to Abernathy and to Rev. Robert Graetz. Graetz has told me he was paid when he went on fundraising speaking trips. A check for $3,750 was paid to prominent Birmingham civil rights attorney Arthur D. Shores, who I assume was consulted on some legal matters. A check for $584 was made out to Hutchinson Street Baptist Church, site of some of the mass meetings held as pep rallies and fundraisers during the boycott.

I didn't go to the auction to bid myself. I merely wanted to see what was up for sale, and to find out who wanted to buy it. It turns out, the auctioneer passed over the lot number during the live bidding. The auction house expected the lot to bring $20,000 to $30,000. A private party purchased it later for $18,750. When I inquired the next day about who had bought it, a Swann staffer told me it was sold not to an individual but to a foundation. He would not disclose the name of the foundation.

———————

The nation is still remembering and still apologizing for segregation. In the late winter and early spring of 2018, Alabama state officials made amends for a fifty-eight-year-old injustice involving students and faculty members at what is now Alabama State University. Twenty-nine black students tried to get service at a white lunch counter at the Montgomery County courthouse on February 25, 1960. They were not arrested as they took seats and refused to leave, but the lunchroom was shut down. The white governor at the time, John Patterson, as chairman of the state board of education, later ordered then Alabama State College president H. C. Trenholm to expel the nine believed to be protest ringleaders, for conduct unbecoming a student or future teacher, and for insubordination and insurrection. Several faculty members were also later fired for their alleged involvement.

It became material for another Fred Gray case, a landmark decision in the Fifth Circuit Court of Appeals that established the precedent that public schools and universities must give students due process before they are disciplined or expelled. That was in 1961.

In 2018 the outgoing interim Alabama education superintendent Ed Richardson, a white man, informed the state board of education that the students' disciplinary records had been expunged. The records of four teachers at the college who were fired for "disloyalty" were also cleared.

Since I began my book project, my uncle has kept me informed of Alabama events related to the boycott and his other legal cases. Usually by e-mail, but often he calls. He let me know about the Richardson decision. The following year, on the fifty-ninth anniversary of the sit-in, Montgomery mayor Todd Strange and Montgomery county commissioner Elton Dean paid homage to the students and presented resolutions to Alabama State University president Quinton Ross lamenting "wrongs from the past." Fred Gray attended the press conference and spoke about the case.

Derryn Moten, chairman of the department of history and political science, spearheaded the move to get the students' records wiped clean. "It is very important that the state acknowledged that the students were wrongfully punished," he says. When I called to ask him about the lunch counter incident, Moten said, "Those students had a constitutional right to protest against segregation. Attorney Gray makes that clear in his brief to federal district judge Frank Johnson [who ruled against the plaintiffs] and to the appellate court," which ruled in their favor.

I suppose the apologies, albeit very late, are all well and good. But what about all the pain and suffering of St. John Dixon and the other eight students who were expelled? And the twenty students who were put on probation?

"Sorry is not good enough," Moten told me. "These people did nothing wrong. They committed no crime." Passionate about the case, he says he's writing a book about the "vindictiveness of the state in continuing to harass and harangue those students." According to Moten, many of them had trouble continuing with their education and getting back on their feet. Dixon's application to a college in California was rejected on the grounds he was dishonorably discharged from Alabama State. And, Moten says, at least one student lost his GI Bill benefits.

The surviving students are senior citizens now, the stain on their college records finally erased. But Moten believes the State of Alabama should still be concerned about potential legal action that could be taken.

As for the four faculty members whose records were also expunged, the late Lawrence D. Riddick, who wrote a biography of Martin Luther King Jr. while he was chair of the history department at Alabama State College, was fired in the wake of the episode. Moten says three other professors at the school were forced out. In her book, *The Montgomery Bus Boycott and the Women Who Started It*, Jo Ann Robinson admits that she and fellow English professor Mary Fair Burks, both leaders of the Women's Political Council, felt pressure and chose to leave the college. Like Riddick, the two women did not live to see their records cleared.

Rosa Parks is forever engrained in our national consciousness as the Mother of the Civil Rights Movement, though her story is one that continues to evolve. Another little piece of that history was reported in the spring of 2018, after the discovery of a long-forgotten box that had been tucked away at the Montgomery County Courthouse. A history housed in court records, yellow from age, bent and folded, wrapped with rubber bands that had long lost their elasticity. The papers included arrest records of Parks, King, and others, found in a cardboard box on the bottom shelf of a huge safe. Circuit Court clerk Tiffany McCord took possession of the documents until a decision was made about what to do with them.

The documents are now on a ten-year loan to Alabama State University, to be preserved, digitized, cataloged, and made available for viewing. My uncle was called over to look through the box's contents, much of which he hadn't seen since the 1950s. Some of the items he didn't remember or had never seen.

I am still learning about our civil rights struggle as I attend events where my uncle speaks. During a visit to the University of South Carolina for a Black History Month program on February 21, 2019, I found out more about Sarah Mae Flemming. She was South Carolina's Rosa Parks. Flemming was a young black woman who was ordered to leave her seat in the front of a city bus in Columbia in June 1954. The circumstances were similar, though Flemming was assaulted by the bus driver. Her lawsuit was overshadowed by the US Supreme Court ruling in the Alabama lawsuit that ended the Montgomery boycott.

"Three generations now know nothing about hardcore segregation," Fred Gray told the audience at the U of SC School of Law. "If we don't teach young people, they'll grow up believing the struggle has ended," he said. His speech coincided with a special exhibit at the university's Center for Civil Rights History and Research, *Our Story Matters*.

With Fred Gray when he spoke about the Montgomery bus boycott at the University of South Carolina School of Law.

Preservation of the history is important. It's one reason I tackled the job of writing this book. My father began to stress it in his later years. It was obvious in Dad's own attempt to chronicle what he'd been through.

My uncle focuses on it in every speech I hear him make. He then usually reaches inside his suit jacket pocket and brings out copies of a brochure of the Tuskegee Human and Civil Rights Multicultural Center—or the Tuskegee History Center as it is often called. He invites members of whatever audience he is in front of to "come on down to Tuskegee to see our little museum." I can see him almost rocking on his feet as he smiles and continues. "If you can't get there, I hope you'll consider making a donation."

The center was initially founded as a permanent memorial to the victims of the federal government's horrific Tuskegee Syphilis Study and to document other lesser-known local civil rights history. At 104 South Elm Street, it is housed in a tan brick building that used to be a bank. A small site, but chock-full of remarkable stories about Tuskegee, Alabama, and surrounding Macon County. As the brochure says, the center "explores the intertwining pasts of Macon County's Native American, European American, and African American cultures." My cousin Deborah is the museum's managing director. She has worked tirelessly to help the museum grow into a much sought-after tourist destination. I do my part by helping with community outreach.

There has been talk of a Presidential Medal of Freedom for Fred Gray. During the sixtieth anniversary of the bus boycott in December 2015, when presidential candidate Hillary Clinton spoke at Dexter Avenue King Memorial Baptist Church, she said she thought he deserved the medal. But then, she was never in a position to award it. Civil rights legend Rep. John Lewis told me he was aware of a lobbying campaign. But that was before Donald Trump became president.

Historian Derryn Moten calls Gray "the most celebrated civil rights attorney alive." He says, "If Trump can give Babe Ruth the medal posthumously, doggone it, he can give Fred Gray one." Wendell Wilkie Gunn was the first African American student to enroll at Florence State College (now the University of North Alabama, UNA) thanks to a lawsuit filed by Gray that forced him in. Gunn, as a special assistant to President Ronald Reagan, served as assistant director for commerce and trade in the Office of Policy Development. In the summer of 2019 he was appointed to the UNA board of trustees. Gunn has been beating the drum to no avail for his mentor to be awarded the medal. He laments, "People say they don't know why he doesn't have one already."

So what's next? I was looking for a way to close out my thoughts on my family's civil rights legacy, and African Americans' struggles, when I came across a printed program from a Montgomery church mass meeting dated March 11, 1957, just months after the end of the bus boycott. The theme of that day's program was "Where Do We Go from Here?" Black people are still asking the same question.

On October 8, 2019, there was a glimmer of hope. Montgomery, Alabama, the city with the dubious distinction of being both the cradle of the Confederacy and the birthplace of the civil rights movement, elected its first black mayor. In a city where more than half the population is black, probate judge Steven Reed defeated white television station owner David Woods, pulling 67 percent of the vote. Addressing a crowd of supporters that evening, Reed said this: "If there was any doubt about what we can do when we come together, when we unify in this city, let the record show tonight above all . . . we build around positivity, around opportunity and all the things that tie us together."

Less than two months after taking office, Mayor Reed weighed in on the verdict in the trial of Officer Aaron Smith. He vowed to look into whether better training of police officers was needed, calling the Gunn killing "a tragedy that we must not forget, we must learn from it, and move forward together to do everything in our power to make sure something like this never happens again."

"Never again" seems unlikely, but we live in hope that, as Dr. Martin Luther King Jr. famously said, the long arc of the moral universe is bending toward justice.

ACKNOWLEDGMENTS

This book would not have been possible without the invaluable assistance of many people. I'd like to thank them all, especially Chicago Review Press, the parent company of Lawrence Hill Books, for taking a chance on a first-time author. Much well-deserved appreciation to editors Jerry Pohlen, Devon Freeny, and Michelle Williams for their skilled guidance and sharp insight. Special gratitude to my agent Sha-Shana Crichton, for her keen interest in the project from the very beginning.

I am indebted to helpful archivists and historians: Adrienne Cannon and Luis Clavell at the Library of Congress; staffers at the Alabama Department of Archives and History, notably director emeritus Ed Bridges; Howard Robinson at Alabama State University; and Richard Bailey, a fine keeper of Alabama's history. I am grateful for resources at the National Archives and the National Museum of African American History and Culture.

The *Montgomery Advertiser* was helpful in my journey, allowing me to contribute to its Alabama Voices opinion column. The civic group One Montgomery provided a wealth of historical information, new friends, and a weekly breakfast of grits and eggs. The Friendly Supper Club also helped me understand modern-day Montgomery.

Special thanks to other writers and mentors who shepherded me along the way. Marita Golden, author and cofounder of the Hurston/Wright Foundation, which nurtures emerging African American authors, steered

me toward the right path after reading an early draft. I also learned much
from authors Bruce Johnson (WUSA9 anchor), Ralph Eubanks, Patrice
Gaines, Glenn "Duffy" Dyer, Gail DeGeorge, and Elizabeth Wilkerson,
and early mentors Nick Mills and Jim Wieck.

What would I have done without caring feedback from my beta
readers, a core group of close friends who read and reread many chapters and drafts of the manuscript and nursed me through periods of
self-doubt and uncertainty? I am eternally grateful to Deborah Gray at
the Tuskegee History Center, knowledgeable and wise, who took my calls
and gave advice any time of the day or night. Thank you to Carolyn
Harvey, Jan Smith, Lark McCarthy, and Natasha Small for kind and
gentle guidance and prodding, constant encouragement combined with
sometimes brutal honesty. I can't thank Lark enough for giving my
book its name during a brainstorming session with girlfriends at lunch,
Carolyn for always being there, especially with a crash course for me
on becoming more computer savvy, and Jan for also graciously hosting
a lovely dinner party for the late US Supreme Court justice Antonin
Scalia and his wife, Maureen, in Florence, Italy, where Uncle Teddy's
court cases were a topic of conversation. She also hosted a dinner for
my uncle when he was honored by the Congressional Black Caucus. The
now secretary of the Smithsonian and his wife attended, as did former
secretary of state Colin Powell and his wife. Lynda Robb discussed the
movie *Selma* and her father LBJ's legacy.

A special shout-out to a gaggle of other boosters and cheerleaders:
Dianna Abney, Reginald and Daryl Stuart, Joyce Wilkerson, Janet Wu,
Randall Pinkston, Maggie Linton, Cynthia Steele Vance, Diane Roberts,
Wendy Wilk Markarian, Kim Sneed, Doris McMillon, Sheila Brooks, Lilly
and Dave Lucas, Megan Beyer, Deborah Heard, McIntosh and Cookie
Ewell, Frances and Earl Williams Jr., Leonard, Eva, and Paula Garden,
Clarence and Eta Holmes, Judith Benkendorf, Beverly Jackson, Barbara
Semedo, Gerald Jackson, Avery Friedman, Dan Cohen, and "newsbabes"
Debra Silimeo, Claire Meyerhoff, Janice Sosebee, Wendy Rieger, Judlyne
Lilly-Gibson, Kate Ryan, Pam Coulter, and Patricia Cooper. Thanks to
my Mobile Heights friends and neighbors Marsha Singleton, William
Singleton, Regina Craig Avery, Edris Stevens Jefferson, Oneita Crenshaw

Sankey, Coralyn Wright, Rose Taylor Harmon, and Frank Taylor (RIP), for helping put Alabama's capital city into context.

Profound gratitude goes out to Bob and Jeannie Graetz and their daughter, Meta, family friends who have navigated a dangerous journey as allies of the civil rights movement. To all the others who eagerly gave their time for interviews I am also truly grateful: Claudette Colvin, Sally Mosher, the Bagley family, Nelson Malden, Ray, Joe, and David Whatley, Ann Carmichael, Christine Calloway, Vera Harris, Valda Harris Montgomery, Uriah Fields, the late Edward and Ernestine Stevens, Alma and Ed Collier, Curtis and Butler Coleman, Alma Johnson, William Boswell, Derryn Moten, and Wendell Wilkie Gunn. To Montgomery's new mayor, Steven Reed, I wish you luck. Thank you for your time.

Thank you to my uncle Fred Gray for answering all my questions, even when the answers were in your book *Bus Ride to Justice*. I appreciate your letting me schlep along to speaking engagements and interviews. And I thank Aunt Carol for permitting the intrusion into your lives.

Finally, to other family members and friends who lent support and put up with me throughout this five-year project, especially my dear brother Thomas Jr., who spent weeks going through boxes and files of pictures in search of just the right ones—it's over now. Much love. Many thanks.

If I left anybody out, please forgive me. It just means the years have taken their toll.